Ignite Your Spirit!
The Time is Now!

Ignite Your Spirit!

The Time Is Now!

A Collection of Inspirational Stories and Reflections

DONNA L. FRIESS, PH.D.

2024

Library of Congress-in-Publication Data

Friess, Donna L.
Ignite Your Spirit! The Time is Now!
Donna L. Friess
Includes bibliographical references.
Biography

Hurt into Happiness Publishing 2024
31506 Paseo Christina, San Juan Capistrano, CA 92675

ISBN-978-1-7358225-2-5

Summary: Inspirational stories by Donna L. Friess, Ph.D., international spokesperson for children's rights. Inspirational stories on life, love, and learning. The stories focus on strengthening one's connections and making wise choices.

1. Women Intellectuals- United States-Biography.
2. Healing from Trauma.
3 .A collection of inspirational stories

Donna L. Friess, Ph.D. rose to international attention when her family had to join together to stop their father's abuse of their youngest family member. The case was a cover story for the *Los Angeles Times Magazine.* It involved a tumultuous 15 month long jury trial. The siblings were guests on the Opera Winfrey Show. Their story has reached over 50 million people. Donna authored Cry the Darkness: One Woman's Triumph Over Incest. This is printed in seven languages. She was nominated for the U.S. President's Service Award in 1996.

Cover designed by Mariusz Jeglinski

Books by Donna Friess

Women Leaders of the Movement to Stop Child Sexual Abuse
A Doctoral Dissertation. An Oral History 1992

Cry the Darkness: One Woman's Triumph over the Tragedy of Incest, 1993
2nd Edition, 2013

Whispering Waters: Historic Weesha and the Settling of Southern California (Oral History) With Janet Tonkovich, 1998

A Chronicle of Historic Weesha and the Upper Santa Ana River Valley
with Janet Tonkovich, 2000.

Circle of Love: A Guide to Successful Relationships, 3rd Edition, 2008

One Hundred Years of Weesha: Centennial 2010. An Oral History, 2010

Cherish the Light: One Woman's Journey from Darkness to Light, 2013

The Unraveling of Shelby Forrest 2014 – a Novel

Capistrano Trails: Ride for the Brand- A History of the Equestrian
Story of Alta California 2018

Growing Up Venice: Parallel Universes– A History, 2020

The Forgotten Apple Tree – A Weesha Story = a Fairy Tale, 2023

The Story of the Mighty Santa Ana River Floods: And their
Impact on the Historic Areas of Weesha and Seven Oaks in the
San Bernardino Mountains of Southern California –A History, 2023

To Order books visit Amazon.com. Also available through Kindle Publishing.

About *Cry the Darkness*

Winner Indie Excellence Book Awards – Women's Issues 2014
Honorable Mention – Paris International Book Festival 2014
Honorable Mention – New York Book Festival 2014
Honorable Mention – Southern California Book Festival 2014
Honorable Mention – London International Books Awards 2014
Honorable Mention – New England Festival of Books 2014

"A real contribution to women everywhere." *Changes Magazine.*

Re-released by Bastei Lubbe Publishing. Germany, 2018

Cry the Darkness has become a classic for those working in the child abuse field.

"It is a wonderful book!" Marilyn Van Derbur, Former Miss America, incest survivor.

"I couldn't put it down. It is inspirational!" *Alpha Gamma Delta International Quarterly*

"It is a gripping story…it keeps the reader moving." U.S. International University *Envoy.*

"A must read for everyone. One of the most important books available. It gives hope. Donna's life story is a beacon of hope and happiness for adult survivors of sexual abuse." Claire Reeves, Founder, Mothers Against Sexual Abuse.

"Cry the Darkness is my most valued possession." Gina, Incest survivor and AIDS patient.

"It changed my life and gave me hope." Sonja, Incest survivor.

"*Tarer I Morket.*" Best-selling non-fiction book in the history of Egmont (Virkelightedens Verden) publishing, Norway, 1990's. Egmont Bogklub.

"An inspiration for those working for victims of childhood trauma." *Changes Magazine.*

"Outstanding Donna! A good reminder that we DO have a choice in how we respond." Judy P., Reader.

For my fellow travelers on the path to discovering wholeness and living in joy

ACKNOWLEDGMENTS

This collection of stories and reflections grew out of my interactions with the Loss of a Loved Ones group members, the Reinvent Yourself participants, and my coaching clients. If it were not for your candor and vulnerability these accounts would not exist. I appreciate all of you. As a result of the topics and issues which arose during our sessions, I often found myself ruminating on those subjects long after our sessions were over. Consequently, I wrote my thoughts into newsletters which I emailed to you over more than a dozen years. I appreciate your bravery as you traveled toward living more fully and happily. This book would not have come together without my husband, Ken's, encouragement and razor-sharp editing skills. Thank you to my sister, Diana Starr, for all of her loving encouragement and excellent technical support. I appreciate the creativity and professionalism of photographic artist, Diana Schmidt of Accent Portraits for the cover photo and Mario Jeglinski for the cover design. Thank you to the early readers for your helpful feedback.

To not grow old, no matter
How long you live. Never
Cease to stand like curious
Children before the great
Mystery into which we
Were born

~Albert Einstein

Contents

Foreword

When I first met Dr. Donna, I was just a student, one among many, in a class full of budding minds. Truth be told, the class I was taking from Donna, was one of my most dreaded. Communications. I hated speaking in front of others and being in a position that I felt was vulnerable. The first day we "really" met, was when she asked me to stay after class. I assumed I was getting dropped because I truthfully was not performing as I needed to be. The first words out of her mouth were, "are you safe?". I didn't even know how to respond, so I mumbled something along the lines of, "well kind of".

From that moment on, Donna played a pivotal role in my life. She showed me what it was like to be vulnerable, to be open and to accept the fact that things weren't okaiy and that it was okay that they weren't. She never gave up on me. Not once. Donna was the voice in my head through every step and every stage. Through the therapy and the growing pains and everything in between. I always heard her words, "are you safe?"

Donna rose from the ashes and has built a life that only some dream of. The truth is, she makes it known that it is possible for anyone to do so. I'm living proof. I sit here and listen to my two kids saying their affirmations each morning before school. "I'm brave, I'm strong, I'm wonderful, I'm special, I'm loved, I'm smart and today is going to be a great day. Woohoo!". I couldn't have ever imagined being where I am today, if I had not ever met Donna. Her words can move mountains, but even more so, her love and inspiration that she brings and so willingly gives, can create masterpieces. Those masterpieces being your beautiful life.

Nikki Reiss
Author *The Line Between*

Introduction

The Genesis of My Journey

The Road Taken

Poetry has a lot to say about the road not taken, well, at least Robert Frost did, and recently I've been thinking about the road I have taken. From my earliest memory I knew that whatever road I would take would be less chaotic than the one my family of origin was following.

Now, at this stage on my path, I have lived a long, productive life filled with many challenges but also with much love and joy. Recently, I have been pondering how exactly I got on the track I've been sticking with these many many decades. It feels luxurious to live long and have the energy and interest to be able to focus on the genesis of one's journey.

Robert Frost chose the less worn road, the greener one covered in leaves. He believed that it made all the difference. Perhaps he could have been describing my journey. This year, my beloved husband, Ken, and I are celebrating our 60th wedding anniversary, I am retired from a full 45 year college teaching career, we raised three happy children to adulthood, and welcomed eleven grandchildren, most of whom are grown. In addition, I've enjoyed my writing and painting path for forty plus years.

I realize my life's choices have roots going back to earliest childhood. As a nine-year-old, I reveled in the task of helping in my grandfather's pharmacy. We called him "Big Ray" and he was the daily after-school babysitter for my little sister, Jackie, and me. Beginning when I was seven years -old, it was my responsibility to wait for Jackie outside of kindergarten at Nightingale Elementary School and take her by the hand and walk to the drugstore which was about two miles away in Venice. Once we arrived at the store we would have a snack and play quietly in the back room with our storybook dolls, unless there was a job to complete.

I felt very grown up when Big Ray allowed me to sort and shelve the newly arrived magazines, comics, and books into their display racks at the front of the store. I can still see my third-grade self sitting on the floor in the corner of the store, surrounded by books and magazines that needed sorting. I loved it!!! (I still love it!) My favorite monthly magazine had to do with psychosomatic illnesses. I had to ask what the word *psychosomatic* meant, and I was thrilled to learn that there was a mind body connection to one's health and behavior. Perhaps, a mighty big thought for a little girl.

That passion for learning about the human psyche has never left me. I studied psychology in my college and graduate classes. I went to seminars on Transactional Analysis. In the 1970's there was an institute for the study of Transactional Analysis (known as T.A.) called "The Frog Pond" in Sacramento which offered weekend classes. Those studies enabled me to learn and teach my college communication students about psychological Mind Games and Life Scripts. I wrote a textbook for them including discussions about these concepts. In addition, I earned a doctoral degree in human behavior.

I always searched for more information on living well in the wake of my parents' abuse and neglect. I have spent a lifetime searching for ways in which to thrive, and to be the best possible version of myself. Starting early in life, I have been driven to understand why people behave as they do. I have been determined to find a place of peace and joy. In looking at where I have arrived, I see that I have done that.

A New Direction

It was difficult to finally retire. I loved being with my students, but eventually I knew it was time. After a few false starts, I did it. Once retired, it became clear to me that hanging out with my three golden retrievers, and riding horses was not quite going to cut it as a full-time occupation.

The very first month of my new life, the City of Cypress Community Relations Director invited me to kick off their year's speakers bureau. It was January 2011 and they wanted me to inspire their residents on the topic of renewal and making positive choices. At the end of my presentation to a large and responsive group, three ladies asked to help me take my materials out to the car.

We talked and walked. They shared their stories with me. They seemed desperate for some direction. Two had recently lost their husbands and the third was going through a messy divorce. After a long while, I left them with my best thinking and some hugs.

On the long drive back to San Juan Capistrano, the conversation with the ladies gave me an idea. I could volunteer to create a free support group, a Loss of a Loved One class, in my own city. My husband had spent many years as a volunteer city official. I was sure he could guide me through the process. He referred me to the appropriate staff. Within a month I was offering a regular monthly meeting through the City of San Juan Capistrano's Recreation Department. It was well attended for nine years before the covid epidemic shut it down. The time was right, I was ready for a change.

Concurrent with the Loss of a Loved One, I began a life coaching practice. As my client list grew, I found myself mulling over some of the problems and issues that had come up. I began writing my thoughts to my clients, often as stories which reinforced my ideas regarding living more fully. Sometimes I wrote about special moments or encounters. My support group members and clients encouraged me.

About the same time, I joined an Orange County women's group called Womansage. I became a board member. Focusing on relevant social issues, the organization became concerned with the difficulties many people were experiencing in the wake of the Great Recession of 2008-2011. Due to economic stagnation in the country at that time companies were shutting down or laying off employees. Lots of people were out of work. The organization felt the call to respond to the need. We developed a free Reinvent Yourself Program.

The program's goal was to prepare participants for finding their way in a difficult job market. It was a ten-week course including life coaching, resume writing, and the development of interview skills. The grand finale was a dinner and fashion show during which the "graduates" showed off their new wardrobes, hair styles and professional make-up. The women reported that it was life changing.

I served as the group's life coach. My job during my four-week coaching segment was to inspire them to grow their confidence, and to learn new ways of thinking and living in order to find meaningful employment.

What is right with you?

I'll never forget what the first meetings were like with each new group. They would be seated around an oversized conference table. Usually there would be about fifteen women, mostly middle aged. They would be sitting quietly and with brittle expressions. They were scared, disheartened, and many admitted that they felt hopeless. I would smile at them and introduce myself. I would ask for a show of hands: "Who was able to drive here tonight?" All the hands went up. "Who can see?" Again, all the hands shot up. "Who is relatively healthy?" Most of them raised their hands. The discussion then focused on gratitude for all that we currently had. I would sort of joke about being grateful for all the problems they did not have! They would laugh.

The next week as I walked into the meeting room, I would be startled to see that everyone was chatting and smiling! The tone of the class had done a 180 as they focused on the positive; what they did have, instead of the negative; what they did not have. I think there is a tendency in our society to dwell on what is wrong to the great detriment to what is right. Anyway, by the end of our four sessions the participants had a significant attitude adjustment. Years later many would contact me and share that they are still close friends with some of the others from their Reinvent Yourself days.

The program was well attended. We offered two ten-week sessions over a period of five years. My contact list grew as I kept writing my newsletters. Readers often reported that my thoughts were an important beacon of hope. At the end of each post, I would ask how they were doing and how had my experience resonated with them. The writings became interactive.

The years passed. I kept sending out my thoughts. It was a connection to people with whom I had worked and with whom I was working, as my own journey progressed.

About ten years into the process, my husband, Ken, began to suggest that I compile my letters and create a book. I would smile and roll my eyes just a little bit when he was not looking. I would think *they are my personal thoughts about growth and healing, creating more happiness. They were not a book. Besides it would be too hard to gather them all up.*

My stories and anecdotes are a distillation of a lifetime of pondering, learning, and ruminations, as I struggled to create the healthiest and happiest life I could after surviving a chaotic and abusive childhood. They are a personal record profiling what I had learned and taught my college students and coaching clients. The reflections are also something of a travelogue of my adventures.

My son Dan and my sister Diana (who is the technical wizard behind my posts) also began to suggest that the stories and thoughts be unified into a book. My readers continue writing to me; telling me that my words gave them strength, motivated them to do better, to risk more, and to take better care of themselves.

Ken, Dan, and Diana continued their lobbying for a book. At year thirteen of my letters, Diana offered to do the compilation and print them out. I was still smiling and nodding, but not taking any of their suggestions seriously. There might have been a bit more eye rolling on my part.

Then suddenly it was happening; on President's Day of 2024, I was making a presentation to Diana's women's group on California history. When she greeted me and Ken before the talk, she handed Ken a thick manila envelope of all the articles I had written over the last dozen or so years.

Ken, still the keen proponent of the posts to a book, gratefully took the thick envelope, understanding that Diana had pulled the articles together. All he had to do was convince me that this was my next project. Not an easy task.

A few weeks later in the dark of an early morning, coffee cup in hand, I sat down in front of our fireplace and opened the envelope from Diana. I read one story, then another, and soon I had read about six of them. It was like visiting old friends. I found myself laughing, smiling and remembering the various incidents. I realized Ken, Dan, and Diana were correct. There was something worth sharing to a bigger audience, and maybe I was not too shy to do it! Maybe I was selling myself short. Perhaps my hesitation was a glimmer of an old dysfunction.

A Hard Look Back

While still pondering the idea of compiling the stories into a cohesive unit, Ken and I had the opportunity to participate in a "sound bath" at our Pilates studio. It was a remarkable, relaxing, guided meditation during which I had a chance to take a long look backward to study my "road taken." I thought again of Robert Frost who claimed that the "less traveled road" he had taken "had made all the difference." In my meditations I focused on exactly how and why I was so determined to choose the road I did?

Lying there on the mat in the darkness, surrounded by the hypnotic sounds of the crystal bowls at high frequency, my mind searched back in time. I saw myself as a seven-year-old in charge of the safety of my five year-old sister. I saw myself as an eight-year-old, the frequent evening babysitter for the child my father had out of wedlock with the teenager who was our babysitter. I could visualize myself striking a match on the gas stove at her apartment, and lighting the burner in order to heat a pan of water so that I could warm a bottle for the infant while also caring for my younger sister. It was a lot of responsibility for a little kid. Unfortunately, it is not that rare of an event even in a country as prosperous as ours.

Our father had us memorize a story to tell others about the paternity of this new baby. We were told to say that her father had died in a "car crash in Chicago." I always remembered the alliteration of car, crash, Chicago. All this was around the time that my father told me that I had become a "real woman." This was his description for having completed his assault of me. It was a great deal to handle for my young self. Also, this too, is not an uncommon experience for many American children.

Our mom was completely focused on her opera singing career, her full-time job, and her college classes. I understood there was no help there. My response was to do the best I could.

Of course I kept my secret. I didn't look for help anywhere else because along with the car crash Chicago story, we were repeatedly told that "sorry sisters end up six feet under." We were young, but we were not stupid. "Six feet under" was a real threat. It was frequently followed up by arms twisted behind our backs as we were locked outside in the dark of night.

I kept my secret. I did well in my studies while dreaming of a life in the future where I could become "normal." I graduated from college, married my high school sweetheart, completed my master's degree, began our family, and entered my full-time college teaching career. I could do it! I did it!

Through the years I was grasping and holding every scrap of knowledge I could about creating happiness. I was happy. I had a beautiful family, a solid marriage, and a career that I felt passionate about.

The Great Upheaval, 1989

Truly, I probably would have rocked along like that 'til my last days on the planet, except I learned that my father was up to his old ways with my four-year-old niece, Kelly.

After Jackie and I went off to college, our father had gone on to marry the woman with whom he had had that baby. He added a big family of six half-siblings.

Agonizingly, once I knew that the four-year-old was being molested, I could no longer hold it all in. I began having panic attacks, flashbacks, disturbing dreams, and my hypervigilant startle reflex became more intense than ever. I was symptomatic for PTSD. I was in trouble.

You might know my story. It is detailed in *Cry the Darkness: One Woman's Triumph Over the Tragedy of Incest.* In a nutshell, I had to tell Ken about my childhood abuse. I felt an overwhelming need to protect my little niece and would need his help. I had kept the secret my whole life.

Ken responded by initiating a police investigation. A subsequent fifteen month-long jury trial dragged on. Ultimately there was a guilty verdict and imprisonment. Many of us sought therapy. For the most part my siblings pulled together as well as they could to stop our father. These days everyone is doing their best, and generally thriving. The little niece grew up; has a loving husband, and a beautiful teenage daughter. My niece is starting a second master's program in creative writing. She too, is on a quest for wholeness.

An Epiphany

I feel grateful to have risen up out of the ashes of my childhood. I continue to work to support others on their voyage toward wholeness and happiness, as I continue on my own journey. During my sound bath reflections, I recalled an epiphany I had one night in a graduate class. The class was Stress and the Human Experience. It was a full class of about 50 older students. The classroom itself was a small auditorium. I vividly remember the first night when the professor posed this question to us. **"Is anyone here the child of trauma?"** Every hand in the room was raised. I was flabbergasted! *Seriously?* I could not believe it!

I had looked around at my classmates, mostly career people who had worked all day. They were well dressed and tired looking. I remember thinking *Goodness how brave they all are!*

That moment has stayed with me across the thirty years since I was in that class. How brave so many of my fellow humans are, going forward in life, doing all they can to have meaningful lives, despite what roadblocks and agonies they have endured.

That memory brought me back to another class during that doctoral program. It was with Professor Herb Baker, one of the most effective and talented teachers with whom I had ever studied. It was an early Saturday morning class. We were all listening intently when suddenly there was a loud bang, maybe a car backfiring. Dr. Baker, a Viet Nam War veteran, suddenly dived behind his podium where he cowered in fear. His brain clearly interpreted danger as he succumbed to his own PTSD reaction. It was heart breaking to realize that our tall, smart, capable teacher was the victim of trauma, doing what he could to get through life. *There are so many of us.*

My coping strategy for the first 45 years was to shove down the bad stuff and do my best. All the while I was studying, listening, and digesting all the research, teachings, and ideas I could to help me live the happiest version of myself.

I realized that Ken, Dan and Diana were correct. My stories might well add up to something of value to my fellow travelers on the road to feeling happier and living more fully. Perhaps, Robert Frost was on to something when he discovered that choosing the road less traveled can make all the difference.

At the end of *The Road Not Taken,* Frost considers the "other more trodden path" and then reflects:

"Though way leads to way,
I doubted that I should ever come back.
I shall be telling this with a sigh
Somewhere ages and ages hence:
Two roads diverged in a wood, and I-
I took the one less traveled by,
And that has made all the difference."

Please join me as you read and experience the reflections along my path. I would like to imagine you curling up in your favorite chair, with a sift blanket across your lap as you take a time out to ignite your spirit and nourish your soul. My hope is that you are inspired to be more gentle with yourself and perhaps try some new things. Maybe there are new people to meet and some adventures waiting for you. One thing I do know is that this is ***your time now*** and there's no time to waste. I think you are brave. I wish you continued joy as you go forward on your own road less traveled.

My best, donna

Section I

Choices: The Art of Applying Our Wisdom and Mobilizing Our Strengths

"We are living the life we have chosen and we control those choices"

~Donna Friess

The Well-Lived Life

July 8, 2023

Last week our oldest son, Rick, a long-distance runner who has long been an aficionado of audio books during his runs, called me. "Mom I am listening to the most intriguing new book. It's by a 102-year-old lady doctor. She talks just like you do about growing one's "juice" in order to fully embrace life. I think you'd enjoy it. I don't listen to too many books where the author reminds me of you. At the end she advises her readers to spend their energy wildly! Mom, I see you doing that."

I smiled as I clicked off my cell phone. Do I talk so strangely? I wondered as I Googled the author and ordered the book. I discovered that she is very much alive and still working! A few days later I was completely immersed in The Well Lived Life by Dr. Gladys McGarey, MD. She grew up in India in camps where her traveling missionary doctor parents ministered to the Untouchables. Gladys enjoyed a unique upbringing. She reports that when her mother passed away at a very old age, that Gladys could not really be sad because her mother lived a life filled with love and community and had accomplished everything she ever hoped for.

That thought has been roiling around in my mind. Dr. Gladys, as she is called, offers six secrets to a well-lived life which include meeting the world with love, and understanding the vast power of community; she says we are truly not alone, that life is about human connection. [Her secrets: We are here for a reason; All life needs to move; Love is the most powerful medicine; You are never truly alone; Everything is your teacher; Spend your energy wildly.

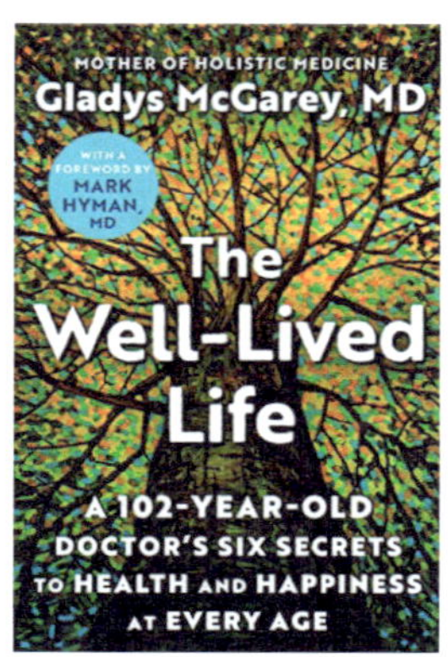

The other morning as I was trekking up a steep incline of the trail on my old horse, Gladys' ideas intruded into my consciousness; the power of the human connection. Gladys spent much of her career doctoring to people in Afghanistan and India. She tells of an experience when she was needed in the mountains of Afghanistan, reachable only by donkey. Though she was hardy she was concerned about the ride up a steep trail, after all, at that point she was 86 years old!

The donkey train started up the mountain and Gladys, precariously perched, was beginning to lean awkwardly off the side of the donkey. An Afghan woman seeing her wobbly plight rode up next to her and grabbed the only halter available, Gladys' bra strap, and held her steady to the top of the trail: the power of community. The women did not even speak the same language!

That story reminded me of one of my most profound travel moments when I too encountered a remarkable sisterhood in the most distant corner of Nepal in 2011. It occurred at the end of a seventeen-day trek through the lower Annapurna Mountains. The final activity of the trip was an elephant safari through the jungle of Chitwan National Park.

Our safari was to search out one-horned rhinos from a wooden perch atop each of three 11,000-pound female elephants. When the adventure was over the mahouts settled the three elephants in the four-foot-deep water of the river. Our guide asked if anyone wanted to sit on an elephant and be sprayed. The spraying was exciting until my elephant started to roll over onto her side. I quickly scrambled off and swam to shore. Later, when all of us had had our fill of being showered by the elephants, Raj, our trek leader said, "So does anyone want to clean the elephants?"

I had no idea what that meant. I waded back into the river to one of the elephants. Raj instructed us to splash water up onto their big backs and gently rub. I began. It was marvelous. Her dark grey hide was very thick and felt rough to my touch. She seemed to enjoy the attention. Before long, growing more confident, I trudged up to her head and began cleaning her enormous ear. I scrubbed rhythmically as she leaned into my touch. As I continued, I studied her beautiful thick eye lashes, the few graceful hairs on her head, and noted the look of contentment in the visible eye. She was so immense. It was wonderful. I could hardly take a breath for feeling the enormity of the moment I was sharing with her. She was still and relaxed. We both seemed to have moved into a kind of bliss. It lasted for long minutes.

After a while my fellow elephant cleaners were climbing out of the water through the mud onto the bank. The rain was coming down and we were all drenched and becoming chilled. Everyone headed back to camp but me. I was still absorbed in my elephant's beautiful head. Finally from the shore, Raj called, "So Donna are you staying?"

That pulled me from my reverie. "Could I?" I asked meekly.

Raj smiled as he replied, "Yes." The group then left while I lingered in the water, truly "soaking in" the experience and the magic. The elephant continued to lean into me and I into her.

Finally one of the trainers came back to help me climb up to shore. I headed up the riverbank to walk back to camp. I bumbled my way along for a while. I was somewhat dazed from being with the elephant, but I was in too much of a state of bliss to actually "get" that I was lost! I continued on. After a while I encountered three Terai women who were harvesting the crops. They saw immediately that I was disoriented. They giggled a bit at my expense. I see now that it was fairly funny. Here was this foreign lady in a soaking wet bathing suit wandering around the perimeter of a massive field, who was clearly lost!

The giggles continued as they gently turned me around and pointed me in the correct direction. We shared shy smiles. By this time I realized I was in a predicament. One lady pulled me in a bit closer and squeezed me in affection. It occurred to me that I was half-way around the planet in a foreign culture, being assisted by beautiful sari dressed women who were tending me as one of their own. We did not share language, or customs, but we did share a bond of human understanding.

That moment and Gladys' bra harness story remind me how much we need each other.

Dr. Gladys believes that when we look for the loving friend in others and spend our energy wildly in the act of living, that those behaviors are part of the secret to a well lived life. She says, "Aligning our life force with community…opens us up to possibilities we may never have considered. Life itself rises up to support us through community." Perhaps we could adopt a goal to live our lives with so much zeal and so fully that when our time is over the best thing our loved ones can say is "he or she lived their life wholly!"

There's No Time to Waste!

February 3, 2023

Recently, I was chatting with my older son Rick, telling him how remarkable my trail ride had been the other day when we encountered a pair of great snowy egrets who had not flinched as we lumbered by. It had astonished me. That reminded me of a rainy day dog walk at the beach last week when a formation of low flying pelicans blew by just over our heads! They had been so stunning that I had exclaimed out loud. I confessed to Rick that, oddly, I feel like I live in a state of constant amazement.

"Oh Mom you'd have loved the speaker we had at a recent firm retreat. He's bestselling author, John O'Leary. He's all about: really living, being fully awake, seeing being alive as living a miracle, and understanding that it is possible for one life to change the world."

Well, that had my attention. I ran out and bought his new book, On Fire, and have been enjoying it.

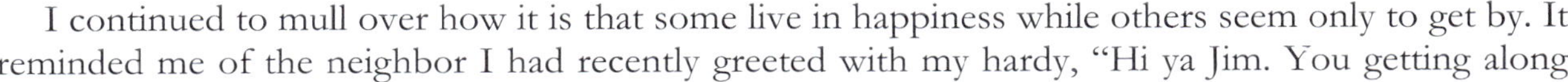

I continued to mull over how it is that some live in happiness while others seem only to get by. It reminded me of the neighbor I had recently greeted with my hardy, "Hi ya Jim. You getting along okay?" His reply was, "just barely." I thought about that. Hmmm. Then I considered some of the most exuberant people I know. What is their secret? I understood my own. Somehow early in my chaotic growing up years, I developed an ability to look past the ugly in my life and see beauty. I found a mental escape route that has become a lifetime habit.

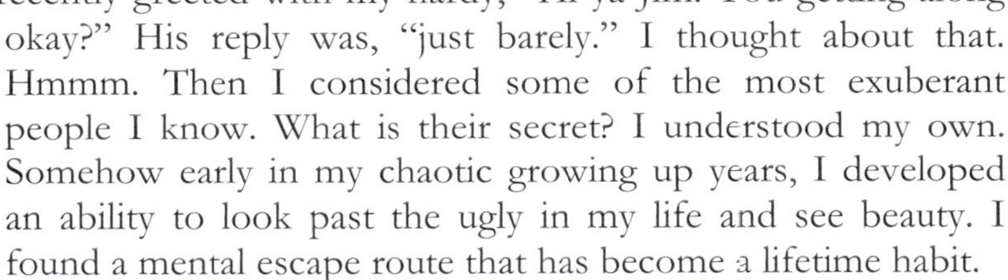

Perhaps it's a function of my recent very big 80th birthday, but lately I have been thinking there is no time to waste. You've not heard from me in some time because I've been helping my friends with health issues and have been attending far too many memorials. Somehow, all this has reminded me more than ever that now is our time on the planet; that there's not a minute to spare. I thought of some of the people in my life who seem to live fully.

One of the most positive and happy people I've known was my dog breeder friend, Linda Isaacson. For the past ten years I have had the pleasure of a most special friendship with her as she was as "gaga" over our golden retrievers as I. We were morning texting buddies, and it was she who was at the core of our crazy golden retriever summer swim parties. Linda found great happiness in everyday life with her family, friends, and certainly the stunts of our beautiful dogs. We exchanged a lot of photos and stories. She led a joyous life and was generous with sharing herself. We unexpectedly lost her in December. Through our deep sorrow, we find comfort in all the love and "Linda-isms" she shared with us. Of course all the while loving the wonderful golden retrievers she brought into the world.

Yesterday I heard from my former teaching colleague Olga Moran, thanking me for donating to her private charity which helps 35 very poor children in a village in Honduras. Olga is another joyous person, always with a smile. I called and asked about her happiness secret. She told me she loves people and years ago when she went home to Honduras she realized that the children in the village were so poor that they could never go to school. She wanted to help them. She began crocheting hats and baking apple cakes to sell to her friends in Zumba class to earn money for the children.

For thirteen years now she has been going to Honduras, taking back-packs filled with shoes, school uniforms, and supplies. It warms her soul. As we continued our conversation, she reminded me that her life has not been easy, she was born and raised in Honduras and came to America to make a life. She and her husband did that, building a family with two children, however, their daughter is mentally challenged and lives in a group home. Olga says that it has not been easy, there's been great difficulty, but her love of people, her constant enrollment in Zumba class, and her ability to give back to the poor children of Honduras, fill her with joy and a purpose. Olga is one person changing the world.

My friend James Littlejohn, Executive Director of the Capistrano Valley Boys and Girls Clubs, a man with a big smile, exudes happiness. He has been an inspiration to me for the twenty-two years we have been friends, as he's easily one of the most joyful people I have ever known. I asked James about that. He said, "Donna, I grew up black, the last of nine kids, in Alameda, California. My mom cleaned and we were on welfare. There were two significant triggers in my childhood. When I was seven years old my sister took me to the Boys and Girls Club and that was life changing for me. The Club gave me hope. When I was about nine years old I walked by a white lady's house. She called out to me, 'You have the most beautiful smile. You put joy in people's hearts.'

James recalled that the lady's comment caused his smile to grow bigger. He had no idea that he could bring joy to others. That compliment was huge in his young life and empowered him to understand that he could have a positive effect on others. It became a lifetime habit for him to express kindness and joy. James' work through the Boys and Girls Club has changed thousands of lives. I will tell you more about these remarkable people in the future.

My global travels have taught me that generally, when children have their basic needs met, their default way of living is in happiness. I recall stopping in the most primitive villages on the Ho Chi Minh Trail and visiting. I would climb out of our tour van and would be surrounded by giggling gangs of half-naked brown-eyed five and six-year-olds. I loved their curious eyes as they studied me. Pulling out my video camera, I would film short movies of them. When they saw themselves, more giggling would erupt. They were in ecstasy! Replaying them over and over, there was so much laughter! I could feel their delight and that of the adults we interacted with through our guides.

Daily, on my dog walks, I look into the faces of the other walkers and generally I see happy. We can choose happy. We can choose to live in amazement and gratitude. We can live purposeful lives. Perhaps as John O'Leary urges, we must remind ourselves to be fully awake to the miracle of being alive.

Keeping Our Eyes Wide Open!

February 22, 2015

Wednesday night I had the pleasure of being the guest of a robust and stimulating book club. The book up for discussion was my autobiography Cry the Darkness. Before long the animated conversation turned to human happiness. Given the enormity of my story, they truly wanted to know how it was possible that I have led a rich and happy life. They specifically were interested in tools for controlling anxiety and depression. As a student of neuroscience and positive psychology, I shared the concept that that we each have a rich internal life. New brain research reveals that we tell ourselves "stories" and it is possible to become mindful of those stories, and change the negative ones.

We can empower ourselves more fully with positive self-talk. In other words, it is possible to reframe a difficult situation from PROBLEM to OPPORTUNITY. If we live in an attitude of gratitude and surround ourselves with well evolved, positive people, feed ourselves properly, and exercise regularly, it can help add up to happiness. Dr. Csikszentmihalyi in his book, *Flow: The Psychology of Optimal Experience*, back in the 90's believed that if we are living through our purpose, involved with work that is meaningful to us, it is possible to achieve the FLOW process which yields satisfaction.

With all of that rolling around in my brain the next day, I set out on my favorite beach trail with the dogs and my wide-open eyes. I soon came upon John, a veteran of Desert Storm, who was busily creating one of those rock sculptures I have been admiring. We chatted. I returned to the walk and as I did I glanced out across the pounding surf to see a Tall Ship fully festooned with its magnificent sails flying high as it cruised along the shore! I stopped and admired its beauty as two of my walking buddies came along to say hi and pet the dogs. As we broke apart and the dogs and I continued, I realized that part of happiness is simply focusing on the beauty around us and finding joy in the simple things, in keeping our eyes wide open for them! I'd love to hear about something joyous you observed lately.

Piecing Together A Lifetime

March 17, 2015

On Sunday Dr. Zavala's Positive Living post included this quote, "For there are no ordinary moments. There are only precious feelings and memories we piece together one by one. We call it a lifetime," Leslie D. Stuart. Having spent a wonderful three-day weekend with my husband, oldest son, and three of his daughters racing the Catalina marathon and smaller races, I took it to heart.

Last week I was the guest on the KUCI radio show Real People OC hosted by Kimberlee Martin. During the hour-long interview many questions regarding my difficult childhood needed to be answered. She wanted the listeners to understand where I have come from in order to get a handle on who I am today. They were tough questions, taking me back to those horrible years.

On my own, hiking the trails of Catalina, I thought more about those questions and how that beginning has colored the who of me today. The best answer I can come up with is that the obstacles of my abuse and neglect have heightened my awareness and appreciation for all that is good and beautiful in the world. And so if I linger too long on the beauty of a sunset, the silly antics of my dogs, or the victories of my many grandchildren, it is because of this. I make no apologies. It is who I am today.

Rising to the Challenge

August 5, 2015.

The other day my friend Christine and I were riding our horses on the trail in the riverbed. We were serene as we chatted, striding along enjoying the power of the horses beneath us, as we breathed in the crisp morning air. We were slowly making our way back home when suddenly a horrendously loud bugle call interrupted the quiet, as it sounded at an adjacent construction site. The food truck had arrived. Instantly Mr. T, under Christine, reared his huge head to take off! As a retired racehorse his DNA must have activated an old memory. Right before our eyes he seemed to shed about twenty years as he morphed into his younger racing self; stomping, tossing his head, lunging and prancing, preparing for his imaginary starting gate.

Oh my goodness! I thought. Christine immediately went into emergency mode as she used all her strength to reign in the mighty thoroughbred, her own survival DNA activated. I was behind them on Pixie, who within a nanosecond also became energized. Both horses, agitated with adrenaline, were instantly prepared to run the race of their lives! The stomping, head tossing, strutting, and snorting continued. We reigned in. The intrusive bugle call sounded yet again! Knowing how dangerous it would be to let the horses have their way, we both pulled back with everything we had, fighting to stay in our saddles.

Overwrought with excitement, the horses' fierce instinct to race continued as we clomped our way home. Maintaining my forceful grip, my mind scanned back to another such experience, only that time I was actually competing in a community cross country horse race. I recalled the practice sessions on my Arabian horse, Windy. In the weeks leading up to the race, when I would arrive at her barn for practice, Windy would be electrified by excitement, her entire body shivering in readiness, her natural urges brought forth by the race. Still holding firm, I smiled recalling those racing days.

Safely back at the barn, Christine and I unsaddled our horses, exclaiming how sometimes out of nowhere a sudden challenge may present itself, and how important it is to be ready. During my teaching years, I saw it with my scared-to-death public speaking students. No matter how nervous they were, they rose to the challenge. I see it now with the widows in my Loss of a Loved One support group, no matter how devastated, they dig deep and find what it takes to go on. I see it with my clients facing the issues of aging and illness, who bravely look ahead. I realize that our own DNA, memories and experiences, must be embedded within and are at the ready when called upon. I admire the fact that we humans, on so many levels, are more prepared than we think. When the going gets tough, we seem to hang in there. New challenges are as close as the next corner, keeping us on our toes, but the happy news is that somehow we can meet them.

The Devastation Wrought by Tropical Storm Hilary

September 20, 2023

When Hurricane Hilary arrived in Southern California on August 20, 2023 as a tropical storm, we residents were as prepared for it as we could be. The news reports besieged us with the seriousness of it for days. My husband Ken, in fact thought the prognosticators were being overly alarmist. In any event, we were warned that a year's worth of rain could fall in a single event.

Down in the coastal regions of SoCal we mostly weathered the storm fairly well, however in the nearby San Bernardino Mountains, disaster befell those of us with residences along the Santa Ana River. The storm got stuck between the southern ridge of Big Bear's mountains and Highway 38 to the south. Perhaps eight inches of rain fell on the Santa Ana River watershed in a very short time. This resulted in a massive flashflood. There was the loss of one life, ruination of three county bridges, the public roads were torn away, and homes were lost. There was historic destruction to at least two mountain communities including ours. The roads, water and power were out for weeks. Due to security reasons, we did not share any of this on social media, though Channels 7 and 5 covered the stories as residents were helicoptered to safety.

Two weeks later, over the Labor Day weekend, my daughter, son-in-law, and I hiked in to survey our home and witness the results of Hilary's fury. We were relieved to find that our home was intact, though our community was not. After a while, we made our way on foot across the swift waters of the Santa Ana River and climbed up the steep banks carved out by the flashflood. We wanted to visit our nearby neighbors at Seven Oaks.

Our hike that day gave us a first-hand reminder of the enormous power of nature. Hurricanes, floods, fires, earthquakes and typhoons occur around the world with all too frequent regularity. We see the horror of it; just last week the tremendous loss of life due to flooding in Libya. That was on the heels of the disastrous earthquake in the Atlas Mountains of Morocco. For us, seeing Hilary's wrath focused on the Santa Ana River headwaters became an up-close and personally grim reminder of, not only the power of nature, but of the resilience of the human spirit. World aid has come to the African continent, and the first responders in the San Bernardino Mountains were unprecedented in their efficiency. Medics were helicoptered in to spend the night with the victims of Seven Oaks, at least four of whom had to be dug out of the mud.

On the day of our visit we chatted with those who had stayed behind at Seven Oaks to protect it and to feed the animals left behind. Living without power or water, their stories were heroic; of strength in the face of calamity.

Once back at our own mountain community known as Weesha, I had occasion to sit by myself on a rock to process everything I had witnessed. I sat next to a producing apple tree, long ago abandoned by the most serious flood of the last century, the massive flood of 1938. I sat with that little tree for some time. The forgotten tree seemed symbolic to me of the resilience and bravery shown by so many people across the globe in one horrendous situation or another. I felt compelled to write about that tree. It is written as a fairy tale. Ken and our son Rick found it moving. You might too. It is on Amazon if you care to read it. In the meantime, have you been inspired by the bravery exhibited by people you know?

What Matters Most?

November 19. 2019

Last year my favorite county beach was destroyed by high surf. The result was that it was closed for over a year. The damaged public restrooms and parking meters were removed, and a wall of massive boulders was installed to push back the surf.

Of course, that just meant that I had to drive further away for my frequent dog walks. A week ago, I finally returned to discover free parking and that dogs are now allowed in the surf during the winter months. I have been ecstatic about this after a lifetime of NO DOGS ALLOWED.

Today, having a free morning, I packed my pups into the Jeep and we were soon frolicking in the enticing but cold waves. After a while, we continued on our walk, where I encountered my friend Randy. I regaled him with my excitement about going in the ocean with the dogs. Randy smiled as he listened and then explained, "You know Donna as we get older, it's the little things that matter the most."

We said our goodbyes, and as the dogs and I walked along, I pondered what Randy had said. Mulling over his remark, I looked up as a gang of Stroller Warriors, maybe 20 mothers and fathers pushing strollers, rolled past me. I grinned at one of the mothers. She had a small child perched on her left hip and was pushing another in a stroller. I wondered if she, caught up in the noise of raising two very small children, could in any way fathom how precious her act of exercising with her family and friends was? I thought maybe, maybe not. I felt a lump in my throat for those long-ago days when my stroller was full of two children with a third tagging behind me, which for me today, is remembered as beautiful music. Surely, these small, every day, acts must not only be appreciated in retrospect?

I continued on, grateful for the two golden retrievers at my side, thinking about Randy's words. It is our ability to assign value to the commonplace that can make a difference: from ordinary to extraordinary...Certainly, dogs in the surf is a small thing, but I am over the moon about it!

I thought about the ordinary. A few hours earlier, for the first time in the two months that my mother's cats have resided in the cattery in our backyard, I was able to hold both of them. Not a very big deal, except that these two old scaredy cats would not even let me see them during the first five weeks of their residency at our home. After a while they would be out where I could see them and not run away, and now they actually let me hold them! I see value in that ordinary act of petting two cats.

If you have been following my posts, you know that I have been struggling with the big changes in my mother's life. Moving her into assisted living, her unhappiness with it, clearing out her big home, preparing it for sale, and then selling it, all have played havoc with my peace of mind. I have been practicing mindfulness and learning more techniques in the area of creating a sacred, still inner space. I am having some success, minimizing the anxiety which has seized me during all this tumult.

Wellness guru Deepak Chopra has a new book out, Meta Human: Unleashing Your Infinite Potential. In the book, Chopra encourages us to discover our inner stillness so that we can heal ourselves. I haven't read his book yet, but I have been looking into the notion of inner quiet. Chopra's "stillness" is the journey into ourselves for the purpose of achieving an inner silence. If you recall from my previous mentions of the brain studies, our brain often jumps from thought to thought like a crazed monkey, or as David Rock says in Your Mind at Work, like a "sniffing puppy." The trick is to focus with enough concentration to stop that kind of random mental skipping. For me, the problem has been my old pattern of trying to "fix" whatever is not okay with my mother. Of course I cannot fix ill health, old age, blindness and immobility. My challenge is to find a way to still the problem-solving part of my brain that keeps working on the issues.

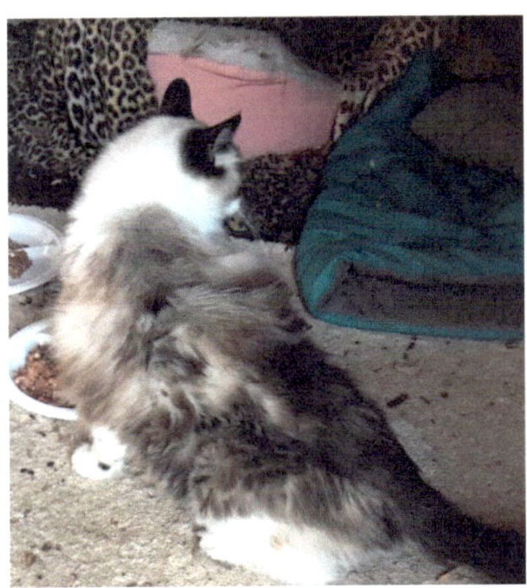

I am learning to follow guided meditation through an app on my phone. I have been making "dates" with myself to sit quietly with the intention of calming myself. I am working on being present in the moment, giving my full awareness to what is occurring in my head and then steering my thoughts back to the "now" and striving to create stillness. When I am able to do this, I feel a warm flush of peace entering my system.

I know that being able to ease my anxiety allows me to be more resilient and more prepared for what comes in the future. For now I am going to continue to revel in taking Lacey and Dixie into the surf, in holding my mother's fluffy cats, and in admiring the young moms rolling past me at the beach. I am celebrating the ordinary, for the fact that oftentimes I find these things to be extraordinary.

Our Days in the Sun: Kicking the Worry Habit

February 25, 2016

Always on the look-out for precious moments, I caught one this morning while the dogs and I were strolling through the park. The rising sun blinded us to the vehicles coming into the overflow parking lot by the park which serves the high school. We waited as a big SUV passed by. As it turned in front of us, I saw my beautiful angel granddaughter, Emily, behind the wheel, my first time to see her driving since she got her license last week. My heart did a little flip and the dogs and I scrambled over to greet her. We walked her to the path, hugged goodbye, and as she set off for her day and I for mine, I was left bathed in love. I had been listening to Barbara Streisand's Memories from Cats on my Ipod where the poor ancient cat laments that all she has left are her memories of her days in the sun. I had been thinking about the fact that we are living our "days in the sun" when I saw Emily. It seems essential to our wellbeing that we revel in them. Several of my clients cancelled their coaching appointments with me this week because they had not taken the steps forward to which they had committed. They were stalled by self-pity, worry, and anxiety.

It is easy to fall prey to the paralyzing effects of worry. To worry is to torment one's self with disturbing thoughts. When we are in a state of anxiety and worry it is hard to appreciate the gifts in life, let alone the precious moments. In Mallika Chopra's book, Living with Intent, she confesses that, "I spin the busyness into chaos by worrying about the future and rehashing the past...could it be that my concern about an unbalanced life is a self-created myth-one I perpetuate by overdramatizing the bad things and under appreciating the good?" I think the answer is "yes" to Mallika and it goes for my clients as well. They are in the worry habit.

Next week I am speaking on "Growing Happiness" to 85 moms. I'm going to remind them of the power of positive habits, that our behavior is a reflection of our thoughts, and that our brains like the status quo. In order to break the dreadful cycle of worry, we must decide to either change our attitude(move to gratefulness), our beliefs (I'm lucky to be alive in America!), or our actions (I'm taking steps forward today!)

We can grow happiness by changing our ways, by learning to say "no" when necessary; by "eating the big frog first" which means to do the chore you hate the most first; to stop procrastinating. Another way is to eliminate meaningless time stealers, and to clear your mind before you go to bed by making a list of what needs to be done the next day instead of troubling your sleep with it. It is possible to be happier, to experience the joy of our days in the sun but worry and anxiety will rob us of the exhilaration of seeing that smile on a young girl's face, or catching the sweetness of certain moments, if we let them. This is our time, let's keep our happiness tanks full to the brim!

A Hundred Year Challenge'

January 20. 2024

Hi, happy belated New Year! I've been receiving a few "where are you?" "Where'd you go?" notes lately. Last August when that hurricane, turned tropical storm, Hilary hit SoCal it devastated the upper Santa Ana River basin in the San Bernardino Mountains and nearby desert communities. It swept away roads, bridges, homes, and a human life. I understood that it was a historic flood. Ken and I have owned a cabin on the river for 50 years. It was very personal to me, and I felt compelled to capture it through the written word, resulting in six weeks of researching and writing. Then the holidays were upon us and last Sunday we celebrated my mother's 100th birthday. My sister and I hosted a beautiful event with live music, a buffet fit for a queen, and 85 of her friends and family. Mom reports that it exceeded her wildest dreams.

I had the pleasure of sharing highlights of her long and interesting life. In thinking about my remarks, my thoughts naturally turned back to my own childhood, circa 1950. An image emerged of being in the chorus of such operas as Regalletto while our mom, the lead soprano for the Santa Monica Civic Opera Association, sang her heart out as Gilda, alone on the stage in the spotlight. It was a culturally unique way to grow up. The reflections led me to research what life is like for centenarians. My musings set me on a path to thinking about what kind of future I want to create for myself.

I had been toying with the idea of having my groceries delivered. I have now scrubbed that idea as I reframe the whole idea of lifting the heavy bags and carrying them up my stairs. Now I see this task as essential weight training. Reframing is looking at things in a new way. Perhaps instead of lamenting our limitations, we focus on all the things we can still do.

The ladies in my Pilates class recently told me about the Netflix documentary The Blue Zone which examines the five places on the planet which have the most centenarians. It has inspired me to walk up more hills and reduce my sugar consumption. I had been working on that when my historian friend, Pam Gibson, recommended a new book she was reading: Outlive: The Science and Art of Longevity by Peter Attia, M.D. Fifty year old Dr. Attia is a

marathon swimmer, having swum from the mainland to Catalina; a surgeon, and a man set on living well as long as possible, hoping for 100. He builds a case backed up by the newest research showing a path forward as we age. A path that could allow us to be at our vital best. He calls it "health span." I am at the section in the book where he challenges us to create a Centenarian Decathlon of physical challenges as we age. His "Centenarian Decathlon" is a framework to use to organize our aspirations for our future years. It is a list of the most important physical tasks we want to be able to do for the rest of our lives. It is a lot about exercise and smart nutrition. Anyway, I have mentally enrolled myself in it! I intend to be a finisher.

Each year at my annual physical exam my doctor, Dr. Lo, asks me the required Medicare questions: "Donna, can you put your bra on by yourself?"

"Dr. Lo, I am riding my horses every week."

Laughing, he replies, "I am required to ask these."

"Donna, can you use the restroom unassisted?"

"Dr. Lo I walk my three huge golden retrievers two miles every day!" He chuckles again and it continues like that…"I have to ask."

I smile and roll my eyes. However, these Medicare questions highlight the very serious physical limitations which most often accompany old age. In preparing the remarks for my mother's event I learned that only 1 in 6000 Americans arrive at their 100th birthday. That is about .00002 percent of the population with no consideration as to what shape those persons are in. The United Nations defines anyone 60 years or over as "older." Some studies distinguish between the young-old (60-69), the middle old (70-79) and the very old, (80+). Apparently, I have already arrived at VERY OLD…NOT!

At its core, The Blue Zone documentary is five episodes of pure inspiration. It is something of a travelogue as well as a show stuffed full of astounding human examples of centenarians who are thriving! I nearly swooned watching a 103-year-old Costa Rican man on his tall white horse guiding an unruly herd of big horned steers into a corral. I couldn't stop grinning as a Japanese woman past 100 shimmied and swayed in a dance for the camera while balancing a bottle on her head. I enjoyed the eighty-somethings on the pickle ball courts of Loma Linda, California. My husband, Ken, tells me that in his alumni class notes for Occidental College class of 1964, that 25% report playing pickleball with regularity!

It's a new year. We are on Flight 2024. Maybe now is a good time to think about what more we can do to mobilize our strength and maintain our vitality so that when we arrive at the next destination, we are prepared to meet its challenges. I for one am excited about the Centenarian Decathlon. Maybe we can do it together? Here is a list of some of my goals:

- Walk my dogs a half hour a day.
- Lift up my future great grandchildren.
- Live in my two-story home
- Open jars
- Bathe my dogs.
- Travel on an airplane.
- Walk up the hill to my home.
- Put on my bra!

I would love to hear your ideas and plans for the Centennial Decathlon. My email is Donna@yourtimenow.org.

The Little Engine that Could!

November 14, 2021

Generally, I pride myself on being fairly well evolved in terms of my inner life, but recently I have caught myself believing some internal messages that limited my behavior in a negative way. I am guilty of some bad thinking. Ugh. I hate to admit it, but it is true.

Last time I wrote to you, I had discovered yoga through an experience with my daughter and three granddaughters at Goat-Llama yoga. The takeaway from that day was that perhaps there was something to this whole yoga thing. That was 43 days ago and I have enjoyed at least one yoga practice each day since then. What have I learned? I realize now with a back that no longer aches and a new spring in my step, that I was influenced by an inner constraint. I had told myself that the exercise I got with the dog walks, horses, mucking, and such was enough. Well maybe it was, but it was NOT enough for my back. I had limited my behavior with a "I am exercising enough" message. However, I had a tendency to stoop over and my lower back hurt a lot of the time, so there was a need for more. Enough exercise was limiting belief number one which I am rectifying by continuing yoga.

My sister-in-law, Kassie, further inspired me when she shared that she had 250 straight days of yoga and recommended Adriene's Yoga channel on YouTube. This has been life changing for me. Adriene offers a meditative experience encouraging her participants to set an intention each day. This is not to suggest that there have not been some obstacles to my daily practice; when I began and the dogs were in the living room with me, River, the puppy, thought that because I was on the floor that we were going to wrestle. Well, that did not work. I locked the dogs up. Today when I turned Adriene on my Ipad, the kittens were about. It did not take Apollo but a minute to jump on my back during "Table Top" pose. Not being one to give up, I ignored him. When Adriene had us move to "Mountain," I was

startled as the five-month-old kitten jumped all the way up to my chest, grabbing hold of my shirt. I staggered a bit, realizing this was not all that productive, as I pressed on. I felt like that Little Engine in the children's story, The Little Engine that Could, as I bravely moved through my poses, thinking, "I think I can, I know I can." Finally, I realized that Kitten Yoga is not my jam. I am locking them up tomorrow.

The next limiting message I have been hearing in my head is, "You don't need to travel any more, you've seen everything. On the last three small group adventures you were the oldest one. It's time to hang it up." I was so cozy at home during the pandemic lockdown with Ken and the animals, enjoying our rural environs, that I had decided enough was enough. I'd stay home in the future. However, I had that Iceland trip planned, paid for, and postponed for two years, so when Iceland opened in September, my daughter-in-law, Jenny, and I went on the trip.

A few days into the expedition I found myself on an amphibious boat cruising around a lake stuffed with ice bergs in the south of Iceland. Hmm. It occurred to me then and has stayed with me, that perhaps I have not seen everything, there is still so much more out there. I certainly had NOT been in an amphibious boat chasing huge pieces of glacier. So, I have booked a trip to the Maritime Provinces of Canada for next June and I am investigating kayaking in the Arctic Ocean.

The point is that we can create life limiting thoughts in our heads, and then act upon them in a way that shrinks our human experience. I was chatting with my husband, Ken, about this and he shared that he sees the effect of negative self-talk on his high school girl wrestlers all the time. He observes girls who must walk off the mat in mid match because they have succumbed to a panic attack. He must constantly work to help them overcome their limiting belief that they are "not good enough." Their negative thoughts paralyze them. This contrasts with his other athletes who seem fearless, listening to internal messages such as "go for it!" or "what do I have to lose?"

Our internal world has a profound influence on our behavior, and often times it is unconscious. Once again, I am reminded of that Little Engine as he sets off up that daunting hill, "I think I can, I think I can…"

Maybe we can take a lesson from that Little Engine. "I know I can, I know I can, and I know that I do not need to listen to my limiting thoughts when they infiltrate my behavior." What limiting messages have you had to overcome? What messages are still plaguing you? You know I love to hear what you are thinking.

Fire Drill!

September 23, 2020

Ah it's Fall! I know you are staying safe, and you were probably isolating a lot during what seemed like an endlessly long hot summer. Such a weird time in our lives!

A week or so ago Ken and I had settled down to watch our favorite Netflix show on a Saturday night about 8 p.m. when we got a call. Four of our granddaughters were on their own for the weekend as their parents were out of town. A brush fire had broken out across the street from their property and the main road into their development was lined with more than a dozen fire engines. Authorities were stopping any traffic in or out of their community. The loud water dropping helicopters were racing back and just above the girls' home earnestly trying to stop the fire. At the same time, the West Coast of the USA was pretty much on fire and we were all in hyper-vigilance mode.

The youngest (15 year-old) sister was starting to freak out for obvious reasons! Her older sisters made the decision to ease her anxiety by calling us, the grandparents, and getting her out of there! Of course they were welcome to evacuate to our home.

Within thirty minutes, the girls had filled three cars with nine chickens, two dogs, two cats (one feral in a cage), a turtle and two snakes, and arrived at our home. Luckily, Ken had built a cattery for my mother's cat which has since found a home. The chickens quickly took over that space. The dogs were nestled in my large home office, while the girls settled the cats. The snakes and turtle remained confined (much to our relief) as we recalled raising our own family with snakes and guinea pigs sometimes living under the dishwasher or behind a drapery! Settled into beds, the youngest began to relax. Ken and I finished our show. Within a few hours the firefighters had the brush fire under control and the immediate danger had passed.

What has stayed with us across these days since the alarming event is the behavior of our four granddaughters. This had been a for real fire drill and they performed like a well

trained Army Special Forces unit. The fifth and oldest daughter, Jill, who lives elsewhere, dropped her plans and hurried to her sisters. She talked to the sheriff, and they had agreed that the girls should evacuate. Jill saw the girls to our home. Knowing her sisters were safe, Jill left.

Preparing to leave, the four evacuees tended to first things first. There was no bickering or questioning the steps in the evacuation. The first order of business had been the well-being of their youngest sibling. Next, valuables, jewelry, photo albums, computers, animals, and essential clothing were stuffed into the vehicles. Upon arrival at our house, the reverse order; securing the many animals and organizing sleeping arrangements. While one sister found a litter box and set up the cats with water and food, another walked the dogs on the back lawn. It was almost as if they had prepared for this for years. Each found a task and carried it out.

One incident particularly impressed me. Our 20-year-old Emily, future veterinarian, who has been taming the feral cat, considered allowing it out of the cage into a closed bedroom. Megan, at 23, was a capable general. She decreed, "No, the cat will be better off in its carrier overnight." Emily, the lieutenant in charge of animals, deferred to her older sister. No push back.

Animals and girls and even grandparents got through the night without further event. The girls didn't sleep much, but they knew they were safe and had done all they could in such an emergency.

For our part, as the older generation, we often worry about the future of our fragile civilization and our precious planet, and then something like this emergency happens and the youngsters step up. Whether they are saving themselves, fighting wars, fighting wildfires, or policing our cities, we see that they come through. I personally feel humbled by the competency of the younger ones coming up behind me.

Once we were the youth. I recall a Spanish teacher in high school telling our class that we were "the do nothing generation." That stayed with me. We were only sixteen years old. That seemed a rude thing to say to us, considering we were barely getting our driver's licenses! As the decades unfolded, my generation and those behind us, saw to some of the important human rights and environmental changes ever known. We were not a "do nothing generation."

During this global lockdown I had so much time on my hands that I looked back at my growing up years and have written about it. *Growing Up Venice: Parallel Universes* is now available at Amazon in Kindle, paperback and hardcover color formats.

In this book, which is the history of some lost aspects of Los Angeles/Venice history, I share my lived experience on the oceanfront in Venice. I grew up during the 1940's, side by side, with a working oil well in one of the most productive oil fields in California. My story visits the Holocaust and Bolshevik survivors who lined the benches along the boardwalk in Venice, the Gambling Ships in Santa Monica Bay, the arrival of the Beat Generation to the Gas House, and the subsequent Hippie invasion. We journey through time past the amusement piers, to the new ethos of Venice, the craziest beach in the world, and to Silicon Beach, a new home to the electronics industry. You might enjoy my tale, certainly a love story is woven through it.

They'll Eat You for Breakfast!

January 19, 2016

Last week on my dog walk, I encountered a woman whom I've briefly chatted with across the years, a woman in her forties who has a nice little dog. As we exchanged pleasantries, I shared that I was excited because my new horse was arriving later in the day. She looked at me and said, "You should not be on a horse." Dumbfounded and perhaps, for once, speechless, I mumbled my goodbyes and the dogs and I continued on.

Really? I thought as I processed that negative transaction and unsolicited dictate. For all she knows I am a world renown trick rider, a rodeo queen, racing champion of the west....I continued to mull over her invasion of my psychological boundary as other such instances came to mind. I recalled my young lady doctor telling me I could not do cartwheels for my granddaughter. "Why not?" I responded. "Because of your age!" She countered. "What's wrong with my age?" Well, that conversation went nowhere! Another time I was having my hair done and was telling the hairdresser about the trip I was taking to Egypt. From a few chairs down a man interrupted and insisted, "You'll be killed. Your family will miss out on you. They take hostages and then you will be killed!" *Who was he anyway?*

Have you had this experience of others around you working hard to reduce the scope of your world?

A basic tenet of communication theory and effective human relationships is that one should never give unsolicited advice. Never! Advice should only be offered when others ask for it, or when one has asked permission, such as asking, "So do you want my take on this situation?" Only then. But in the instances I have cited, those people were not offering advice, they were giving out dictates. Ugh!

Dr. George Bach in his wonderful book, *Stop! You're Driving Me Crazy*, teaches about mind rape, the strategy wherein others force their way into our head and tell us what to do or what we are thinking or feeling. Dr. Bach believes they pull this stuff on us due to their own chronic low self-esteem. By trying to somehow lower us, they are attempting to raise themselves up. They place themselves in a position of one-up, telling us what is best for us. This is passive/aggressive behavior. It includes elements of the psychological game called "Blemish," where the instigator strives to put a blemish, a negativity, on another. If confronted they will fall back on something like, "you are afraid to look at the truth," or "you are in denial." When you think about it, it takes a lot of nerve for someone to butt into our business! These crazy makers are incredibly annoying, but perhaps using Dr. Bach's lens and seeing that they are toxic people, we can better insulate ourselves from their invasiveness.

One of the most interesting classes I have ever taken was at UC Irvine with Dr. Robert Bramson, author of *Coping with Difficult People*. One day in class I asked him about a toxic person I was forced to interact with. He heard me out and then said, "She'll eat you for breakfast!" Yikes I had thought, I know... His advice: work to keep away from the toxic difficults! My best thinking, when you encounter one on the dog trail, just smile and keep on walking!

Being Pulled in All Directions

December 8, 2015

Early the other morning my dogs and I were coming out of the field where they had been running free, heading home. As I cinched their leashes on, I noticed a woman struggling with her two big dogs. Each dog was pulling her hard in the opposite direction. She noticed me and crossed the street to keep away from us. Clearly she did not want the dogs to meet. I had Adele crooning to me from my Ipod and did not think much about her, though I could hear her yelling through my music. My group kept up our pace as the noisy skirmish continued across the street. Finally she halted and called to me. I unplugged my ear buds and smiled as she called out, "I want your dogs! Mine are stubborn. This one wants to walk in the middle of the street!"

My dogs paused politely as I, ever helpful, asked, "Did you ever try a pinch collar?" The dialogue continued for a few more sentences until she again stumbled forward with her recalcitrant duo. I plugged back in. My brown eyed doggies looked at me as if to say, "Oh my, they have bad behavior."

As my grand girls as I decorated the tree my mind went back to that woman being pulled in every direction. Her morning walk was anything but an enjoyable meditative experience in the crisp morning air. If the holidays are beginning to have you feeling like you are being pulled in ways you'd rather not be pulled, now is a good time for a boundary check.

An important aspect of healthy living is to respect your own personal boundaries and the boundaries of others. If one is not taught to set boundaries he or she might not even be aware when they are being violated. I know that we don't like it when someone in a doctor's office sits down next to us when there are a dozen open seats available. Our psychological boundaries are like that as well. We feel uncomfortable when others cross them by telling us what we should think or how we should feel or have us agreeing to things we do not want to do. Here are a few simple tests to check the state of your boundaries:

1. Do others behave as if I don't have a life?
2. Is "no" unknown in my vocabulary?

3. Do others take my belongings without asking?
4. Am I afraid to tell my loved ones the truth, which is that I don't want to?
5. Do people ask me to do little things which I resent doing, but I do them anyway?
6. Do my family members expect me to drop everything when they need something done?
7. Do I feel guilty even considering not doing what everyone else wants?
8. Do I sometimes dread the holidays because I don't get to do what I want?
9. Am I taking care of everyone but myself?
10. Is it bothering me thinking about this?

If you answered "yes" to some of these questions it could be that your personal boundaries have become blurred with some of the people in your life. If the holidays are beginning to have you feeling like you are being pulled in ways you'd rather not be pulled, now is a good time for a boundary check. It is an important step toward self-care to protect yourself. You don't want to be like the woman with her unruly dogs, being pulled in every direction. This is your time; you are in charge of your life. Our happiness is up to us. My hope for you is that this holiday season is rich with joy and blessings.

Rising to the Challenge

August 5, 2015

The other day my friend Christine and I were riding our horses on the trail in the riverbed. We were serene as we chatted, striding along enjoying the power of the horses beneath us, as we breathed in the crisp morning air. We were slowly making our way back home when suddenly a horrendously loud bugle call interrupted the quiet, as it sounded at an adjacent construction site. The food truck had arrived. Instantly Mr. T, under Christine, reared his huge head to take off! As a retired racehorse his DNA must have activated an old memory. Right before our eyes he seemed to shed about twenty years as he morphed into his younger racing self; stomping, tossing his head, lunging and prancing, preparing for his imaginary starting gate.

Oh, my goodness! I thought. Christine immediately went into emergency mode as she used all her strength to reign in the mighty thoroughbred, her own survival DNA activated. I was behind them on Pixie, who within a nanosecond also became energized. Both horses, agitated with adrenaline, were instantly prepared to run the race of their lives! The stomping, head tossing, strutting, and snorting continued. We reigned in. The intrusive bugle call sounded yet again! Knowing how dangerous it would be to let the horses have their way, we both pulled back with everything we had, fighting to stay in our saddles.

Overwrought with excitement, the horses' fierce instinct to race continued as we clomped our way home. Maintaining my forceful grip, my mind scanned back to another such experience, only that time I was actually competing in a community cross country horse race. I recalled the practice sessions on my Arabian horse, Windy. In the weeks leading up to the race, when I would arrive at her barn for practice, Windy would be electrified by excitement, her entire body shivering in readiness, her natural urges brought forth by the race. Still holding firm, I smiled recalling those racing days.

Safely back at the barn, Christine and I unsaddled our horses, exclaiming how sometimes out of nowhere a sudden challenge may present itself, and how important it is to be ready. During my teaching years, I saw it with my scared-to-death public speaking students. No matter how nervous they were, they rose to the challenge. I see it now with the widows in my Loss of a Loved One support group, no matter how devastated, they dig deep and find what it takes to go on. I see it with my clients facing the issues of aging and illness, who bravely look ahead. I realize that our own DNA, memories, and experiences, must be embedded within and are at the ready when called upon. I admire the fact that we humans, on so many levels, are more prepared than we think. When the going gets tough, we seem to hang in there. New challenges are as close as the next corner, keeping us on our toes, but the happy news is that somehow, we can meet them. I would love to hear about your challenges.

"Neither Sticks nor Stones…"

March 2, 2015

I am looking forward this week to the monthly meeting of the Loss of a Loved One support group which I facilitate, as well as the kick-off to a new ten week class for Women in Transition through Womansage. As the life coach for these programs, my brain is gearing up to lend a hand. I know that life has thrown these women some curve balls. I know they are often nervous, scared, and excited to begin their self-actualizing journey. As my ideas come into focus, I recall some of Kathy Guzman's thoughts in her article I found online, "Against All Odds" in which she points out:

To stand alone in the sunny meadow - facing the sun and living a peaceful existence while there are stones being thrown at you from the shadows - is a test of courage and fortitude that we must all be prepared to experience. The actions that others take are out of our control... Sometimes, in our own stillness, we can find the strength to push through - without scars and nightmarish recollections - but rather with dignity, pride and the certainty that sticks and stones are just that -sticks and stones - and they will not dent the armor that is our true character.

Her words take me back to the 1970's when Dr. Eric Berne's "I'm Okay-You're Okay" ideas were just becoming popular. For some months I flew to Sacramento to a place called The Frog Pond for weekend classes to master Dr. Berne's skill set. In one class the leader was talking away when suddenly a student stood up and screamed, "You don't know what you're talking about! You're a fake, an imposter! I have wasted my money taking this program!"

We class members were dumbfounded. We'd never before seen such behavior! As we looked more closely at the shouter, we noticed that he was wrapped from head to toe in white muslin. Across his chest was huge glittery sign that read: Certified Crazy Person. We glanced to the leader to see his reaction. He was laughing out loud. It was a gag!

They were illustrating a new interpersonal skill; that when people say mean things (sticks and stones) we must learn to REFRAME their toxic behavior and turn it around.

We must negate their power. We can secure our armor in place by discounting whatever horrible thing has been said or done. That stunning role play has stayed with me across the years. When my clients are hurt by the verbal jabs from others I remind them to reframe it, to find confidence in their own dignity. It is one of the techniques for becoming mindful; taking control of our reactions and emotions so that we are not blown away by others. Eleanor Roosevelt used to say, "Remember no one can make you feel inferior without your consent." She understood that we must take control of our feelings, instead of simply reacting. You know the blindsides will come, of course they will, we live in the world. They add to our education and strengthen our character. It is in these moments that we grow and come to understand who we are, and how important it is that we center ourselves to live in peace. We are far tougher than we may realize.

Holiday Resolution: More Fun and Less Fuss

November 5, 2015

Last week I was standing in line at Vons when I realized that the music playing was Jingle Bells. As the others around me groaned, the lady in front of me lamented, "It isn't even Thanksgiving yet! I feel so much pressure!" I smiled with her as I considered this common sentiment.

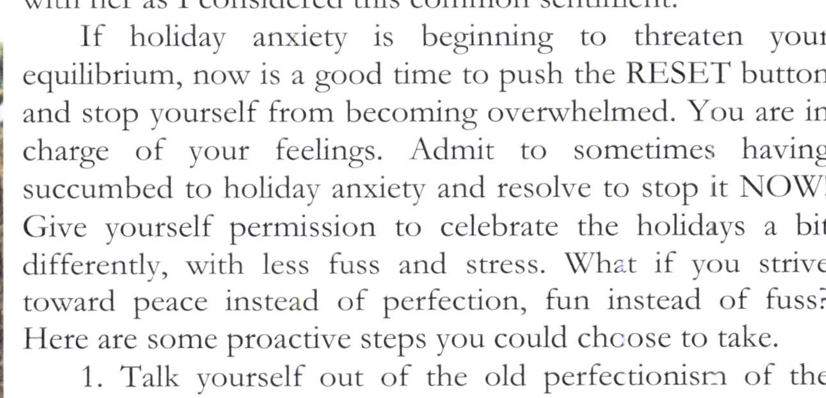

If holiday anxiety is beginning to threaten your equilibrium, now is a good time to push the RESET button and stop yourself from becoming overwhelmed. You are in charge of your feelings. Admit to sometimes having succumbed to holiday anxiety and resolve to stop it NOW! Give yourself permission to celebrate the holidays a bit differently, with less fuss and stress. What if you strive toward peace instead of perfection, fun instead of fuss? Here are some proactive steps you could choose to take.

1. Talk yourself out of the old perfectionism of the past. Just because you have done things a certain way forever does not mean that you have to continue. What parts of your rituals could be trimmed away or changed all together? My single friends enjoy "Pie for breakfast," a Thanksgiving tradition where everyone brings a pie and from 9-12 a.m. they enjoy fellowship and pie. Any angst of being alone on Thanksgiving is banished.

2. If the holidays are a painful reminder of the past, change up what you do. Plan ahead by becoming proactive to protect yourself: visit a mission, take a trip, greet people in the hospital, go to church.

3. Start today and make lists for gifts, food, shopping, and events to attend, so that you do not have to keep all of that in your head. Slowly chip away at your list.

4. You are allowed to say "No." Take care of yourself by declining invitations and expectations that are just too much for you.

One of the most meaningful books I ever read was *Chasing Daylight: How My Forthcoming Death Transformed My Life*, by Eugene O'Kelly. O'Kelly was a man who stopped for nothing, go go go! He made millions and flew hundreds of thousands of miles a year, missing out on a personal family life. When he learned at age forty that he had just weeks to live, he transformed his life. His last weeks were his best because he stopped and appreciated life. He said, "I collected more precious moments in those weeks than in all the previous years of my life." He learned how to really live life. Kris Allen's song, Live Like You Are Dying, carries the same message. Now is our time. It seems a waste to spend it wigged out because we have allowed too much to be on our plates or we are mired in grief over the past.

I don't think happiness is found spinning around, faster and faster on a treadmill. I think happiness is found through a life of gratitude, through feeling hopeful, by taking time to reflect on the positive in the world, and by taking care of ourselves. The holidays do not have to be a marathon of shopping, wrapping, too many parties and fatigue. They can be a time of peace and joy as we celebrate this wonderful life we have been given and our many blessings. Happy Thanksgiving!

So Maybe There <u>ARE</u> Limits

May 7, 2014

Husband Ken and I had a reality check Sunday as we completed our 13.1-mile Orange County Half-Marathon event. The story began a year ago when our son Rick and Ken challenged any of our grandchildren to complete their first marathon. With rewards in mind, Jake and Jill completed theirs last year, this year Megan, turning 17 years old and younger sis, Emily, were up for the challenge. It was a lot of fun participating with our grandkids, so Ken and I were in. As a daily power walker, I thought little of it as we signed up, paid our entry fees, and took the girls the day before to pick up race packets and go to dinner; little of it. In fact, I teased the girls about "carbo-loading" as I ate a salad and a half tuna sandwich sans any bread.

As in the past six half marathons I have competed in, I got up at 4:00 a.m., ate a scrambled egg, tied my shoes on my feet and, with Ken, met up in the dark of early morning with son Rick and his two girls. The gun went off and Rick and Megan began their full marathon. An hour later our starting pistol sounded and Ken, Emily, and I began our half-marathon. We soon spread out; I in my ipod zone.

As the miles clicked by, I admired the beautiful Corona State Beach, Newport Harbor, and the sunrise, all the while keeping up my usual steady power walking pace of four-miles an hour. As I passed mile ten, I noticed that I was not interacting with the many cheering us on along the way as is my habit, nor was I now jogging past my competitors. Still, I thought little of it, hoped Ken was right behind me and ate my three snacks. It was a lovely race, even though my legs were starting to complain. It was not until I was across the finish line that the troubles began.

I hear my Ironmen sons complain of 'BONKING,' but they do such huge events, it did not occur to me that I could do the same. The finisher medal was placed around my neck, and I made it about ten steps to a table along the fence of the corral, where suddenly I was over taken by nausea, dizziness, and white lights in front of my eyes. I knew that was not good. I sat.

Ken came in ten minutes behind me and experienced more of the same. This was a big lesson for us. We were blasé about the event, overly confident, and did not consider the seriousness of power walking over 13 miles in the heat, at our age. One of the causes of "Bonking" is depletion of the blood-glucose levels. I had snacks but they were not carbs. Ken had no snacks.

Recovered the next day, Ken studied the race results: the event raised three million dollars for charity, 22,000 people participated, only .37 % of all the contenders were 70 years or over. HMM..........maybe our age mates are more realistic, set more feasible goals, and do not take chances with pressing the limits, or at least they CARB LOAD THE NIGHT BEFORE!!

Our grand girls easily finished the event, loved it and said, "this is just the beginning of their running life." For Donna and Ken, we enjoyed participating with the family, but we learned a big lesson about being overly confident and the importance of one's fuel.

A Wise Person Chooses His Battles!

April 16, 2014

My husband and I are caring for our grand dog Buddy while our youngest son and his family explore western Canada. Last night I let Buddy and our three dogs out one last time before bed. For a moment all four dogs seemed to disappear into the inky darkness. Suddenly there was a noisy scuffle. I turned on the powerful outdoor light and saw that Buddy had caught a skunk; a very big black and white skunk! Quickly, realizing what he had caught, he released it, and in that instant it turned its huge and fluffy tail toward him and let loose! Horrified by what he had done and the stickiness of the odorific spray on his face, he rushed into the garage and frantically rubbed himself on his bedding in a vain attempt to rectify his condition. Tessie, his co-conspirator, did the same. Lacey and Zoe stood off to the side watching all the commotion, shaking their heads in wonder.

000Shamed by their new smell, he and Tessie lurked in the corners of the garage. I tended to them as best I could, considering the lateness of the hour, and the odor seeping into my home. I bid them goodnight as they slunk into the shadows.

The next morning I went to Buddy's pen to let him out. He shamefacedly hung his head, contrite over his foolishness. I had texted our son to share the excitement. His response was that "Buddy tangles with skunks about twice a month, he knows all about them, but never seems to learn." So his surprised innocence was no longer working on me as I understood that it was the thrill of the confrontation that Buddy enjoyed.

Out in the big yard this morning, he and Tessie went looking for more trouble. Hoping, I am sure, for a rematch with their worthy opponent. As I sat drinking my coffee, it occurred to me that sometimes humans do the same thing; engage in a conflict, perhaps over the smallest thing, for the excitement of the exchange. It is true, the adrenaline flows and the muscles are ready for action, but later one might feel foolish for the silliness of the altercation. Often the motivation is the thrill of the fight, not to actually win a point of argument; besides one never knows when they might get "skunked!"

The old saying, "One must choose one's battles wisely" may apply here. For now the thrill-seeker named Buddy is casing my yard for more excitement!

Putting the Brakes on Magical Thinking

January 9, 2017

Happy New Year! I hope the holidays were kind to you. This year our family tried something different, a Santa Auction. Each of the 34 participants (we have a big family!) brought a gift which they then had to "sell" to the group. Each bidder had about $200 in over-sized Santa Bucks. We were nervous about trying something new, but, happily, it was a big rowdy success! It was hilarious watching as family members pooled money and bid hundreds of "bucks" on the item of their dreams! A basket of Almond Roca and a Starbucks card easily going for hundreds!! My daughter and I were proud that it was a hit, as we had ventured out of our comfortable old White Elephant tradition to try something new.

With the New Year, maybe this is a good time for you to try something out of your comfort zone. Maybe set a new goal. I found my 2016 goals list last week and was pleased to see that I accomplished all of them. I've been trying to work less and play more. For years I have written "more balance in my life." Woo hoo I made it!! What do you want to do?

One "comfort zone" that many people fall into is the zone of Magical Thinking. It is easy to unconsciously slip into it and it can be an unpleasant place to go. In Loss group last week the discussion centered around the disappointing fact that for some, extended family members such as grandchildren or siblings do not pay as much attention to us as we imagine they "should." This disappointment can easily fester into hurt feelings, to irritation, to anger, to withdrawal, leading to unhappiness.

Magical Thinking is fantasy thinking. It is the mental "chatter" that goes on inside our heads, the dreamy stuff of reverie. There's nothing wrong with a bit of it, but it can become mixed up with reality and affect a person's expectations. Relationships are fertile grounds for it. All we have to do is listen to a song, turn on a TV sitcom, or watch a romantic film and fantasy is delivered right to us, happily ever-afters and all! Magical thinking can contaminate our thoughts so that they are not grounded in reality. This thinking can become toxic if it affects our sense of what we can realistically expect from others. Here are some common fantasies:

- "I'll get as much as I give."
- "Relationships are 50-50."
- "Love conquers all."
- "Every problem has a solution."
- "If I love them enough, they will change."
- "They will love me back the same as I give."
- "There's only one true soul mate for me."
- "If I am agreeable there will be no conflict."

If we can recognize some of this fantasy thinking we can label it and put a stop to it. We can become more realistic in what we expect. The harsh reality is that our loved ones lead very full lives. Our siblings might be working, raising families, worrying about money, dealing with health issues, while our children and grandchildren are struggling with their own concerns with lives more jam-packed than we can imagine. I know that my grandchildren work to maintain high grades, participate in Greek life, compete in sports, maintain friendships and romances, and work hard at earning money, as they hone skills for their future. They are thinking forward. It is important for us to remember that they have a lot going on and not let our feelings get hurt if they don't always have as much time for us as we'd like; and to understand that it does not lessen how much they care for us.

Good Food and a New Friend: Happiness and a Child's Perspective

August 28, 2018

Greetings my friends! I have missed writing to you. Last week our nine-year-old granddaughter began third grade in a much bigger, new school. I have been watching her adapt to this enormous change. Two of our older grandchildren are facing big changes as they prepare to leave home to go off to college. My husband, Ken, also began a new chapter in his life this summer by reentering the world of high school coaching. Life presents constant challenges. We cannot help but face the need to adapt to new situations as life catapults us forward. I have been thinking about you and hoping that you are taking the best care of yourself that you can.

As I picked our third grader up from school on Friday, after just four days in her new world, I asked all about it. I could not help but smile as she told me about the food and the many choices available and about her new friend, Ceiri. As our conversation continued, she added, "Ceiri is new too." I see that of all the possible reactions she could choose, she is focusing on the positives. I see her child's wisdom: good food and a new friend. After all, what more is happiness than appreciating our blessings, having something to look forward to, and finding new passions to wrap our brains around?

I've had the "pedal to the metal" challenging my brain by writing a new book. It is the horse story of our quaint town, San Juan Capistrano. I told you a bit about this last year. In early 2017, during my mission docent studies, I was electrified by a charming book describing the 19th century lives of the Mission San Juan Capistrano parishioners. The stories had been told to the resident priest, Father John O'Sullivan and published in 1930. The book, Capistrano Nights set fire to my imagination. A powerful urge overtook me. I knew that somehow, I wanted to contribute something unique to the history of San Juan Capistrano, but I did not want to repeat what others had already written.

I thought and thought until one day when I went to purchase grain for my horses and I discovered, to my chagrin, that the tack and feed store was closing down. The owner, Fred Love, a long-time cowboy and friend, was moving away, forever. He had stories to tell, and they needed to be saved.

San Juan is often called the "Horse Capital of the West Coast" or the "Horse Capital of Orange County." The community seems to have defied all odds and preserved its historic character and equestrian culture. How is that possible? That's when the idea struck me. If I hurried, I could gather up the lived experience of those involved with horses before their stories were lost. Perhaps, I could find the answer to the mystery as to how San Juan has remained a charming Western enclave while the rest of Southern California has succumbed to concrete, glass, and steel.

I felt like I'd heard a shot fired at the starting line! So that is why you haven't heard from me. I dug in deep, interviewing, researching, and writing. I learned so much. When I started the project, I had no idea that my studies would take me to a 190,000-year-old horse fossil found in San Juan Capistrano! My book, *Capistrano Trails: Ride for the Brand*, takes the reader on a ride from the horse's Ice Age beginnings, through the Mission Periods, the Rancho Era, to the dynamic horse friendly place San Juan Capistrano is today; a place that cherishes its Old West heritage. If you are interested, it is available at Amazon.com in Kindle format, black and white print version, as well as hard-back color print.

I hope you have had an enjoyable summer practicing mindfulness and taking the best care of yourself that you can. My hope is that as life thrusts you forward, you have been finding new satisfying ways of being. When I was a young mom with three active offspring and a full-time career, my grandmother shared advice with me that I have kept close to my heart. She always reminded me, "Donna, no one can take care of you, but yourself."

Are you taking the best care of yourself? Are you resting enough, eating foods to support health, keeping your body fit, and being around people who inspire you to be your best self?

Carving out New Habits of Excellence

September 28, 2016

Through careful planning Ken and I booked a lovely five-night trip into Yellowstone National Park last week. We had a great time watching the herds of bison roaming on the plains; one mama buffalo was nursing her baby along the road. A mother elk and her two calves were quietly grazing along the parking lot by our inn. They wandered closer. I had no sooner whispered to Ken, "I guess their defense is running away," when suddenly a park staff member in a hushed stage voice called to us, "back up quickly!" We did. He explained that the mom elk will charge when threatened and can toss a human twenty feet into the air! That stopped us in our tracks!

It was a fine get-away abundant with wildlife, geysers and boiling sulfur mud pots. Very early Friday morning we left the Old Faithful Inn and headed down the mountain in time to catch our Friday afternoon flight to get us home for Ken's many Saturday morning soccer obligations. Our flight was delayed; then delayed again and again as we sat ever hopeful of getting home in a timely manner. Finally, as dark fell the agent announced, "All flights cancelled!" As we struggled to find a room in a town booked for a special event and re-rent a vehicle, we grumbled. Ken was upset, but managed to get his friends to cover coaching the two soccer games and we found a room.

In the dark of 5 a.m. the next day, we once again made our way to the airport. I happened to be sitting next to a handsome thirty-something clean-cut man who appeared to be a veteran. He was using cuff crutches. He and I chatted about our postponed trips. He said, "I've learned to take things in stride, I am going fishing at Coos Bay in Oregon." We talked about his fishing prowess. As it happened, once on the plane, his seat was just behind ours. As the woman who was to be his seatmate appeared, she saw the crutches and asked, "Do you want the window as it might be easier for you than getting up. What happened?"

He responded, "Sure" as he moved over. "I have ALS."

She looked confused.

"Lou Gerhig's disease," he clarified.

She said, "Oh good." (Clearly not comprehending what ALS was or perhaps she did not hear him).

He muttered, "Not really..."

That exchange has stayed with us these several days since we have been home and it quickly put into perspective how small our problem of missing our flight was in the great scheme of things. Once home, I reviewed ALS, as I knew that it was rare and serious. I learned that in a majority of cases it is fatal within two to four years.

I had noticed the young man's wedding ring and could imagine a lovely young woman kissing him goodbye that morning. I could visualize him tucking in a little child or two and saying good night to them the night before. My heart breaks for him, but there he is making absolutely the most of life in the time he has left. He had mentioned to me about another fishing trip in Boston when he met with his doctors. Clearly he is not going down without a fight.

Since I have last written to you, I have met my new class of women in transition . I've heard their stories of profound despair and feelings of hopelessness. I empathize. What they suffer is real. Many ended their stories saying they were "stuck." I see that. The new research in neuroscience shows that by understanding how our brain operates we can increase our ability to change its thinking, our thinking. That science teaches that our brains are hard to control, but that the brain has a deep need to be in control! In other words, it can take over, mulling and mulling around in thoughts of despair, thus causing many people to be held captive in the arousal state, running an awful, silent internal narrative of desperation. In Loss Group, one year, a new person announced to the entire group, "I am helpless and hopeless." She stated her internal message out loud. Neuroscientists call that story a narrative, it's what one tells oneself; it can easily become a life-limiting habit.

Steven Covey in, *The 7 Habits of Highly Effective People,* says, "Our character, basically is a composite of our habits... habits are powerful factors in our lives because they are consistent, often unconscious patterns that daily express our character and produce effectiveness or ineffectiveness. In Transitions I am working hard to guide the participants toward seeing what their assets are instead of focusing on their deficits. The first night I asked if any of them had her health? Most of the hands went up. "Can you see?" All the hands went up. "Can you drive?" All the hands went up. Then I asked, "What is right with you?" That took some thinking as often there's a tendency to focus on what is wrong.

I am hoping to guide the women toward taking control of their thoughts and celebrating their many assets, seeing their possibilities, as they set goals and strive toward moving forward. It is not an easy task as our habits mean that we have deep neural maps for thinking and doing certain things. It is possible to change those maps and create new ones, but it takes effort and being conscious of what one is thinking. We know that one's attitude is what frames one's state of mind, one's happiness. It seems to me that it is essential that we focus on what we HAVE instead of what we do not have. The young man at the airport was going fishing while he still could. He was embracing his assets. Aristotle said, WE ARE WHAT WE REPEATEDLY DO. EXCELLENCE IS NOT AN ACT, IT IS A HABIT. That young man was practicing what he probably always practiced, embracing life.

The Magical Power of Rest: Restoring You!

May 5, 2015

I vividly remember my little girl-self racing up the front walk to my grandmother's house across the street from Farmer's Market in Hollywood. My younger sister and I would eagerly finger the doorbell which would lead to our favorite grandmother. We would be filled with anticipation, standing on tippy toes to look into her front bedroom window. Almost always, she would be lying down, resting, probably before one of her late night Arthur Murray balls. The fact is that our grandmother was modeling resting to us in a very real way. She knew that to do all she did, and it was a lot, she had to rest. That value has sustained me across my life while I managed 120 rental units, was a political wife, mother to three active children, held down a full-time college teaching job and mastered portraiture. In more recent years rest has sustained me as I volunteer in my community, facilitate a loss of a loved one group, meet with private clients and turn out books.

I admit that in those early days I was sometimes the object of a ridicule, (I still hear other couples saying, "We're out with Donna and Ken, gotta' get our girl home early…"). If there was a layer of criticism, I ignored it. Over time our friends came to understand that Donna makes rest a priority. Just yesterday, as I greeted my coaching client, she hugged me hello remarking, "Donna you must have 48 hours in each day!"

I just smiled as I thought not really. It is just that I listen to my body and take time to recharge my internal engine. When I was a young, exhausted mother, blazing the feminist conviction that a mother could do it all; hold down a career while raising good kids, that same grandmother frequently admonished me, "Donna, no one will take care of you except yourself."

I began to take that to heart. I got some housekeeping help. I scheduled weekly massages, I learned to say no to non-essential activities, above all else, I rested. An article by Emma Derman Teitelon in the elephant journal, April 14, 2015, resonated with me on this important subject. Emma notes that the people she sees are depleted, uninspired, and exhausted. She says this is because of a "deep rejection of rest…when we rest it is easy to feel unworthy. In stillness it is easy to question our value." She goes on to discuss the social addiction to speed. Imagine drive-through dry cleaners, pharmacies, banks, Starbucks! Oh, that's right, you don't have to imagine, they are everywhere! Somehow many of us women have come to revere the mandate of "doing it all," aspiring to becoming superwomen. This is in direct violation of our feminine need to reflect, to be, to contemplate. Also, it is not possible without paying too high a price.

Perhaps we can do a lot of it, but we must rest. There is no doubt about the mind body connection. If one is to be at one's creative best, connected to the inner life force, it is essential to rest. We cannot be our authentic selves when we are depleted and exhausted. You know that when you do too much, your body finally screams, "time out!" You become ill. Let us not wait until then. Let us live the longest and fullest lives possible, let us celebrate the quiet, enjoy the pulse of our own hearts, for in that stillness we regenerate ourselves and there is simply more of us to go around.

"You're Up for a Party!" – The Power of Reframing

February 2, 2016

This morning as the dogs and I were about to enter a fenced trail where they could run free, a young woman and a dog came jogging out. We waited. "So, three dogs, huh?" she asked, slightly out of breath.

"Yes! I smiled. "What does that say about the psychology of me?" I responded half joking.

With a big grin and a cheery tone, her answer was easy, "That you're up for a party!"

What??? As I continued, I thought, that was interesting. In the woman's simple **reframing** of my many dogs, an epiphany flooded into my awareness. Really? I had long supposed that my canine passion was more about something left over from my less than delightful childhood, about my inner child longing to be whole. I flashed on the day before as the dogs and I went off to coordinate the refurbishing of one of my rental units. The music in the Jeep was up high, Lacey with her head partially out of the window, had her ears flopping in the breeze, Zoe's tail was thumping, and Tessie was keeping beat to the music. (Well, maybe not...) But we were a happy gang going off to work. "Hi Ho, Hi Ho!"

Hmm. Going off to work felt like fun.... Making the bed this morning to the backdrop of three huge dogs wrestling all around me was fun... They were certainly having a party; and a raucous one at that!

Maybe the lady was right, maybe one's old take on something is just that, old. I know that reframing is one of the most powerful personal tools one can have. It is a skill that grows out of adversity. It is the ability to look at something from another perspective. Resilient people have it in spades. It is their ability, when in distress, to reduce the appraisal

of perceived threat and to increase their coping effectiveness. For example, if your feelings are hurt because your friend forgot your special day, it could be that by reframing it, you can see that something else might have been going on. The forgetfulness might not have been personal. **EVERYTHING MIGHT NOT ALWAYS BE ABOUT US!**! (That is a complicated thought to digest!) In Loss Support group we use reframing to shift to gratefulness, to celebrate all the years we have had with our loved one....It helps stem the agony of loss. It is possible to examine our old beliefs and reframe them. We have the power to draw new conclusions from what we know. The jogging lady did that for me. Now instead of thinking I am a bit over-the-top running through life with three big dogs, I see that I take my party with me wherever I go! How fun is that?

On Letting Ourselves Off the Hook!

October 13, 2018

Two weeks ago I made a mistake which resulted in my being whisked away in an ambulance. I have been interested to notice how much grief I have been giving myself for contributing to getting myself hurt.

Eric Bergstrom, the wonderful host and producer of the Cox Cable show So Cal Safari was at my home to film the opening scene for his episode on the horse story of San Juan Capistrano. He had wanted to do such a show for a few years, and when he saw my new book, Capistrano Trails celebrating our town as "horse capital of Orange County," he was eager to get filming. He thought it would be fun if he and I opened the show on horseback and then rode off as the show continued.

It is common for horses to fill their bellies with air as one is cinching up the saddle. Dancer, the mare I was going to be on, had done that; she'd puffed herself up. The camera lady was adjusting her equipment as my friend Christine and I brought the two horses up onto the back lawn from the barn where we had saddled them. My main concerns were that I get my lines right and that Eric would be safe sitting on Blaze.

Satisfied that Eric's saddle was secure on Blaze, I mounted Dancer. That was when the trouble happened. The saddle slipped and I crashed five feet down on my right elbow and landed on my back. I failed to re-cinch her girth after she expelled her belly full of air.

I knew immediately that I was injured as I could feel that the bone in my lower arm was loose! I managed to get up and stumble over to a patio chair. Alarmed, those around me considered our options. I suggested finishing the filming. Eric was clear that we would reschedule. Duh!! I asked for him to call 911 and in no time the wonderful medical team at Mission Hospital Emergency Department had my situation under control. Within two hours the dislocated elbow was reset and Ken brought me home with a cast.

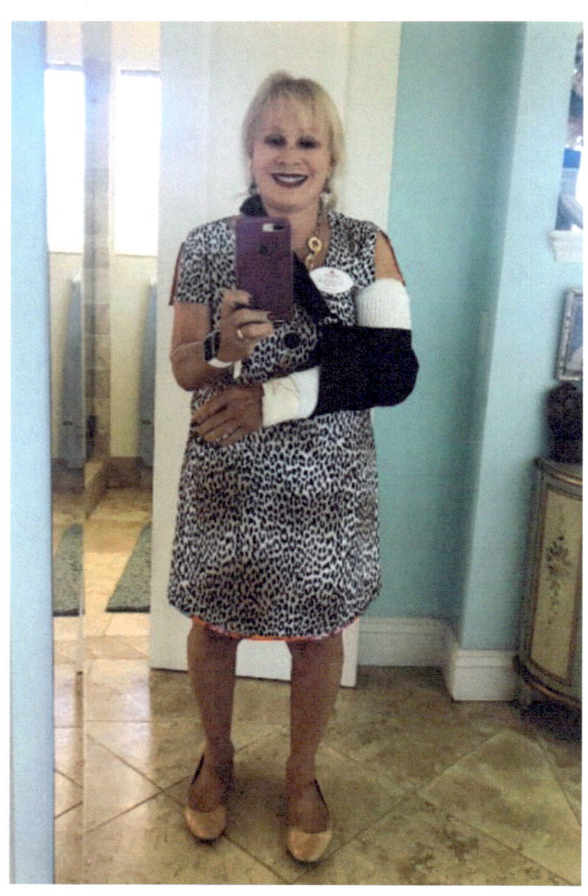

The next day, my daughter-in-law Jenny came to check on me. I shared the whole story with her, emphasizing how much I was blaming myself for not more fully securing Dancer's girth; that I was beating myself up for making such a dumb mistake. In an effort to help me chill out she declared, "Donna, no one thinks you are perfect."

Those words were a wake-up call, because they revealed a serious unwritten, possibly unconscious assumption underlying the reason why I was giving myself so much grief; You were not perfect! Bad Donna!

Through Jenny's statement, I came to understand how right she was. I was critical of myself for being distracted, for not being perfect...for being human. Maybe you have fallen into this trap yourself? Perhaps it's hard to get real and remember that we are only human, not super people.

I always loved Helen Reddy's "I am woman, hear me roar" song where she "brings home the bacon and fries it up in the pan." Superwoman is venerated, but truly she is not a superwoman, she's just a gal trying to do a lot, and sometimes she makes a mistake. I am going to write some Post Its and stick them around the house. They will say: "It is okay to be human!" "People make mistakes." "It's okay to make a mistake." And "Re-cinch the blasted saddle!"

Anyway, that's my epiphany for the month. I will admit that looking up into the concerned faces of four handsome firemen and two strong paramedics wasn't the worst situation I have ever experienced!

I love to hear from you. What have you been doing to keep yourself in check from thinking you have to do it all and to do it perfectly?

P.S. Eric Bergstrom will reshoot the scene and it will air in January, 2019. It is So Cal Safari, a Southern California Television Production.

CAPISTRANO
TRAILS

Section II

Resilience: We Can Do the Hard Stuff, Getting Out of Our Comfort Zones and Being Brave

"Goals are dreams with a deadline."

~Author Napoleon Hill

Stepping out of our Comfort Zones

May 19, 2015

What fun I had observing the joy on the faces of eight teens as they raced the stormy surf at the Wedge in Newport Beach last Friday evening. We were there through a new program at the Boys and Girls Club, one forcing the youth to experience new things, to vacate their comfort zones. The eight youths laughing at the ocean's edge chose to go, while three spots remained unclaimed out of the 100 club members who had the opportunity. Perhaps trying something new just seemed like too much, but for those with us, they were bursting with excitement having never before been to Newport Beach. They had opened the door to new possibilities.

The researchers into what brings human happiness put taking up new challenges and living through one's passion high on the list. Dr. Willliam Glasser, father of Reality Therapy, loved to say, "We choose the life we are living." If your Happiness Tank is not filled to the brim, why not start now to move forward, perhaps into the unknown, to take on something new? We all have different strengths and talents, and we may not reach the highest pinnacle but there is joy and excitement in the journey. I love the quote, "It is not the destination but the journey that brings happiness." You are in charge of your life. Only you can take care of yourself, and only you know what that little voice in the back of your mind is whispering about what to do next.

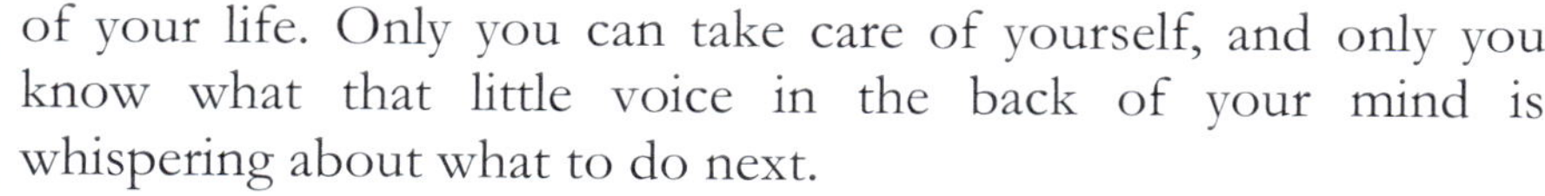

It is a big world out there. Why shouldn't you be among those who choose to step out of the comfort zone and into something new? Those of you who have followed my posts know that I was very apprehensive about leaving my comfortable world of teaching, but after 45 years it was simply time. I had to make a move. It was the right move. Maybe it is time for you to make a move too. It would be awful to come to the end of life and regret not being bold enough to go for it.

You are Old, But You are Fast!

May 16, 2019

I am still cracking up laughing at the hilarious 4th graders who were in my mission tour this week. It has been my pleasure the past few years to be a Mission San Juan Capistrano docent, leading tours for both adults and fourth graders through the grounds and buildings which tell the story of the Mission Era and Native Americans. Sometimes a certain group of students becomes unforgettable like this one. This class consisted of about 20 boys, three or four girls, and six parents. When I met them I could tell that they were excitable. I knew they had just endured a two-hour long bus ride from the inner city of Los Angeles to get to the mission. They were wiggly, pushing, talking, and jumping around. I started with my usual welcome spiel about this being a mobile classroom and being respectful etc. I sensed this group was particularly boisterous which is not unusual, this time of year with summer coming, and with a predominance of ten-year-old boys. I took a deep breath and got them into their imaginary "Time Machines" and we set off going backwards in time.

We began the tour at the cow hide. I fought to keep their attention as they touched the fur and wondered if it were a bear? With so many stimulating artifacts about; a stack of dirt at the adobe brick station, the wine vat, an old cart; the boys' attention was all over the place! I thought to myself, "herding cats?"

At the wine fermentation vat I managed to grab their awareness, and got them all stomping on imaginary grapes to make the "wine." Still boisterous; excitement was flowing out of them. As our tour continued, I noticed a shift. Their hands started popping up. They wanted to share. "I read about that in my social studies book!" "I know about the acorns..."

So many hands in the air, so many wanting to tell me what they knew! I watched as their excitement morphed from being in a new place, to the thrill they were experiencing in making connections to their classroom lessons. It was exciting for me as I was witnessing education in real time, before my eyes. They were engaged in learning. The process was rowdy and boisterous and beautiful and inspiring. It was magic....they were applying what they already knew and they were bursting at the seams doing it. I was in every teacher's dream.

You can imagine how captivated they were by the 240-year-old soot on the ceiling of the padre's kitchen, and how breathless they became staring at the golden alter in the Serra Chapel, bathed in the sounds of the Gregorian chant. As the tour progressed I could see more connections unfolding for them. By the time we got to the bells in the sacred garden they could barely contain themselves because they understood what they were seeing.

As the tour wound down, I was on a tight time schedule needing to get them to lunch before their next activity of making adobe bricks. They knew I was rushing to pack it all in and they began saying, "We don't care about lunch. We want to stay with you Miss Donna and learn more about the mission." "We are taking you back with us!"

As I power walked them to the lunch tables, I was laughing at their suggestions. One young man skipped up ahead to walk with me and exclaimed, "You are old, but you are fast!" That really made me smile!

I delivered them to lunch on time and congratulated the teacher and parents on their wonderful kids. As I left the mission, I could feel a giant grin on my face. I told the front gate staff that I had just become ten years younger! The students' energy had been contagious.

As the seasons of our lives change, I think it is important that we put ourselves in the path of new opportunities and experiences. Perhaps now is the time for us to live life a bit differently than we did during some of the earlier seasons?

My husband is coming along well in his recovery and has gone back to coaching high school girls' wrestling. We are looking forward, laughing as we think about being old while walking fast!

My Evening with Mrs. Clause

December 16, 2019

Sometimes I can hardly believe the crazy places I find myself inhabiting! It stems from my philosophy of "saying yes" and "putting oneself in the path of opportunity." That personal mantra has taken me, among other things, to the heights of the Himalayan Mountains where no inhabitants have ever seen a car, and to being forced to leap off the back of a big female elephant who felt like rolling over in the river in India! There's an element of surprise humming quietly in the background of my life. You may not be that shocked then to discover that last Saturday night my job was to be Mrs. Claus' helper. We weren't at the North Pole, but it was an extraordinary experience which I will hold close to my heart.

It was Mission San Juan Capistrano's second year for our big opening night of the holiday spectacular "Capistrano Lights." I was the docent assigned to "Mrs. Claus." The stage was set. The staff and the volunteers were ready. The musicians had warmed up, our 35-foot-tall musical tree was in perfect working order, Monsignor McKiernan was standing by to share his poem, the tamales were heating, and the

lights were twinkling, as we anticipated the arrival of 2300 guests. I had a little knot of excitement in my stomach as I was not sure what being there to help Mrs. Claus actually meant. I supposed it was about crowd control. I was wrong.

Our own Acajaman tribal member, Jaque Nunez, was volunteering her energy as Mrs. Claus. She was all made up in a white wig, night cap, Mrs. Santa red dress with a strand of lights blinking around her neck, granny glasses, and a big warm smile. As the little children began to come around, we could see that they were shy of meeting Mrs. Claus. Jaque would gently call to them, "I have been waiting just for you." Slowly they would approach and she would bring them in closer, all the while whispering encouragements. The shy little ones would soon warm up to her, while their eager parents stood back beaming their joy. I quickly understood that my role could be to record the magic that was taking place in front of us.

"Would you like for me to take a photo of all of you with Mrs. Claus?" The cell phone cameras would immediately appear as the family members posed with their children. More smiles. Sometimes the parents would hang back, a shyness of their own resisting the moment. I would grin one more invitation and be rewarded by their excitement to be a part this special time with their children and Mrs. Claus.

As the evening moved forward Mrs. Claus' joy for each child continued, and I got a better handle on my job of recording memories. Mrs. Claus greeted and chatted with literally hundreds of children, while I snapped their photos. Even though photos with Mrs. Claus might seem insignificant in the broader scheme of life, it was a night I will remember, for the fact that it was an example of people adding value to their lives and creating happiness.

In retrospect, I realize that it takes effort to create our own happiness, to put ourselves in the path of opportunity, and to take the risk of saying yes in life. I see that we must be actors in our own lives. We cannot wait for opportunity to find us. Last weekend was a very stormy time. It was raining on Saturday night when those families bundled their children into the car, drove to the Mission, found a parking place, and made their way into the historic landmark. They took a risk to make memories and to create cherished holiday traditions. Those hundreds of smiles told me it was worth the effort. I also think about Jaque and about myself. We could have been at home in front of our fireplaces, but we, too, were adding value to our lives by being a part of something bigger, something for the community.

I think happiness does not come to us serendipitously but is created through our actions. The holidays are a time of the year in which we can get caught up in unnecessary details, when we might succumb to feelings of being overwhelmed. Perhaps mindfulness can be applied to the season. We can ask ourselves, "does this effort add to my happiness or detract from it? With a small effort we can create our own value and only take part in activities which add joy.

For me, spending five hours with "Mrs. Claus" and greeting hundreds of guests, personally added to my happiness. Enjoying Jaque Nunez in action fills me with admiration and wonder.

I feel grateful to be alive. I feel grateful that both my husband and my mother have come through scary health issues this year. I think the more we can live in gratitude and mindfulness, the happier we will be.

Capistrano Lights is open through January 6th. I invite you to bring your family and friends to enjoy our historic landmark, the beautiful ruins of the Great Stone Church, the lovely Serra Chapel, the most historically significant building in all of California and the beautiful lights.

Learn Like You Are Going to Live Forever

January 30, 2020

The other day at Mission San Juan Capistrano I strode across the courtyard in my docent attire, eager to meet the tour group waiting for me. There were about thirty fourth graders and ten adults. I greeted them with a big smile and introduced myself. Then I asked where they lived.

"We are from Brea, in North Orange County."

"That's great! You've come a long way," I responded, "and we are so happy to have you here. Does anyone know what "brea" means?

My question was met with silence. I looked at the group. They looked at me. I grinned into their expectant faces. After a moment, I announced that it means "tar." Their astonished expressions grabbed at my heartstrings. Without losing a beat, I went on to explain how the Native Americans, who had built the Mission, used tar to line their canoes and baskets to keep them watertight, that they could even boil water in their sturdy containers. The hills and canyons of Brea have been rich sources of tar and petroleum for centuries. I knew that the early ranchers avoided buying up the tar-filled acres because the gooey substance clung to the sheep's feet and soiled the wool. The settling farmers of Orange County were oblivious to the value of the "liquid gold" beneath the ground.

That did it! I could feel their eagerness to learn more. I bundled them into their imaginary time machines and off we went. The rest of the hour-long tour zoomed by, fueled by their interest. When it came time to part ways, I asked each student to share what aspect of their visit had meant the most to them. In sweet whispers so many replied, "Everything!"

Needless to say, witnessing their excitement of discovery filled me with awe. It also humbled me to think that as a career educator I had found a rewarding niche for myself in retirement.

That encounter prompted me to focus on the idea of life-long learning, and what it can mean. The day before, I had attended an art history class at the Mission. We learned in some detail about the Mission's extensive art collection. We were taught about the paint mixing techniques used by the medieval master's in liturgical art. The ancient works tend to be dark as the minerals they had to work with were from finely ground rocks and minerals mixed with linseed oil. I listened to the lecture and took notes. It was not until many hours later, when I was watching a YouTube video on those long ago practices, that an epiphany flashed through my brain!

Connections flooded my mind. As a porcelain artist, I realized I have been utilizing the same techniques as the old masters for over four decades. We carefully mix the powdery minerals with a binder, like linseed oil, we call it "mixing medium," to create our paints. We then fire our painted pieces in a kiln to adhere the paint to the porcelain.

What fascinated me is that I sat through the entire lecture about 18th century painters and did not connect their techniques to my own. When I did, I was exuberant! My discovery nearly bowled me over!! I continued to ponder my ideas: about the excitement of discovery, and its connection to human happiness.

Today, I was in the produce aisle at Trader Joe's with my ten-year old granddaughter, Caroline. I reached for a container of banana nut squash zig-zags. That action caught the attention of the woman standing next to me. "How do you eat those?" She inquired.

"Well, I cook them in the microwave."

"In their plastic container?"

"No, I place them in a covered glass dish."

"Do you add butter?

"No, just a few tablespoons of water."

"For how long?

"Maybe three minutes."

I turned, Caroline smiled, and I began to push our cart away. The delighted lady exclaimed out loud (clearly talking to herself), "Oh I just love learning new things!"

Caroline and I exchanged a knowing look. The lady was pretty funny, certainly she was persistent, but her remark speaks to the fact that learning new things, discovery, is a huge turn-on and probably an element in maintaining one's happiness.

Anyway, this is something I'm going to continue to ponder. I particularly appreciate Mahatma Gandhi's thoughts about life-long learning. He said, "Live as if you were to die tomorrow, learn as if you were to live forever."

Other Worlds May Be Closer than We Think

February 22 ,2024

This past President's Day weekend, my husband, Ken and I were reminded that whole other worlds sometimes are just a short distance away.

I was invited to speak to my sister Diana's women's group in Palos Verdes. I eagerly accepted, reminiscing about how special that area has been in our lives; it is where Ken and I first met when I was just a girl of 14. I was accompanying my girlfriend, Lee. We were visiting her family's friends for a week in Rolling Hills. The husband, a leader of a group of Boy Scout Explorers, invited some of the scouts to meet us. Ken was among them. That was the start of a lifetime together.

Soon after meeting Ken, I returned to my home thirty miles away. Too shy to talk on the phone, we exchanged letters all year. When my friend Lee and I returned to Palos Verdes the next year Ken had developed more courage, arranging an outing. We were quite surprised when he and a buddy showed up with horses! The plan was to ride over the steep hills and look at the oceanarium known as Marineland of the Pacific which had opened three years earlier in 1954. It was California's first themed amusement park. Having only heard descriptions of Marineland, we were happy about the day's plans to actually see it, but quite hesitant about seeing it from the back of horses, sitting behind boys we were just getting to know.

Ken and Donna 1962

Swallowing our pride, Lee and I climbed on the back of those horses behind the boys. It was an exciting few hours. When it was time to ride back up the tallest hill, I was not about to put my arms around this boy I did not know very well. As my horse started up the incline, I slid right off its rump. After that we all just walked next to the horses up the slope. These are some of our favorite memories. Many years later we married in a church near where we met and moved to Orange County where we have spent sixty years, raising a family and building a life.

When this invitation to speak arrived, Ken immediately offered, "How about if I drive you and we will make an overnight adventure out of it?" Indeed we did just that! We packed our bags, organized care for our many pets and set off, quite oblivious to the idea of entering another world.

An hour later, we arrived in Ken's adolescent growing up neighborhood on the Palos Verdes Peninsula. It warmed my heart to see horses out on this holiday weekend, and to make a stop at the site of our wedding. We delighted in discovering the many colorful peacocks, preening on corral fences and unabashedly strutting down the middle of the roads! I took many photos.

The driving tour continued to Malaga Cove where Ken had attended middle school, and where we encountered more beautiful peacocks. We hiked a bit to enjoy the views of Ken's old surfing spots while he regaled me with tales of his shipwreck adventures climbing aboard the crashed freight ship, the Dominator, which was beyond salvage, stuck on the rocks where it had run aground in 1961.

We drove on, admiring the extravagant views of Catalina Island sitting just to our right. We soon drove into the entrance for the glamorous Terranea Resort on the site of the earlier Marineland Park. A quick Google search taught me that eons ago this area of Southern California had once been connected to the Channel Islands. We parked and Ken pointed out the trail we had taken on that long ago horse ride.

We continued over freshly asphalted portions of a very topsy turvy road. I learned that it is constantly moving and being repaired, as much of the soil in the Rancho Palos Verdes area is unstable. In fact, the home in which we had met in 1956 fell down the hill years ago and had to be demolished.

We drove into the legendary Wayfarer's Chapel parking lot only to be turned away by a guard. The historic building is red tagged. It is coming down, the earth beneath it moving to the point that the glass windows are cracking, and the structure is unsafe.

Ken told me stories of the beautiful Portuguese Bend Club that had once stood at the nearby beach, and how it had been destroyed by sliding earth. Today all that remains is its memory; there's very little sign of it; it was taken long ago by the moving earth as have many dozens upon dozens of homes.

At day's end, we found a seaside restaurant near our hotel and settled into a candlelit dinner. We talked excitedly about the history of the area, the unfortunate movement of the earth, and about the remarkable fact of so many wild peacocks roaming about.

We learned that there are a few other areas in Southern California where early flocks of peacocks were set free to proliferate over time. Research revealed that businessman Elias J "Lucky" Baldwin (Baldwin Hills is named for him) imported a flock of peacocks from India in 1879 which was probably the start of the Southern California peacock population. It is generally believed that Baldwin's daughter gifted 16 of the family's peacocks to Palos Verdes developer Frank A.Vanderlip who owned a massive 1600-acre estate on the peninsula around the turn of the twentieth century. An ornithophile, he kept aviaries on the peninsula property filled with exotic birds. Upon his passing the peacocks were set free to roam the hills, and to live on over one hundred years later.

The next day, I arrived early to my meeting excited about my presentation, but also interested in what the locals thought about all those loose peacocks living side by side with humans. I asked a few of the ladies who lived close by. They smiled, sighed, and agreed that they enjoyed them. However, they were quick to point out that the birds are a point of great controversy, that about half of the area's residents find their squawking and vast amounts of excrement to be disagreeable.

My talk was on the "Colonization of Alta California." I came attired in the image of the historic figure of La Dona Ysidora Pico Forster, the former matriarch of a massive Alta California rancho. I wanted to grab the listeners' attention and help them to understand that they are part of California's astonishing story; its rise from rural outpost to a world class powerhouse economy. I was warmly welcomed by a full audience of interested, attentive listeners. It was a wonderful day.

On the journey home Ken and I got back to reminiscing, recalling our own experience with some neighboring squawking peacocks. Our neighbor across the creek had kept them, and while we heard them clearly, they were far enough away as not to be annoying. We enjoyed having a peacock link.

As we pulled into the driveway of our home, we marveled at the idea that we had only been gone a bit more than 30 hours and had discovered a whole different environment just a short trip away. Our takeaway is that if we make the effort and get out of our comfortable routines, there's much to discover, often very close by.

Why not you?

February 4, 2014

Hi there. During the celebratory minutes after Superbowl XLVIII on Sunday, the lovely female TV interviewer asked for Seattle Seahawk quarterback Russell Wilson's take on the day, after he guided them to an incredible victory against the Denver Broncos. Wilson, small for a quarterback, told the story of discussing his size and abilities in terms of making it into the pros with his father who remarked, "Why not you?"

That comment instantly resonated with me. Russell Wilson would not be expected to dominate against the big league tough guys, but he did not listen to the naysayers and has not just made it into the NFL, he is a star. He said "yes" to football, even though he was signed as a pro baseball player. He said "yes" to the Seahawks' decision to make him the starting quarterback. Russell Wilson is all about YES! In a newspaper interview he elaborates, "I believe that God made me 5-11 for a reason. For all the kids that have been told, "no," that they can't do it, or all the kids that will be told 'no.'"

Do you ever think about all that would not have been accomplished if others had listened to the "nos"? Maybe no America, after all we are an experiment in individual liberties. Maybe no walking on the moon, no exploring space, perhaps no artificial hearts, no organ transplants, no to real civil rights, surely no lady interviewer on the football field! The list would be long.

Russell's message can apply to us. Why not us? What more do you want to do? Of course it will take determination, focus, and hard work, but what are you dreaming about that you still want to do in the world?

Remember that Starfish story where the youth is throwing back the starfish which had been washed up during a storm? The old man naysayer comes along and sees the expanse of beach littered with starfish and says, "there are more starfish on the beach than you can possibly save before the sun comes up." The youth continued to throw them back one by one as he said, "I can make a difference to this one!" With that the naysayer bent down and began to help the youth. Before long others joined in and all the starfish were saved.

I love that story because it reminds us to take action and to insulate ourselves against those who would discourage us in following our hearts and realizing our dreams. Russell Wilson went for it. He reminds us "why not you and me?"

From Yoga on the Sand…to Life Changing Experience

July 29, 2023

If we are open to it, one of the great adventures of being alive in the world is that we just never know what can happen if we just say "yes"! Last Sunday one of those unbelievable experiences caught me completely by surprise. Yes, I had wandered into yet another unknown, but of course I did not expect anything life changing to happen. It was during our annual family get-away-vacation to Avalon, a tiny city on the Island of Catalina.

On the second day I was chatting with a seasonal local and she invited me to "Yoga on the Sand," a free program offered by the City of Avalon on Sunday mornings at 8 a.m. I had told her I would go. On Sunday morning I was sort of stalling, sipping coffee, in our hotel room when Ken urged, "Just go. It might be fun. You might get a story to tell!" Hmm I thought. Okay.

I walked the short distance to the front of our hotel and there on the sand were two big City of Avalon canvas pop-up tents. Towel in hand, I walked over and said hi to the three women setting up; the City representative and the two leaders. All three greeted me so warmly that I immediately felt at ease. I spread out my towel. They chatted with me as they set up Tibetan sound bowls, a sound system, and began spreading lavender scents around the area.

Within a short time a group of perhaps ten people gathered beneath the awnings and started stretching as they lay on their towels. Soon "Air-e," introduced herself. Dressed in a long skirt, and sleeveless top, she introduced co-leader "Lumina." Lumina was dressed in loose Indian yoga pants and a tank top stating "Breathe." Her flowing body art proclaimed her devotion to alternative healing methods. Both women exuded peacefulness, warmth and love.

Air-e opened her session and soon asked each of us to share a recent "crappy and a happy" moment. The sharing brought us together. Then we were directed to select a card on which to focus our thoughts during our yoga practice. I selected a card at random. When I turned it over it said, "I radiate positive energy from my being." Well that seemed prophetic. Our group went through a demanding hour long practice. As it ended we were invited to stay for a "Sound Bath." By now Lumina was working her Tibetan bowls and more fragrances were filling our atmosphere. Intrigued I stayed. I had never before heard of a "Sound Bath."

The Sound Bath began. Lumina walked between those who remained, spreading lavender and sage scents. We lay with our eyes covered and enjoyed the explanation of how the sounds vibrations affected our bodies and our energy fields. Gongs played. Cymbals chimed; sounds and fragrances flowed. We were led deeper into our meditation. As an inexperienced person in such things, I was a rapt student. She directed us to see the "light" of all the people across our lives who have supported us. Our direction was to focus on their "light." I was so relaxed that I did see "lights" in my imagination. Perhaps some hypnosis was taking place. The strongest light that came to me was from thinking of my husband Ken. I became more aware than ever of how much he has encouraged me across our long life together. As my mind began to explore all past and present people who have supported me, I felt a rush of tearfulness, of appreciation for the support I have gotten. I thought of my grandmother, my model for grandparenting.

The hour continued like that. The wind picked up as the sounds continued their vibrations, I could hear the waves lapping against the sand. My hands and feet felt tingly and I was deeply relaxed. It felt like my heart rate had slowed down. It was an emotional experience for me. Two more of the "lights" I became aware of were from my childhood girlfriend, Leanne's, parents. I lingered in that appreciation for all they did for me during my troubled childhood. They were a refuge. I felt transported as I took a broad look at my life and thought about changes that I could make.

After a long while the sounds and vibrations brought us back to a more awake state. My hands and feet still tingled. The wind continued. The others left. I stayed on my towel, as I was rather shocked that I had had such a powerful experience. It was a visceral immersion in gratitude. I wondered if the others had such an experience? I looked around the area thinking perhaps Lumina also had a wind machine? No. It was the natural environment. The breeze had picked up while I was in my deepest meditation. I don't know what that was about? Air-e and Lumina came to me, encircling me in a group hug. They asked if they could have some photos with me. They took my phone and put their contacts in. When I got back to our room I told Ken all about it; that it had been life changing in that it has inspired me to look more fully into such guided meditation and certainly to continue the experience of sound baths, and to think about my life.

I have long believed that living in gratitude is a solid path toward happiness, now more than ever I believe that. It seems essential to me that we understand that we must be in charge of the life that we are living; that putting ourselves in the path of the unknown may present opportunities and experiences we could never imagine. Maybe I stepped a bit out of my comfort zone on Sunday by going to Yoga on the Sand, but what wonderful rewards I was gifted. I like the sign over my sink that reads, "It is not the destination but the journey that brings happiness." What a wonderful internal journey I experienced on Sunday! Now I am Googling meditation retreats and Sound Baths. I'm excited.

Goat Yoga and a New Perspective

October 8, 2021

Goodness, I find myself at this "well seasoned" stage of life once again reevaluating my choices, creating a new action plan, and purpose statement. Really? Again?

This has come about in the wake of the long lockdown due to the world wide pandemic. Honestly, I got so comfortable staying at home, entertaining myself with the animals, writing, reading, and exercising that I had sort of decided that I was through with all my running around the world adventuring on big trips. I had kind of thought I would simply mellow out my life at home with my husband and family. That was what I was thinking when suddenly last month a very long postponed journey to Iceland was back on.

I admit I was hesitant. Iceland is far away, and the prospect of being squeezed into a crowded airplane while Delta Variant raged on did not inspire me. However, my daughter-in-law and I had paid our money and Iceland was ready for us.

We met up with our dozen or so tour mates and enjoyed the hikes and sights of an eco tour; glaciers, geysers, an active volcano, waterfalls, and more. It was all marvelous, but the higher and further we hiked, the more I was hearing my trip mates commenting on how "spry" I was and that I was an "inspiration." Mind you the travel mates, excepting my daughter-in-law, were well into their 60's and 70's. As the most senior in the group, I felt a sting of being outed as "other." These "compliments" felt "ageist" as they kept coming to me, making me uncomfortable. I admit I began to feel annoyed. Probably the comments were well intentioned but they hit a sour note and were not really welcome.

However, the majesty of the vast volcanic lava fields, the expedition through ice bergs in an amphibious boat, and the enormity of hiking to

Europe's largest waterfall, were telling me a different story, that there is still so much more to see and do. Then I saw this REGRETS OF PEOPLE WHEN THEY ARE DYING chart by Barry Selby on social media and I began to question my earlier thoughts.

All that was roiling around in my brain on Saturday when I joined my daughter and three granddaughters for Goat and Llama Yoga in San Diego. It was a sprawling class of 30 under a shade at a farm. Not having practiced yoga in a decade I thought I was situating myself at the back of the class where I could hide out. I was wrong. I had inadvertently put myself in the front row a few feet from the instructor, thus challenging me to do my best, to rise above my reticence. Class began. I contorted into the poses, the goats came out, the llamas came out, but my attention was focused on the where of my arms and legs. By the end of the class my back, sore from all the plane rides and driving 1500 miles around Iceland, felt good, really good.

My takeaway from Goat yoga was that I must keep it up, maybe without the goats! I have committed to a practice every day and have been loyal to that decision. In addition I have reevaluated my earlier plan, I am not giving up traveling until I have to. I do not want any regrets. I don't want to get to the end of my life and say, "yes it was a good life, but I regret that I succumbed to the expectation that older folk should live a smaller life."

Also I am changing my perception of what it means when people offer to help me, comment on my stamina, and set me apart. I am going to graciously accept the help when my fellow shoppers at the grocery store want to lift the water or the bag of carrots into my cart. I am going to smile and say thank you. I am embracing who I am, but I will not let it shrink nor annoy me. I am changing my ways. I will make a conscious effort to not let others define me. This is our time now. If we can go for it, why shouldn't we? I think we need to embrace the attention, say thank you, and keep on keeping on. If any of what I have recently been experiencing resonates with you, I would love to know what you are thinking.

Lean Into Your Life: The Power of Yes

March 15. 2016

On Friday I was making my way north into Los Angeles to be the guest at my nephews' Grandparents Day, when I passed by two elementary schools. The crossing guards stopped our cars as a few dozen pint-sized cowboys and girls crossed in front of us. I smiled as a kindergartner, glad in pink cowboy boots and pink western hat, walked in front of my car. Laughing out loud, I scanned across the more than four decades that our family has been involved in Swallows Weekend, with three generations of us marching in the famous San Juan Capistrano parade. As I cruised up the freeway I marveled at our human ability to find meaning in life, for creating incredible institutions and rituals.

On Saturday, we joined the 20,000 celebrants gathered along the parade route. Laughter and music and the enticing aroma of bar-b-cue filled the air. The eager expressions on the faces of the spectators as they thrilled to dancing horses, brilliantly costumed Aztec dancers, and massive Clydesdales pulling antique fire engines, revealed how totally present they were in the moment. That is what we have, each individual moment. Life does not just "happen," we have to make it happen. The massive crowd and the hundreds of marchers were making a joyous life happen at the moment.

Placing ourselves in the path of opportunity is key to growing our happiness and living to our full potential. I met our new class of Women in Transition for the first time a few weeks ago, and already I can see the change that has come over them. They are moving forward even against serious life challenges. They have put themselves in a situation that can lead to opportunity. They adopted the Power of Yes. The parade participants chose "Yes" to marching, the spectators chose "Yes" to join in. Your life right now is the result of your past decisions, but you do not need to be bound to them. If you are not happy with where you are, you can alter your course today, this minute. You can choose "Yes." You can move out of your comfort zone and try something new. Sheryl Sandberg, CEO of Facebook and recent widow, implores

people, especially women, to LEAN IN (the title of her book) to our own power and abilities. She says, "We hold ourselves back in both big and small ways by lacking self-confidence, by not raising our hands, by pulling back when we should be leaning in."

On my dog walk this morning, my neighbor Kay and I chatted a moment, "Donna next year let's ride our horses in the parade!"

"Wow, that's an idea!" I responded.

I didn't say "No," perhaps I will lean into that! Mark Twain once said, "courage is the mastery of fear, not the absence of it." What opportunity is knocking at your door? This morning I had a post and delightful photos from my former Transition client Sonia, who is in the Peace Corps right now in Africa. Sonia has leaned in. What more do you want to do? Maybe you want to march in the parade next year? Take a trip, learn to Salsa dance, or volunteer at the hospital? It is up to us to make our individual lives meaningful, to find joy even against difficulty. You are powerful. This is your time.

No Regrets – The Importance of Taking Action

March 2, 2023

The other day I was scanning through CNN on my iphone, when I came upon a Jane Fonda interview in which eighty-five-year-old Jane wanted to "clear everything up" before dying. That caught my attention. The interviewer was probing into Jane's take on life, regrets, and more. Jane has always been of interest to me. Back in the 1970's during her years of notoriety as "Hanoi Jane" she was a popular figure on the college speaking circuit. Visiting Hanoi as she did was against American foreign policy rules. It turned her into a controversial figure, a sort of anti-hero. College students were intrigued by her, and our college booked her as a speaker. As the chair of the speaker's bureau, I had the responsibility for hosting and introducing her to our packed auditorium. Before I could get lost in that old memory, I began to watch the interviewer who was inquiring about her regrets in life.

Jane Fonda began to talk about motherhood and the mistakes she felt that she had made with her three kids. "I was not the kind of mother that I wished that I had been to my children. I have great, great, children; talented, smart. I just didn't know how to do it."

Wow. A knot settled in my stomach. That was a lot for her to admit. My parents did not know how to raise me and my sister either. The interview was hitting home. I continued to watch as she explained that since her children's childhoods she has studied parenting and has since learned what she should have done, that she had not done then. These days she says she is practicing "showing up." She is trying to get things done now while there is still time.

A few weeks ago I wrote to you about the many losses I sustained in December and that it caused me to take action understanding that I have NO TIME TO WASTE. I booked a trip to Panama Canal and am leaving this week, made a date and visited a retired colleague friend and his wife whom I had not seen in seven years, and bought airline tickets to bring my niece out from Chicago for a visit. I had not seriously interacted with her in 23 years. I am taking action. I do not want any regrets.

Years ago, Pulitzer Prize winner Anna Quindlen's book, Loud and Clear (2001), really resonated with me. In that book Quindlen admitted her own regrets which were similar to Jane Fonda's. Anna regretted that while she was raising her three children SHE DID NOT ALLOW HERSELF TO BE MORE IN THE MOMENT. She confessed that she was too other focused. Now grown she can only look at old childhood photos of those children, but in so doing she does not feel any real recognition. Her regret is that she did not pay more attention, that she was not there in the moment with them.

For many of us our lives have been or are on "turbo thrust." We have a lot to do and stay busy. Busy or not, I am dedicating this year to finishing up "unfinished business" so that I have no regrets. My long weekend visit with my thirty-eight-year-old niece was pure joy; and getting to know her remarkable fourteen-year-old daughter, Scout, was stunning. Some of you may know that when this niece, Kelly, was just four years old, it was necessary to accomplish an intervention to protect her from further abuse. It was life upending for me, certainly the hardest thing I will ever be called upon to do. I risked my marriage, my career, and my life, and we got her to safety. She is currently finishing a master's degree in social work, policy and administration.

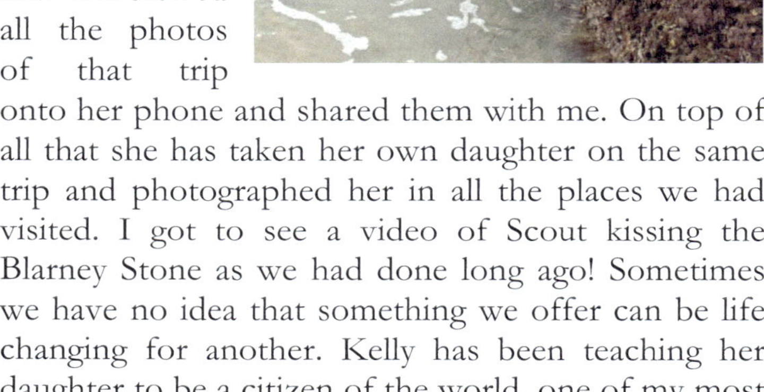

When Kelly was fifteen, I took her on a trip to Ireland. As the later tumultuous teen years came, she moved out of state and we mostly lost contact. During our visit last weekend I discovered that the Ireland trip was life changing for her. She has saved the shampoo bottle and the trip itinerary folder all these years. She had transferred all the photos of that trip onto her phone and shared them with me. On top of all that she has taken her own daughter on the same trip and photographed her in all the places we had visited. I got to see a video of Scout kissing the Blarney Stone as we had done long ago! Sometimes we have no idea that something we offer can be life changing for another. Kelly has been teaching her daughter to be a citizen of the world, one of my most important goals for my loved ones. Had I not taken an action and brought Kelly and her daughter out to my home, and spent many quality hours with them, I would not know any of this, and I would have continued to live with "unfinished business;" and I would not enjoy a solid relationship moving forward.

What about you? Do you have some things hanging that could use closure? Do you feel like there might be some regrets bugging around the periphery of your consciousness? We have time to finish unfinished business, to take action and get some of the "bucket list" items accomplished. My husband, Ken, at 80 says he has no regrets about events in his life, good or bad. The things on his bucket list are things he would like to do again! My heart is full for the actions I have recently taken.

Ancient Rituals and Cultural Encounters: A Powow in the Heart of Downtown

August 15, 2022

Sunday morning as I was mucking out my horses' stalls the mission bells began their familiar rhythmic tolling across our valley calling our town's parishioners to Mass, a sound that has been heard for the past 250 years. Continuing my labor, a smile played upon my face as my thoughts drifted to the day before. I'd had a hair appointment in town and found a parking spot next to our Historic Town Center Park. I recalled that as I climbed out of my car, the air was vibrating with the melodious throbbing of tom toms coming from the park. A shiver of excitement washed through me. I knew I had to get to my appointment, but I hoped that whatever the event was in the park would still be going on later.

After an hour or so, I left the salon still hearing the drums, only they were much louder. I hurried toward the sounds thinking it must be something to do with our very active band of Native People. At the park, I slipped into the crowd of a few hundred and watched six men in the center of the park dressed in native dress. They were stomping in time with the loud drumbeats. Another shiver ran through me. I had somehow stumbled onto a powwow! I soon learned that representatives from many Native American nations from across California and beyond had traveled great distances to join in. I learned that this was the first powwow to be hosted by our local Acajacheman nation.

My work as a mission docent, teaching school children about our first people, has heightened both my interest and appreciation of them and their important role in our town's history. For over ten thousand years, tribal people inhabited this area of Southern California; long before the Spaniards arrived. The California Teaching Standards for fourth graders require a unit on Native Americans. It is my honor to guide our visiting

students through the mission, teaching about the skills, culture and lifestyle of the earliest people. Mission San Juan Capistrano welcomes more than 50,000 students each year. The children love to hear about the hunting, fishing and agricultural practices of the first inhabitants. The fact that the City of San Juan Capistrano has recently supported the construction an outdoor Acajacheman Village museum, located nearby, adds to the children's excitement.

At the powwow two friendly women were standing next to me. They seemed as spell bound as I. We smiled hello. Soon we chatted a bit and introduced ourselves. They were local residents, mother and daughter. The daughter told me she had been married for thirty years to a Native American, and that he was the "fire keeper" of his tribe in Northern California. As my eyes widened in interest, she elaborated. "Yes, we had a sweat lodge on our property. The elder men held a weekly healing ritual at our home." She laughed, "The tribal leader would call my husband and report how many rocks he would need to have heated for each week's ceremony. One time my husband had to have 145 heated rocks ready! It was a fascinating way to live."

As the crowd grew, the circle of about ten drummers kept up their persistent beat, participants could be seen getting into their intriguing colorful costumes. The older men donned something like an enormous bustle of turkey feathers attached below their waist in the back. Younger men and boys had less ornaments. The women were beautiful in long skirts, skins, shawls and headdresses. One dancer, Teeter Romero was carrying a basket with smoking incense. Teeter is often weaving baskets at the mission.

My new acquaintance, helping me to understand what I was seeing, whispered against the beating drums. She explained that turkey feathers are highly revered and represent abundance and strength; that the elaborate bear claw necklaces worn by some of the men are considered to contain spiritual powers.

Before long a colorful processional of perhaps 50 dancers of all ages circled the inside of the arena as welcomes were made. Domingo Belardes, a well-known member of the local Juaneno Band of Mission Indians offered a prayer. I knew that Domingo headed up the newly refurbished Blas Aguilar Adobe, one of the last 1790's adobes still standing in town, which has become a museum displaying Acjacheman history and artifacts. Later I learned that it was the Blas Aguilar Adobe Museum which sponsored the event.

As the program continued, we met Roy Two Bears who was bearing the Eagle Staff. Many others were introduced. Stories of the sacred Acjacheman lands on which we were standing were shared. I understood the purpose of such powwow gatherings. They are about honoring the rich ancestral culture through stories, songs and dances. It is also a time to socialize, strengthening the bonds of community.

I sat down on the grass in the shade of an awning at the edge of the circle. I did not want to miss a minute of it. As the participants danced around the circle, my friend and representative of the Acjacheman people, Jacque Nunez, recognized me and blew me a kiss. I felt a bit fevered by the thrill of it all. I could not help but think that this was happening in my very own hometown. I swelled with pride to live in a community which respects and reveres its native people. On a recent trip to the Los Angeles Natural History Museum I was humbled to view a portrait of Jacque hanging on the wall in the First Americans exhibit. She is a recognized spokesperson for the Acjacheman people, frequently presenting lectures in schools and in the community. One of her favorite topics is: "The Acjachemen Nation is Alive and Well."

Across my life I have been earnest in seeking out and appreciating other cultures and ways of living. I have been blessed to travel to many parts of the world in that quest. My experiences are many and include dancing the Jumping Marriage Dance with the Masaii in Tanzania; dishing alms into the food pots of the Buddhist monks in Cambodia in the dark of early morning; stepping inside primitive shelters visiting families along the Ho Chi Minh Trail in Viet Nam while chickens and pigs rubbed past me inside the humble abodes, to the giggles of scantily dressed bare-foot boys and girls tantalized by my presence. Across my adventures I have been awed to find that my fellow humans are mostly joyous and eager to engage, no matter the setting.

Interacting with people in dramatically different cultures in other parts of the world has been a driving force in my life, meaning more to me than I can say, experiences I keep in the deepest part of my heart. Like so many others with whom I have interacted, the powwow celebrants beamed with joy and welcome. I could feel how much this all-day event meant to them.

Later, during a break in the festivities I shyly asked one costumed dancer, a man, if I could have a picture with him. Smiling he agreed. Grinning with pride, he proclaimed, "I am Apache!" For my part, I am thrilled to live in a world where it is possible to meet all kinds of people who are free to live their lives in their own ways and to share those ways with others. I am particularly grateful to live in an historic community which respects our First Americans and views them as an integral part of life in San Juan Capistrano.

What cultural experience have you enjoyed that caused your heart to skip a beat? I'd love to hear about it. For now, I best get back to finishing my mucking..

On Being Alone: The Powe of One

January 5, 2022

Happy New Year!

For the second time in two years, our coveted tickets to see Hamilton were cancelled due to Covid. Frustrated, my daughter, her husband and I purchased admission for that particular Sunday, January 2, to see the well-reviewed Jane Goodall exhibit at the Los Angeles Museum of Natural History. On the eve of our departure both of my companions fell ill. I considered aborting the trip. After all it is a long way into the city, and I almost always travel with a companion. I realized of late that I had developed a habit of going places with others. I decided I would go alone. Off I went to Exposition Park in Los Angeles.

Upon entering the museum and providing my vaccination card, I was admitted to the spellbinding Goodall exhibit. Wonderful technology allowed a video presentation of Jane explaining to us the importance of anecdotes, observation, and the immense power of the single individual. Goodall fervently believes we can save the environment if we each work together toward that goal. I was inspired. The exhibit further explained that paleoanthropologist Louis Leakey was instrumental in starting Dr. Goodall on her chimpanzee project in Tanzania. On a 2011 trip to Ngorongoro, Tanzania, our family had been captivated by the 3.5-million-year-old fossilized footprints of an early hominin discovered by the Leakey family. The Leakeys had been on my radar for years, ever since Richard Leakey was a guest speaker when I taught at Cypress College, and I had the privilege of hosting him.

After an extended time in the Goodall exhibit, I made my way to the Becoming Los Angeles rooms where I encountered photos of the oil fields on Venice Beach where I grew up. I had never seen these powerful views before. They were remarkable in that they showed the density of the 1930's and 40's oil wells on the beach shore where I grew up in the 40's, sandwiched between derricks. As I continued to appreciate the beginnings of my birth city, I became more rapt when I came upon a portrait displayed on the wall of my friend, Jacque Nunez from San Juan Capistrano. Jacque is a Native American and a prominent spokesperson for indigenous people. She has dedicated her life to representing the important contributions of Native People.

I realized that had I been with companions, my tour of the museum would have been far different. After a way too short three hours, I drove myself to Venice Beach where I spent most of my childhood, and where Ken and I visited many times researching for my Venice book in 2020. However, the pandemic lockdown limited our access. I wanted to walk around and take it in with its current bells, whistles and quirks.

I parked on the beach lot at the end of Washington, and walked the few steps onto the fishing pier. I was astonished to discover that I had serendipitously caught the King Tide at its lowest point!! Controlling my impulse to jump up and down with joy, lest others think me strange, I quickly pulled off my shoes and set out walking south on the wet sand toward Ballona Creek. It was a venture I had not taken since 1964, in the summer of our marriage when Ken and I lived in an apartment over the fish market at the pier. The extremely low tide revealed dozens of perfect sand dollars, scallops, razor and large clam shells set among muscle remains and seaweed. I was immediately transported back to my shell collecting, beach walking girlhood on this very stretch of sand. I was delighted and became lost in my old ways of being at the beach, on the edge of the continent, which included a whole lot of alone time, thinking, and being in nature with myself.

When I got home I shared my adventurous day with Ken. Smiling at me he said, "You know Donna, I wasn't so sure about you driving alone all the way into the inner city, but I am glad you did. I see now that you still know how to be alone. I'm proud of you."

Continuing my pondering, I recalled two things one of my favorite authors, Pulitzer Prize winning journalist Anna Quindlin has to say. She urges us to live more in the moment while she wishes that she had simply paid more attention to her children when they were young. She regrets that she kept so busy. The other idea of hers I admire is how important it is for us to be alone with ourselves. I realize that's what my Sunday was about, a day of being alone with myself. Perhaps when we allow ourselves personal time we have the luxury of thinking about bigger things such as the environment.

I have been writing and thinking about my new year's resolution for a while now. I resolved to have more open spaces in my calendar, but maybe that is not really it. Perhaps I simply need more conscious alone time. I know that when I am alone to think, creative ideas flow to my consciousness. So my new year's resolution is to carve out more alone time and to give myself permission to live more in the moment, to set the To Do list aside, and be more with myself. I want to find ways to do more about the environment as well. How about you? Are you taking time to be alone with yourself, to celebrate the power of one? What kind of New Year's resolutions are you contemplating? I am interested in your thoughts on this subject.

I wish you a wonderful, healthful, peaceful new year filled with respect for yourself.

Sometimes the Silver Lining has Mildew

04 Sep 2021

Greetings as summer winds down. Recently, I learned a lesson that sometimes joy comes with a price tag that's not readily apparent!! The incident reminded me that "no good deed goes unpunished." On a warm summer day Ken and I adopted a litter of 8-week-old kittens. Our home front gang of cats had gotten so old that we joked that they were carrying around their AARP cards instead of hunting critters on our rural property. Ken was insistent that we adopt more cats.

Striking out at the shelters, I turned to Craigslist where I found three male Bengal kittens up for adoption. I made arrangements to meet them and perhaps adopt them. Ken and I met the kitty lady in a motel parking near Knott's Berry Farm.

We parked in front of the motel, which had seen better days, where we were offered easy viewing of the woman loading the kittens into a personal metal shopping cart at the back of a fenced parking lot. Kittens on board, they were wheeled toward us.

We said our hellos, admired the strikingly beautiful young cats and quickly agreed to adopt them. We placed them into our cat carrier, thanked her, and headed home in the 5 pm. traffic.

I was over the moon!! Shangri La! I had never seen sweeter kittens, nor had we had any kittens in over a decade. As we made our way down the 405 Freeway Ken said, "Donna you do realize that the motel is a county reimbursed homeless shelter, right?"

"Huh?"

Ken continued, "I saw four adult people going in and out of that room where the lady was organizing the kittens. Do you remember that she mentioned that they had a dog and the parents of the kittens with her?"

I didn't say anything, but I thought that's a lot of folk and animals in one room. We dropped the topic and discussed the kittens' transition at our home. I did not think more about it. As the days unfolded we discovered that we had the most loving, happy kittens. They were used to be being handled, leaping into our laps for petting and love. We were smitten. The granddaughters and my mother came to meet them. We were all beyond delighted with the new additions. Our days were filled with fun as we played with them, especially after the vet gave them gold stars during their wellness visit as their vaccinations began.

A couple of weeks passed and my son and his family returned from a Lake Powell houseboat vacation. He casually mentioned that his youngest daughter had come down with ringworm on the boat. They used an antidote and the spots cleared up. I assured him that it could not have been from the kittens as they had passed the veterinary inspection.

However, my son had planted a seed of doubt in my mind. I began to study what I thought were "poison oak" spots on me more closely. Oh no! I realized that I had not contracted poison oak during my horse ride, but that I had 12 ringworm lesions on my face and body. I looked like the Zombie Apocalypse! There were panicky calls. I managed an emergency dermatologist appointment; oral and topical medications were prescribed, and I frantically called the veterinarian, The vet immediately prescribed medicated baths for the kittens and oral medication. We cancelled all our plans and commitments for the next two weeks. I was contagious!

That was the turning point where the bliss had morphed into something else entirely. Conscientiously, our 12-year-old granddaughter, Caroline, and I began our nursing duties. We played YouTube videos on how to bathe small kittens. We followed the directions. As we dried the kittens after the first round of baths, we could hear suspicious rasping sounds in their tiny lungs. They had inhaled water. Real worry began to set in. No longer was ringworm the focus but we were concerned that our "cure" had threatened the lives of the kittens. We tucked them in for the night and hoped for the best by morning.

I had a terrible time sleeping for concern over the kittens. The next day, their breathing was still rough and they had developed coughs. I sounded the alarm and the veterinarian worked us into her busy schedule. I worried. The doctor diagnosed pneumonia and prescribed morning and night administration of antibiotics on top of the oral anti-fungal medication. We began a ten-day regime of administering three oral syringes of medication per day to each of the three kittens. I was a bit frantic. I spent my time vacuuming, running loads of laundry and disinfecting the kittens' area.

Slowly, the babies recovered and my lesions and those on the granddaughters healed as well. I no longer looked like a Zombie and the kittens returned to their playful selves. We are all recovering. The kittens never did show any symptoms, the doctor described them as "asymptomatic" and told the story of being an intern in an animal shelter where all 30 of its cats had ringworm. She said it was a nightmare to resolve.

My dermatologist was more philosophical saying, "Well this is the price we pay for loving our critters." I am still cleaning like a maniac, but we seem to have turned the corner. The lesson I have learned from all this is that sometimes the silver lining has a mildew beneath it. Would I do it all over again knowing what I know now? Hmmm... Of course I would!! They are precious and I know we will have years of enjoyment. Eventually they will be old enough to take over the hunting tasks our older cats have abandoned.

Did your summer go okay? Are you staying healthy? I would love to hear how you have been doing.

Waking a Sleeping Bear

May 18, 2021

California is racing toward the less restrictive yellow tier; all around us we can feel the stirrings of new beginnings, as our world returns to taken-for-granted lives where we could hug one another and visit in-person. Closed down for fifteen months, I almost feel like a bear blinking her eyes open as she staggers out of a long, dark hibernation.

Last evening, my husband, Ken arrived home after a victorious night of wrestling in which his high school girls' wresting team sailed undefeated to another South Coast League Championship. Their sights are now set on the CIF-SS Dual Meet Tournament. What seemed almost impossible months ago became a reality, the girls have been allowed physical contact. I have watched Ken and his co-coach struggle all year, trying to keep the teen wrestlers engaged in the combat sport when they only had imaginary opponents. The coaches used creativity and ingenuity to help pass the agonizing months of no contact, social distancing, and mask wearing. Somehow they succeeded.

How have you fared? Were you successful in holding yourself together during the deprivations of: no contact, no outings, no parties, no activities? About five weeks ago, fully vaccinated, my daughter hosted a belated 21st birthday outdoor dinner party for her son James. I was the beneficiary of my first grandchildren hugs in over a year; I felt embarrassed when tears appeared on my cheeks. It shook me to see how much those hugs meant to me. I had been practicing "a stiff upper lip" in the absence of physical contact with my loved ones.

Hopefully, such an event as a worldwide lockdown will not be upon us again. It has been such a complete time-out in our lives that there are lessons to be learned on how we can do better moving forward. What did you learn? Last week, I met with a much younger, single, lady friend for dinner. As we were seated, she removed her mask, and offered that the pandemic taught her that she is unwilling to live the rest of life single. She is going to start a dating campaign and find a life partner.

Well, that certainly opened a serious conversation on the important understandings we have gained from this crushing time. For a vast majority of us we had never heard of Zoom meetings before the spring of 2020, much less understood the advantages of them. We have learned that we can work from home. Probably in-person office hours will never be what they were in the past.

On a more intimate level I found that not being so involved out-of-the-home allowed me to have the zest to act on my creative thoughts. As you know, I woke up the second month of the lockdown with an idea to write about growing up in the 4th most productive oil field in California, on the beach in Venice. I wanted to preserve that piece of my lived history. The months researching and writing that book felt like a pleasure trip because I had the LUXURY of time. I was not trying to cram in writing between teaching college classes, raising a family, or leading tours at the mission. I had nothing but time, glorious time, and because I did not feel rushed, it was an extremely pleasurable writing experience.

Across my life I have not been a "foodie." My son-in-law's favorite story to tell on me is that upon all of us arriving in Rome one year, hungry and wondering where to eat, I pointed to a Chinese restaurant across the square. He is still laughing at the idea of being in Italy and me thinking of chow mien! Admittedly, I eat to live, not so much living to eat. However, cooking during the lockdown, three meals a day for 15 months got me more interested in things culinary. I bought an Instant Pot and fell in love with it. When I joined a Facebook Instant Pot cooking community, they welcomed me in as a fellow "Foodie." I was beside myself with joy for this new designation in my life. I have thrown myself into it all; reading recipes, studying ingredients and how they relate to one another. All this has led to a new orientation toward mindful eating. The result, Ken and I have each lost more than 20 pounds during this lockdown.

Another thing I practiced was creating pockets of silence within me. I've carved out long moments of quiet where I let my creative right brain hemisphere have at it. The daydreaming and mulling have allowed me to come up with some new ideas for my art and writing. It has helped me to be still.

Excited about this topic of Lessons Learned from the Pandemic, I did a bit of research asking others what they too have learned. Some of the responses: "to recognize the value of the people that surround you. The pandemic really makes one think about what others bring to your relationship and how important they are." A friend who lives alone reports: "I have learned even more than ever how important staying positive is and recreating your life in a way to stay safe and active."

"The pandemic has taught us that we are way more flexible in our routines than we imagine, but that we still want our routines back as soon as we can have them. We are all very resilient, but we really do prefer to be around people."

Other insights: "If I can live through this, I can live through anything."

"I had to find my inner introvert because I love people."

"I learned to do handyman jobs and how to prepare for on-camera Zoom meetings and that you can get a pitcher of Margaritas to go!"

"Slowing down is important. Time with friends and family is most important. Work is secondary. Covid put a spotlight on our necessities and made everything else seem silly. Outdoor activities really are fun, and I don't need to be around people all that much to be happy. Thank God for the Internet. Lockdown would have been a completely different experience without it."

Simmering Below the Surface

March 27, 2021

Recently, I experienced some emotional triggers which have given me pause. Yesterday, for example: dressed in my mission docent costume, mentally prepared to deliver a bang-up history tour, I parked my car in downtown San Juan Capistrano. I glanced up to see three big flags in front of the new hotel next to the mission, all flying at half-mast. Suddenly the painful reminder of the two recent mass killings filled my soul. It felt like a knife in my heart. I took a few deep breaths to get hold of myself. That grim reminder was sobering. As I walked the short block to the mission I fought down the despair of the senseless violence of the last week. By the time I met the tour guests, I had pulled it together.

Later, I had time to reflect on my emotional reaction to those low flags flying. I checked in with myself. I recalled another such trigger; it was seeing cars in the parking lot of the local elementary school after so many months of mandated lockdown. I had been embarrassed that day to feel tears falling down my cheeks as I noted teachers' cars; a bit of "normal" was coming back. It caught me off guard.

I kept studying this phenomenon of my interior life, tears at seeing cars in a parking lot? Bummed by flags? My thoughts flashed to the past weekend and how dazed I felt being hugged by my loved ones!! Our daughter and son-in-law had hosted a backyard 21st birthday party for their youngest son. I received hugs! There were 15 of us there, and finally, because Ken and I are both well vaccinated, they felt safe hugging us for the first time in a year. I appeared to keep my cool, but as a hug-starved grandmother, the sensation of gathering up love was layered with more intense emotion than I care to admit.

I think for many of us, perhaps for most of us, we have been in a mental state of "guardedness," waiting for the next thing to pile on. I think we have been far more stressed during the last year of lock down, our worlds upside down, than our conscious self allows. We are brave, resilient people. We put on our "Can Do" masks and move forward. Of course we do. It is who we are, but I think for many of us there is a simmering vat of emotion seething under the surface. Perhaps now as the world begins its slow return to normal, with 90 million of us vaccinated, and predictions that by summer all who desire vaccines will have them, we can begin to let our guards down.

I am coming to understand that I have been through something extremely challenging, something difficult. During the 15 months of the trial against my father, over 30 years ago, I understood the need to take care of myself, to treat myself gently. Maybe by admitting that we have endured a year unlike any other in our lives we can give ourselves permission to be vulnerable humans. Maybe my tears at the parking lot, the agony of the flags at half mast, are a simple expression of my humanity.

Perhaps more than ever we must take back up our search for precious moments, for finding joy in the littlest of things, like looking at the passengers in the car next to you at the signal and smiling because they are singing their hearts out, or getting a kick out of something others say. I had a fourth grader on a mission tour the other day, and I asked, "Max, I hope you are not getting information overload!" Max looked at me with his sparkling eyes and exclaimed, "That's impossible, I live for facts!"

I laughed at his charming candor. The world is a beautiful place, admiring a stunning sunset or the way light plays along the carpet in your home, precious moments are waiting for us. My horse-riding companion, Christine, and I burst out laughing the other day when, on horseback, we had to almost dodge the dozens of swallows who were frantically diving into the mud near us to build their nests.

Of course living in gratitude for being alive can help us return to some kind of normalcy. I would love to know how you are holding up and your plans for keeping yourself happy.

Enchanted Tide Chasers

March 1, 2021

As the worldwide pandemic has moldered on with California being particularly locked down, my husband Ken and I have been motivated to discover new ways of living our lives. He is still seeing his high school girl wrestlers a few days each week, and I am just getting back to leading tours at the mission, but it still leaves many hours in which to find creative ways to live.

Our new "thing" began serendipitously back in January after my emotional reaction to the January 6th Capitol insurrection. We began, in earnest, looking for active ways to keep me settled down. More than ever we started taking little adventure trips around our county, particularly to the seashore. Our first such visit was on January 12th to Doheny State Beach. We nearly opted to stay cozy on the sofa watching the news, but forced ourselves to go out and we were glad we did. Our timing happened to coincide with an extremely low tide. The tide was so far out that huge rocks far beyond the surf line were exposed. With great delight we hopped from rock to rock, laughing and snapping photos of the flocks of seagulls which refused to be scared away. Later we walked around the harbor and discovered several Black Crowned Night Herons, Blue Herons, and an Egret sunning on the hand railing next to our path, they were far too at home to fly away. I had entered a birder's Eden and was dizzy with excitement as I snapped dozens of photos.

That trip got us excited to begin studying the tide charts. A few days later we ventured to Crystal Cove, just south of Newport Beach. At the trail head we were chatting with a man, explaining that we were following the tide charts. He looked at me and exclaimed, "Are you a surfer?" I smiled, "No, just a nature lover." Ken got the biggest kick out of that; he loves the idea that his septuagenarian wife could be taken for a surfer!

These many weeks later, we have both downloaded the tidal app into our cell phones. We think of ourselves as "Tide Chasers!" We have adopted a new habit. We are having the best time following low tides while getting our steps in every day. Part of the thrill is that we never know what we will discover. Late yesterday, at Salt Creek we came upon a sunset photo-shoot of a very expectant mother, her small child and husband. She was on the wet sand in a long lavender tulle and lace gown, cupping the enormity of her expectancy while holding the toddler's hand. The husband smiled down at his budding family as the photographer snapped away. Tears filled my eyes. It was beautiful.

Leaving them, Ken and I proceeded down the beach when two single-passenger motor-gliders buzzed twenty feet above our heads, dizzying all us spectators with their crazy dipping, and soaring antics. They came by three different times. It was wild fun to watch them! Walking and chatting about the gliders, we soon encountered several elaborate drip sand castles, one with rock towers adorning it, and endless flocks of seagulls!

As the sun began to sink behind Catalina Island, some kind of magic seemed to settle across the area. Spectators began arriving and staking out their sites to watch the sun's spectacular Technicolor goodbye. We realized this was becoming a consistent experience: hundreds of spectators assembling each evening up and down the coast. It seems that the setting sun has become a new kind of pandemic spectator sport.

The Covid-19 restrictions have brought on new ways of being, not all of them good.

According to some of the posts I see on Facebook, the threat has led to depression and feelings of isolation and desperation. People live with grief, and loss, and worry. These past twelve months have been extremely traumatic for most Americans, and specifically devastating for others. Our suffering is real.

Neuroscience has discovered that it is possible to change the way our brain is thinking when we are "stuck." Being "stuck" means that our brain mulls a negative thought over and over while it is trying to problem-solve. After that January 6th Capitol incident, I could feel myself being pulled down. This can lead to the arousal state of feeling overwhelmed. We can change that pattern but we must take action to do so. My daughter, Julina, sent me an interesting quote yesterday. "Crisis does not create character, it reveals it."

We humans are resilient. We can be mindful that we must take action to feel better. Habits come from deep neural maps for thinking and doing certain things within our brains. It is possible to change those maps and create new ones but it takes effort and being conscious of what one is thinking. Steven Covey in, *The 7 Habits of Highly Effective People*, says, "Our character, basically is a composite of our habits…habits are powerful factors in our lives because they are consistent, often unconscious patterns, that daily express our character and produce effectiveness or ineffectiveness." We need the good kind of habits!

I think it is essential to focus on what we HAVE instead of what we do not have. Aristotle said, WE ARE WHAT WE REPEATEDLY DO. EXCELLENCE IS NOT AN ACT, IT IS A HABIT. I invite you to walk outdoors and embrace nature in a new way. Look for a moment of joy. This morning I saw an egret sitting on top of my neighbor's gazebo. Really? How delightful! Maybe you can become a sunset aficionado, taking photos of its color show, or a recorder of all you see on the walking trail, or a lover of birds or wildlife? For now Ken and I are enchanted by all that can be discovered at the seashore as we chase the tides.

Getting On Up that Trail!

January 26, 2021

I learned a difficult lesson two weeks ago about the impact of our past upon our present. In an attempt to live in the now, many of us actively ignore or suppress old, painful events. Why wouldn't we?

A gallows put up by Trump supporters. Photo: ANDREW CABALLERO-REYNOLDS / AFP

In all innocence last week, I wrote to a friend who is a self professed "Foodie." Not knowing that many Foodies, I thought he would be excited about my new Instant Pot and the world of fun which it has opened up to me. My new Instant Pot Facebook friends have welcomed me into their "IP" community as a fellow "Foodie." I knew my friend would appreciate my newly discovered passion. He also happens to be a rabbi as well as an experienced marriage and family therapist. I dashed off a detailed Instant Pot email, and as a P.S., I confessed that I had suffered a meltdown and an unexpected return of my PTSD symptoms during the horrifying insurrection at the Capitol two weeks earlier. I admitted that I was still a bit shaken by my unexpected reaction to the violence.

He immediately emailed me back, skipping past the Instant Pot message, saying, "Such a strange time. Every therapist I know has been totally overwhelmed. These times have unmasked formerly dormant and, for many, unrecognized traumatic stressors. It reminds us that these wounds never really resolve but sit beneath the surface waiting to be triggered."

Oh ugh I thought as I read this. I had hoped, believed even, that my peaceful, secure life filled with creative work, loving people, dogs and horses, had cemented over my ancient childhood agonies. Of course I understood that the dark side of my growing up years, suffering profound abuse at my father's hands, had left scars. However, as time has passed since the trial thirty years ago, that sent him to prison for his crimes, I have tended to white-wash the enormity of the trauma. Hence, I was ill prepared for what unfolded on January 6th as I sat down on the couch with a fresh cup of tea in hand to witness the certification of the Electoral College vote.

Protestors climb onto the Capitol in Washington. Photo: JASC ANDREW/JASON ANDREW/The New York Times/

As I watched angry aggressors scale the walls of the Capitol, beat Capitol police officers with flag poles, use stun guns on the necks of others, and throw a heavy fire extinguisher into a crowd of defenders while chanting "Get Pence," I felt my composure begin to slip. The camera scanned to the gallows that had been erected and showed plastic handcuff ties hanging from violent assailants' pockets. Glass was broken, a fatal shooting occurred, and the inner sanctum was breached. Violent mayhem was playing out before me. Helplessness washed over me as tears filled my eyes. They rolled down my cheeks. Old feelings of despair overwhelmed me. I could not stop a personally devastating situation. Was our country falling before me?

Before long, Ken, my husband, who had been working at his computer, entered the room. Seeing that I was overcome, he turned off the news, and tried to understand what was wrong. It took him about one second to realize that I had been catapulted back into deep-rooted feelings of my past horror. He got me out of the house, onto my horse, and up the trail. He walked beside my horse. Before long I felt better and could finally talk about it.

I was stunned to learn that those archaic, helpless feelings were lurking beneath the surface of my happiness. I had no idea that our democracy was so fragile, that such a breach was even possible. I had no clue that I could be rendered defenseless against an attack on our way of life. In the last few days, I have learned that others experienced similar reactions. One woman we know awoke at 5 a.m. the day after the terrorists' attack and was repeatedly physically sick to her stomach. Other friends have confided that they cried all day on January 6th. It seems to me that we need to more fully recognize what lies beneath our surface; that we need to respect our pain that has gone before.

The temperature on our national political stage has turned down some, and perhaps as a country we are getting back toward something more acceptable to most. I know that a whole lot of fun is going on in social media with the Bernie Sanders memes, and that millions of us are still celebrating our young poet Amanda Gorman. I think one of my takeaways from all of this is that dramatic events on the national and international stage can profoundly affect us. Being human, we do not have to pretend we are okay when we are not. We can admit to real feelings. We can understand that perhaps there is no such thing as "cementing over them."

We have been through a lot. Isolation alone is hard on our spirit. Sheltering in place, not seeing or hugging our loved ones, unable to gather and celebrate with each other, or worship together have been incredibly traumatic. Mixing in rising death rates, the weakening economy, and extreme political unrest adds up to a recipe for astronomical stress levels.

More than ever it is important that we take extra special care of ourselves, that we find new ways to engage our minds. Probably no one would have imagined that I would go crazy playing with my new Instant Pot, but I have. It is an adventure! Even my children are sharing their favorite recipes with me. I'm making dishes I only dreamed about and learning new techniques. It's exciting! The future cannot help but hold events that can trigger our old feelings, but we can acknowledge those feelings, and use our tools for mindfulness and maintaining our resilience. We can focus on the positive in things, celebrate our daily victories, and nourish our bodies. These actions are key to feeling better. We know that daily exercise and interacting with positive others (and finding fun where we can!) are ways to keep ourselves moving forward. Perhaps we need to find time to leave the Instant Pot to do its thing and get on up the trail!

Staying Sane During this Insane Time

November 17, 2020

It has been interesting to me in conversations with my husband, Ken, to reflect on how his 50 San Clemente High School female wrestlers are handling coming to in-person classes knowing that there is only a small chance they will get to wrestle at all during this year of Covid-19. He says they keep showing up and that their spirits are pretty good. He and his co-coach create alternate activities for them. On Veteran's Day they had a voluntary "meet" with Dana Hills' girl wrestlers on the beach in Doheny where they participated in sort of a socially distant "fitness Olympics" with the other team. From the photos it looked like a great turn out and that the girls were engaged and enjoying the competition.

So Ken and his co-coach are being creative. Maybe that's part of the solution to how we can stay sane during this insane time. There's no argument that keeping safe during this pandemic is a huge challenge. My daughter who teaches 7th grade English feels like she is talking to herself when she teaches her students on Zoom. Sometimes she resorts to dancing to keep their attention. I know that my grandchildren are struggling to understand the materials in their classes while staying engaged. It's hard not seeing our loved ones or hugging them. Millions of Americans have lost their jobs. Depression is rampant. Food scarcity is real, but we still have hope. We know a vaccine will be coming soon.

Living on the "corona-coaster" I hear some of my associates saying they miss people they don't even like. Others report that "they are bored with being part of a major historical event!!" For me, personally, I am at a place where running errands and walking the dogs are big highlights which count as "going out." Of course all of us get that it is up to us to figure out how to accomplish contentment when our old activities are shut down. We are now forced to become even more inventive in how we live our lives.

My sister Diana, after months of lockdown with all four of her family members working from home and going to school on-line, had a genius idea. It was very difficult to execute,

but she was successful. She finally found a cabin high in the San Bernardino Mountains which has good Wifi and needed work and a family to love it. They closed escrow. Last week they enjoyed their first snowfall while working on-line from 7200 feet elevation. They are bewitched by a new life.

Others in my life have discovered the thrills of RVing and are planning road trips around America. My friend Mary is taking two art and drawing classes on Zoom. She is full of more energy and excitement than ever as she faces new art challenges. My daughter, Julina, has taken up Pickle Ball and is playing several evenings each week. For my part, you know I wrote that memoir-history book, Growing Up Venice a few months ago. That led to me embracing my Los Angeles roots and joining the Los Angeles City Historical Society. I kept pulling on that historical society thread which led to me becoming a part of their board of directors. It's captivating to meet new people (on Zoom) and to think about new ideas.

Our challenge is how to adapt to this crazy period in the world. We know time is slipping by quickly, like warm sand through our fingers. We cannot afford to waste any of it; it's too precious and too fleeting. You may recall that brain science has discovered that we humans have some 50,000 thoughts per day, and that about 80% of them are negative. They kept us safe during the cave-man days, but negativity can tear us down in today's pandemic. It can freeze us into inaction. We need to be actors in our own lives to live to the fullest. Here's a remedy to overcoming negative thinking's detrimental effects:

Practice Mindfulness: Acknowledge judgmental, critical, irrational, and fear-based thoughts and then poke holes in them as you would a bubble and watch them disappear.

Exercise Daily: Our bodies desperately need the good endorphins which are generated through movement. My septuagenarian mount Everest climbing friend always says, "Motion is Lotion."

Find Something New to Focus Your Thoughts Upon. Join a new group, take up a hobby, discover some different recipes, plant a winter garden, start a virtual book club, take up yoga or meditation, adopt a puppy.

This is our time now and it's more important than ever that we make the best use of it. You know I always enjoy hearing from you. Happy Thanksgiving.

Turning a Forced Time-Out into a Gift

September 10, 2020

Hi! I've missed writing to you. I took such a drastic action to fill up these months of Covid-19 lockdown, that my hands have been really full. If you follow me on Facebook, you may know that Ken and I adopted an 8-week-old puppy, River, a few weeks ago. River is keeping us hopping! Caring for her now structures our days and nights. When I am on the patio for the 2 A.M. potty break, I have to laugh, realizing that I certainly did take an extreme action to occupy myself! But there's something more to my late-night visits to the cool outdoor air. They have allowed me to appreciate the stillness of darkness and the beauty of not being so busy all the time.

I guess I am seeing my life in new ways. I'm reveling in the LUXURY of just being. I am enjoying every minute of River's development. Last week I heard her bark for the first time. A few days ago, I carried her in my arms into the pool and watched her dip and splash her little front paws. Last evening, Ken placed an empty bottle on the ground so that River could check it out. She was so adorable, barking at it, then leaping up in the air, running around, and leaping and barking some more. It was fascinating to her! Finally, she was brave enough to touch the bottle and drag it under our chairs. Ken and I watched, adoringly, like young parents, all the while throwing balls for Dixie and Lacey.

It's not all smooth sailing. There was a dust-up when she too rambunctiously approached two of the cats. They were less than impressed, got all big with their hair on end, and went after her. She cried and ran behind the sofa. I rescued her. It was a hard lesson for her. She was consoled later when each of those same cats rubbed against her.

I hope you are making the most of this unusual period in your life. It seems we must play the cards we are dealt, so that even with a bad hand, we can make it our time now. Because of the difficulties in the world, we have been forced to step out of our sometimes crazy-frenetic schedules. We can rail against the circumstances or use this occasion to renew and reinvent. Perhaps we have been given a gift of time?

One of my favorite research books on the science of human happiness is: Flow: The Psychology of Optimal Experience. In his book, the author teaches us that happiness is nothing more than living in the FLOW of the moment when we are engaged in something meaningful to us. We can feel happy making a cake, conditioning for a 5 K run, or growing zucchini. One of the big tricks is to live in the present doing things that give us a little thrill. This requires that we become mindful of our thoughts, and pin down our dreams, and make the effort to fulfill them. I hope that you are doing just that, finding joy in some of the simple things during this unusual time in history.

I love when you write to me. I have written a new book. It is the best of my childhood, growing up in the fourth most productive oil field in California, on the Venice Peninsula. I have captured some aspects of Los Angeles history that could be lost forever. *Growing Up Venice: Parallel Universes* is on Amazon in paperback, while we are waiting for the color hardbound copy to be available in a few weeks. I'll let you know when it's ready. I am looking forward to hearing from you and learning what you have been doing to stay sane during this insane time.

Locked Down and Gloved Up!

April 4, 2020

Under cover of early morning darkness today, masked and gloved, I sneaked into Von's Market, accepting a freshly sanitized shopping cart from a worker at the door. As I passed the colorful Easter candy display, I felt a sharp pain, like a kick, grip my stomach as tears sprang to my eyes. No Easter gathering this year. I pushed the cart forward and worked to shed the jab of the emotional toll this lockdown is having on us.

Introverts, please put down your book and check on your extrovert friends. They are not okay.

The day before, on the walking trail with my dogs, a man approached from about thirty feet away, and seeing me, lifted a mask to his face. I quickly veered out into the empty street. He lowered his mask and gave me a brief wave from a great distance.

THEY SAID A MASK AND GLOVES WERE ENOUGH TO GO TO THE GROCERY STORE

THEY LIED, EVERYBODY ELSE HAD CLOTHES ON

Something like four billion of us on the planet are under mandatory lockdown. In the 200,000 years of anatomically modern humans, there has never been such an isolation occurrence. Firstly, across human history the populations have been much smaller, and certainly no opportunity for mass communication. You and I, right now, are living history.

We Baby Boomers grew up learning about the agonies of the Great Depression, hoping no such thing would befall us. The recent strong economy and low unemployment rates have lulled us into a sense of safety and comfort. That view has suddenly been shattered.

Ken and I have been deeply respectful of the CDC guidelines. Staying in, spraying down grocery bags, sanitizing the groceries, and leaving packages on the porch for several days. Our schedules are pretty open. For the most part we are doing okay. Across our long marriage my chief complaint has been that I wished my husband were home more. Well he's home now and I have plenty of time with him. Guess what? I like it! The other day, when I returned from a walk, he was so proud because he had been sewing!! (I know, Ken sewing is pretty wild!). He proceeded to demonstrate his creation. Using a clean white dusting cloth and a paper coffee filter, he had manufactured a serviceable mask. He was so proud!

Anyway, we've completed a few projects around the house, read some books, and of course done a lot of cooking, but what surprises me is how exhausting it is not doing that much. Do you, too, feel a strain of exhaustion?

It occurs to me that many of us are in a type of grief mode. If it is not grief, certainly it is anxiety. The economists agree that we are headed for a deep recession. The financial unknown out there alone is plenty to scare us, and certainly the daily CORONA VIRUS

DEATH REPORT is enough to do in the strongest of us.

Our losses are lurking under many different layers: not seeing our loved ones, having our freedom of movement curtailed, losing our daily schedule and its familiar comforts of coworkers, the mental challenges of work, and feeling the sting of missing our friends. Others of us are beginning to experience the agony of actually losing loved ones to this virus.

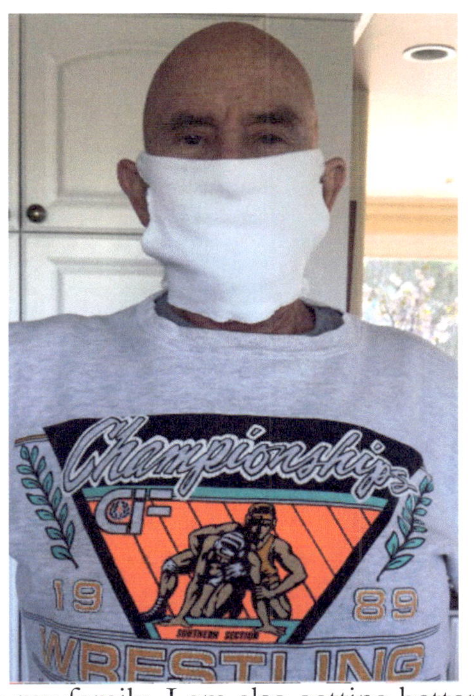

As a survivor of child abuse I have had a default "setting" for "hyper-vigilance." What this means is that I am unconsciously preparing for the next assault. It's possible that you also may be unconsciously gearing up for the next blow. This is a hard way for us to live. Our reaction to the world pandemic may be the only aspect over which we have some control. Perhaps this is a good time to work on training our brains. For me, I now recognize that I feel exhausted because my world has upended. Going forward I am going to respect that fact and give myself a break, maybe even a nap!

So recognizing how stressed we actually feel is a good first step. Deciding to control it is another positive move. This is a good time to calm our minds through meditation, walking, yoga and relaxation techniques. Maybe we should limit the time we watch the news. Every time the economists discuss the next most dire prediction, I feel my anxiety climbing.

I downloaded Zoom and am having "meetings" with my family. I am also getting better at remembering to use Facetime and being grateful. Brain science has proven that when we live in gratitude our happiness levels elevate. In addition, when we help others, we tend toward feeling better. The local food banks desperately need our help, as do elders who need grocery deliveries. Our friends need phone calls and texts. My beautiful daughter-in-law texted me this sign: INTROVERTS PUT DOWN YOUR BOOK AND CALL YOUR EXTROVERT FRIENDS. THEY ARE NOT OKAY!! Yes, we can help our friends and neighbors.

Certainly there is no silver bullet that is going to rescue us anytime soon. The laboratories around the world are working as fast as they can on a vaccine. For now we are keeping our distance and wearing masks. It seems to me that it is our job to respect how truly stressful this is and give ourselves permission to understand that: this is a really big deal! In the meantime my family and friends continue to share outrageously hilarious videos and photos. I love the Chris Mann Youtube parody on the right margin. The other night my friend sent this question to me: DOES ANYONE KNOW IF WE CAN TAKE SHOWERS YET OR SHOULD WE JUST KEEP WASHING OUR HANDS?

Puppet on a String

October 14, 2019

It is easy to fall into living on auto pilot. One never knows when a life-changing event will occur and old, worn-out, ways of living life might resurface. It has been interesting for me to realize that even with all the studying and therapy I have enjoyed across these many years, that my old dysfunctional behaviors want to leech into the present. About a month ago I made my usual morning wellness call to my nearly 96 year-old mother, who is legally blind, lacks much mobility in her walker, but still lived on her own. I discovered that she was too ill to call for help or even to shift the pillow under her head. She lives less than a mile away. I immediately went to her bedside and got help. There was a five day hospital stay, a surgical procedure, and according to the doctor, a very close brush with death. He thought she had only hours before succumbing had there not been medical intervention.

My sister and I dug in fast and visited assisted living establishments. We found a roomy one-bedroom apartment with a terrace in a nice facility. Over the course of several days my granddaughter, Kate, and I physically moved our mother's personal items into her new place. One of the biggest stressors, upsetting her the most, was what to do with her fourteen-year-old cats, one of which is diabetic. After some sleepless nights, I realized that I could have a cattery built on my property. I would take over the cats' care. My husband, Ken, agreed to build the cattery. We soon transferred her cats to our home. I took a deep breath. I thought we had gotten her and her cats to a safe place and settled.

Immediately, however, the calls started coming in on my cell phone. I seemed to get at least one call a day where she urgently needed something. One day she called complaining about the establishment's weak coffee. I dropped everything and jumped into my car and brought her stronger coffee. I reacted like that for over a week, jump jump jumping. On another day when I thought she had finally adjusted to her new life, I went to take her to lunch only to be sat down in a chair and lectured on why she should be allowed to live independently elsewhere. It was not a very pleasant lunch.

So after weeks of sketchy sleep and an anxious stomach, I have had to almost slap myself on the side of my head to stop my "auto pilot" puppet behavior. Across the years, even with her limitations, I have supported her insistence on living independently in her two story house full of stairs. Her recent scrape with death proved that she could no longer live alone.

On a recent Sunday morning, after another comprised night's sleep, I was sipping my coffee and staring at the fire, my stomach still in knots, when I realized that I had fallen into my old survivor behavior left over from my childhood which had been less than ideal. I was trying to "fix" everything, trying to make everyone happy, so I would be safe. I had an intervention with myself. I explained to that little girl who lives inside of me that she is NOT in charge of everyone's happiness. I gave her permission to stop reacting like a puppet on a string. It is not easy to quiet her down as our mother is very unhappy and is insisting on living elsewhere independently. There is a lot of "noise" and it's hard not to react.

I have been blessed with empathy, I feel what my mother is going through, giving up her home, her beloved pets, her vision, her mobility. I feel all of that, but I must understand that I cannot fix it. We must not allow ourselves to be made to be responsible for someone else's happiness. It is hard enough to accept responsibility for our own. Of course this will all be resolved somehow. I must remember to set personal boundaries and keep my eyes open so that I do not slip into old patterns. I must not allow Donna to be a puppet on a string!

I have come to see that I have been guilty of failing to place proper boundaries around myself. I see that I have allowed another's unhappiness to affect my own, and that I have permitted the little girl inside of me to run roughshod over the adult. I am forcing myself to examine my own behavior. I must remind myself of the negative impact of allowing rigid roles from the past to dictate one's behavior. Those old roles can strangle us. I am doing better. I am setting limits even though the stress continues.

I hope that by revealing my struggle that you might heighten your awareness to some of the emotional traps that are out there, and understand that navigating the sometimes-tumultuous waters of life is not always easy sailing.

Surviving the Holidays

December 8, 2016

While the advertisers shout out Black Friday deals and the malls shimmer with their glittering holiday cheer, it might be important to remember that for many the season can be loaded with emotional landmines. Even the most positive may succumb to feelings of anxiety or depression. The enormity of gifts to gather, a house to decorate, or the food to prepare, could cause the most hearty to feel overwhelmed! Memories of past years, perhaps with one's original family, or the loss of a loved one, could also trigger the grief response. Some of the participants in my Loss of a Loved One support group have expressed the idea that they wish they could fast forward through the holidays to January 2! Truly it can be a tough time.

Anxiety can be controlled by making "to do" lists and scaling back. The lists get it out of our heads and the scaling back makes it easier. Simply admitting how you feel can be a relief. Many of us tend to "should" on ourselves by demanding that we must do what we have always done to make the holidays "perfect" for our loved ones. Often they don't even notice if a certain dish is homemade or store bought, or whether something is beautifully wrapped or is in a Dollar Store decorative bag! If you suffer the "Be Perfect" admonition why not dump it right now? Your friend Donna here is telling you that we don't need to be perfect! Where can you slim down the details in your life to make your experience less nerve wracking? What can you change?

If you or your friend have recently lost a loved one, this first holiday season can be particularly difficult. Here are some survival ideas:

- Be proactive. Plan some activity or ritual that will help you get through the day. Perhaps it is a trip, hosting a gathering, taking a walk in the afternoon, doing something to break up the traditions from the past.
- Take time to think about your loved one and talk about him or her with a trusted confidant.
- Create a new tradition. My friend enjoys a morning of eating pie at a friend's house each Thanksgiving. Perhaps there is a game to play, or an art project the family or friends could enjoy such as decorating cupcakes, stockings, creating a gingerbread house, making ornaments.

- When invited somewhere consider whether you want to go or are you going to be polite. Answer conditionally, "May I tentatively say yes, and if I feel up to it that day I will come?"
- Let one trusted person know how you are really doing behind the social mask of cheerfulness.
- Carry out one of the traditions or rituals of your loved one to honor him or her.
- Most important of all know that it is okay to cry.
- Take good care of yourself by eating properly and sleeping properly and avoiding excessive use of alcohol.
- Live in gratitude. The prescription for negative thinking is to be grateful for all your blessings.
- Make a goals book and begin to look forward. What more do you want TO DO, TO HAVE AND TO BE in life?

Mark Twain said that courage is to face our fears and go forward. You can do that even though the holidays may bring more than social gatherings and beautiful music. I would love to hear your idea for Surviving the Holidays.

A Trip Inside Cuba 2016: A Study in Everyday Contrasts

July 16, 2016

I didn't know what to expect as we embarked on our Cuba "Face to Face" adventure two weeks ago with 17 other travelers. What would the next eight days reveal? Would we be looked down upon as Americans, ignored, or welcomed? I hoped I was doing the right thing by encouraging my daughter and granddaughter to go with me.

Our travel group got off to a shaky start in Miami. We were belted into our seats on the charter airline to Cienfuegos. Some of the passengers could view the luggage and cargo being stowed in the plane. After a while those same passengers could see suitcases being taken off, apparently the plane was over its weight limit. That is when the riot broke out. Passengers were screaming in Spanish to the non-Spanish speaking flight attendant, Pola, who in turn was demanding that the most vocal of the leaders, a hot tempered woman, be removed from the plane! Others shouted, "We have rights!" It was an ugly scene with perhaps 20 passengers fully engaged in the battle. We watched in amazement at a spectacle we had never before seen. After a very long half hour or so of yelling, the captain ejected all of us from the plane. There was more shouting as our little group circled the tour leader. "You are a coward!" one of our new, not very well mannered, tour mates yelled. He demanded that the tour manager decide whether we were all going to get back on the plane or stay in Miami until everyone had their luggage.

Some four hours later, we all got back on the plane, taking our chances on whether luggage would arrive with us or not. As it turned out six of our group of 20 had no luggage and never did get it until the next week. Upon arrival in Cienfuegos, while the plane was in motion taxiing to the gate, about twenty passengers got up and started removing their bags from the overhead bins! They were walking about on a moving plane! Yes, a strange and shaky beginning. Clearly I was already privy to a bird's eye view of a dissimilarity in cultural norms. Well, I wanted an adventure, I just didn't know it would be in the very first hours!

My elderly mother, a devotee of the Sunday travel section of the newspaper, had been warning me for months that Cuba was not ready for tourists, that I must carry my own roll of toilet paper and take shampoo and soap, that it was Third World. So what a lovely surprise to discover that the rooms were clean and up to American standards and that we did not need toilet paper. They have lots of toilet paper! However, we did need a certain inner toughness as Cuba is a study in contrasts. Here are a few:

1. Government workers make $12 a month. All Cubans are given a monthly ration card for five eggs, a pound of coffee, one pound of sugar, soap, etc.: the essentials. It did not seem like much, and the women in line in the ration store told me it was not enough, but everyone we encountered seemed well fed and adequately dressed. The government provides free education, mandatory through the 9th grade, excellent free medical care, and housing on paved streets. However, the citizens are not free to travel to other places.

2. Our luxury air-conditioned motor coach speeding through the lush green countryside was another contrast as I noted the ubiquitous horse drawn carts and water buffalos working in the fields of sugar cane.

3. We visited Girone, the beach at the Bay of Pigs where our American forces invaded Cuba in 1961. It is the home of the anti-American war museum where we watched a black and white news film depicting that losing invasion. We were continually referred to as "Yankee Imperialists." Two hours later, my daughter, Julina, and granddaughter, Jaycelin, and I were swimming in the Bay of Pigs with another tour mate when some children came to join us.

Soon the little band included about twelve Cuban youth ranging from perhaps six years of age to 25. We floated in the warm water for an hour or more laughing and teasing in a mix of English and our inconsistent Spanish. Two of the youngest climbed on my shoulders (once an abuela [grandmother] always an abuela, I guess.) That impromptu face-to-face was a delight as we learned more about their lives. One youth, a 25-year-old engineer, shared his dreams and opportunities with us. Their excitement about us and the warmth toward us were in stark contrast to the name calling in the war museum's film.

4. The Cuban government is tightly monitoring visitors as it is "hyper-sensitive about sovereignty" as we were told during a university professor's lecture. The government does not want Cuba to become a tourist place like Cancun. We were permitted to visit only under the controlled conditions of meeting Cubans "face to face." Careful records were kept of our visits to a boys and girls club, several senior centers, art studios, community clean up campaigns, music projects, mural and literacy projects, and more. Our visit included a lot of dancing, singing, listening and eating with the Cuban people, and never a mention of Guantanamo Bay.

5. To my delight my granddaughter had us rent a bright pink 1950's classic Ford Fairlane for our visit to the newly opened American Embassy. My eyes filled with tears at the sight of

our American flag waving freely. Today there are still four United States laws in place stating that Cuba is the enemy. However, it did not feel that way. The Cubans seemed to be very excited about us as Americans, and very interested in our politics!

6. Our eight days were filled with colorful and poignant observations. Standing near Ernest "Papa" Hemingway's favorite typewriter at his home held meaning for me as a writer, but the fact that no one seemed to know or say that he may have run guns for Fidel was striking. There were monuments and pictures celebrating Che Guevara all over Cuba, but we were told that he died in an airplane crash, when in fact he was probably executed. I observed oral history being rewritten...

7. The last afternoon of the trip is imprinted on my memory. I was resting in my comfortable waterfront room in the Nacional Hotel, when I heard a light tapping on my door. I opened it to find the middle-aged woman who was the maid for my room. She spread her arms wide and I stepped into her embrace. She hugged me and kissed my cheek goodbye. Was she digging for tips? I don't think so. Earlier in the week I had been in a too warm room and she had helped to move me. At that time I offered her two CUC ($2.00). She would only take one. We encountered many helpers along the way who would only accept the minimal tip they thought was appropriate.

8. A last common practice we discovered revealed another aspect of the Cuban character. When we would ask a person for directions, they would stop what they were doing and escort us to our destination, sometimes a few blocks away. What a generous and accommodating people!

We found them to be warm, welcoming, articulate and surprisingly informed about our politics. They don't have freedom to travel, to watch more than the four government sanctioned TV stations, or to hear world news from several points of view. They do not have freely accessible Wi-fi nor the material goods that we take for granted, but their hearts are full of love and they very much wish the embargo would go away. I'm glad I made the trip. I don't see how Cuba can remain the same for too long with the influx of Americans eager to meet their neighbor.

One of the most important life lessons my travels have taught me is that happiness resides within the individual. Over and over again I see my fellow humans delighting in the smallest gifts of life when by our standards they seem to have so little. It warms my heart.

Let's Plunge Head-First into this New Year

January 5, 2016

In the frosty darkness of New Year's Eve a sturdy band of about thirty of us braved the freezing chill to venture outside into the orchard at our mountain home to partake in the ancient Anglo-Saxon tradition of Waes hael - "to be well, hale." We gathered around the trees dancing and singing, "Here's to thee old apple tree; hats full, sacks full, great bushel bags full. Hurrah!" Then we sprinkled the waissail mixture of mulled ale and wines on the sleeping trees, a practice from antiquity. Perhaps our dances to scare away the worms and bring good wishes for a plentiful crop were more subdued than in eons past, nonetheless we enjoyed the ritual linking us to our bygone roots.

As we sang, my musings slipped from the past to my personal goals for this fresh new year. I was warmed by the deliciousness of new beginnings. Then I thought of you and that Kris Allen song, Live Like You Are Dying, which reminds us how precious our days are. I hope you are happy with the way you chose to live your days in 2015. If not, for 2016 why not reaffirm the importance of mindfulness and finding the positive in situations. Happiness experts tell us that we are the happiest when we are pursuing something that has meaning for us. As we ring in this new year, let's commit to living with the best choices possible, to strive toward our most joyful selves, to live with meaning. If you aren't that satisfied with the life you are living right now, you can turn things around quickly by making a transformative decision for the future.

My great wish for you waes hael, that you be well and enjoy the comfort of your spiritual life, that you thrive within the warm embrace of your family and friends. It is your time now. You have the power to create wonderful days. I hope that you plunge headfirst into this brand new year with all the excitement and energy at your command.

Life Starts Outside our Comfort Zone

October 27, 2015

My daughter Julina and I enjoyed a wonderful Saturday at the Mindful Her event with headliner Mallika Chopra held at the Crystal Cathedral in Garden Grove. As we rolled our yoga mats out onto the wet grass, we could not help but smile to see a hundred others doing the same thing in the shadow of that magnificent structure. As a student of the new brain research, I am deeply rooted in the idea that we humans can feel better if we adopt MINDFULNESS STRATEGIES. This event solidified my thinking.

Mindfulness is the practice of being present in the moment, giving your full awareness to what is occurring and accepting it without judgment. It requires that we are conscious and aware - that we learn to choose our response instead of simply reacting.

As a life coach, I am working to help my clients to have more purpose in life. Many feel too scared and nervous to move forward. The necessary action steps just seem too hard. When we practice mindfulness we acknowledge our negative feelings and let them pass through. It is human to be nervous and scared. Life is hard, but difficult does not have to dominate our behavior. It is possible for us to manage our internal world. The first step is awareness of our feelings, the next step is to rewrite what we are telling ourselves about them. If we are thinking, "I'm too old to get this job" rewrite the narrative to, "I am a hard worker and I know I can contribute to the workforce."

Our bodies believe what we are thinking. To move forward and get unstuck, change the internal messages you are creating. Your body responds to those negative messages, hence the sleeplessness and anxiety. I love this Iceberg Metaphor. What we are thinking is unseen, it is below the water line, but it is powerfully influencing our behaviors, that which is seen above the water. If you want to move forward, check what you are telling yourself, acknowledge that you are afraid and do it anyway. Give yourself a deadline. The difference between a dream and a goal is that a goal has a completion date. Courage is the bridge between our scared selves and taking action. You can do it. Start today. Life starts outside our comfort zone!

One last thought, I attended the conference to learn more about using meditation as a mindfulness tool. One break out section was about "Getting Your Calm On." I listened intently to four different ways to meditate; how important it is to empty our minds and BE.

The next day, I got up in the dark of early morning, settled my dogs around me, poured my coffee, and turned on the fireplace. As I stared into the fire I had an epiphany! I laughed out loud! I have been staring into that fire every morning for thirty years and never realized that I have been meditating all this time! I have always known that my quiet time is the part of the day when I still my mind. It is non-negotiable. It energizes me. It keeps me on track.

I invite you to practice telling yourself positive messages so you feel better, to still your mind every day, and when you feel scared to take the action step, do it anyway.

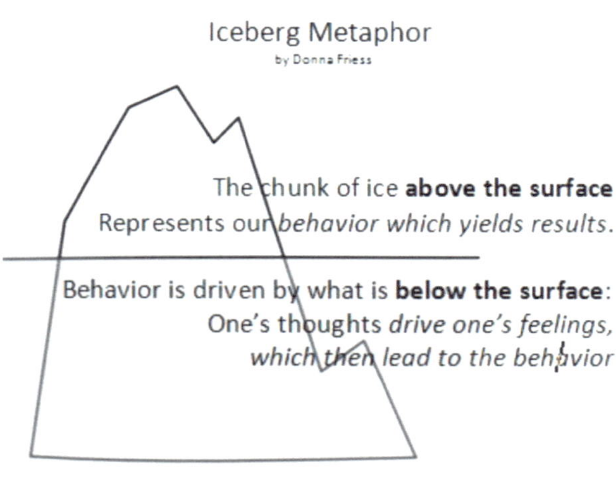

The Big Yellow School Bus

September 1, 2015

As the big yellow school buses again appear on our neighborhood streets, and the school yards fill with the music of children at play, a wave of nostalgia flows through me, recalling my own excitement at the beginning of each new school year. For 45 years I thrilled to the challenges of learning the names of my eager new students and preparing to excite them about communication. Those years are now in the past.

Smiling to myself, I acknowledge that momentary yearning as I place my boogey board in the back of my Jeep. It isn't the worst thing to pursue new challenges and to have the freedom to do so. But the longing for that other life is tangible and I'm not alone. More than ever my coaching clients are contacting me for help as school starts, perhaps it is a trigger for them, as they too look back on another life they once lived. This is normal, but anxiety may seep in around the edges as we struggle to figure out new ways of living life, especially for the newly retired, the empty-nesters, and the recent widows.

It is up to us to imagine new and meaningful ways to live. Happiness experts teach us to live in gratitude, to take up new challenges and activities, to have something to look forward to. We are in charge and we can choose happiness or desperation, it is up to us.

One of my all-time favorite books is Flow: The Psychology of Optimal Experience, in which the author teaches us to set goals, live in the present, and to immerse ourselves in compelling activities. This requires that we become mindful of our dreams and make the effort to fulfill them. This is our precious time and we need to continue to make the most of it. The Pacific is warmer than usual this summer and there are some waves out there waiting for me. Perhaps they are waiting for you as well. We can choose joy.

A Confident Young Lady

August 7, 2017

Hello my friends, you have not heard from me for a while as I've been working on my new book and traveling, but something happened the other day that I simply must share with you. You know I am constantly scouting for precious moments.

Last week, a big family group of us gathered at Catalina for our annual reunion which coincided with Ken's 75th birthday and our daughter's 49th. We enjoyed days of swimming, boating, and celebrating . On one of the days, all the dinghy drivers were away from my son's boat as they were wake boarding, leaving only myself and my daughter and son-in-law on board. Ken called from shore looking for a ride out to the boat. I looked at my son-in-law, Justin, he looked at me. We called up to Julie sunning on the flying bridge, she answered, "between the three of us we can figure it out!"

At that moment, seven and a half-year-old Caroline walked out of the cabin. I asked (kidding), "Caroline do you know how to run the engine on the dinghy to go get Poppa?"

"Well, I'm not the best..." she replied as she walked over to her life vest. "I will need this." She explained matter-of-factly, as she donned her life jacket.

She did not lose a beat as she settled her aunt and uncle into the rubber boat, took the wheel, turned the key, and started the engine. The adults cast off, and with great confidence she motored through the very busy Avalon Harbor to the pier to get her grandpa. Uncle Justin sat next to her to ensure that the journey went safely.

I was speechless with wonder, sporting a huge grin on my face,as I watched the event from the stern of the boat. Soon they returned. As Caroline climbed out of the small craft, she exclaimed, "Mimi that wasn't bad for my second time running the boat!"

Well I should say not!!!! I thought, keenly aware of her young age, as I assured her that it was a stellar effort. What amazed me was her high level of confidence. She wasn't afraid. She wasn't tentative. She just went for it. Perhaps one of the greatest gifts we can pass on to our children and grandchildren is the confidence to become masters of their universe.

In that same spirit, yesterday afternoon her father, my son, drove her to Rawhide Camp (her first time away from home on her own) where she will stay for the week learning horsemanship. She will have two cousins there, but not in her age group. She is by herself but has the personal fortitude to know that she will meet new friends.

Through my life coaching and grief counseling, I frequently encounter people who are paralyzed by indecision. They say they are afraid to move forward. They seem to fear that they may fail. Well they might, but so what? They might succeed as well! I believe that the greatest design project in existence is that of figuring out the best version of our own lives. It gets tricky because life is constantly changing. One of the concepts I teach is that we humans are infinitely resilient. I believe that we are strong and capable. Many of us sell ourselves short, worrying that we might look bad or that success might not be ours. We cannot succeed if we do not try. Little Caroline gets that. If there is something you've been wanting to do, I encourage you to go for it. I loved Ralph Waldo Emerson's thought, "Make the most of yourself, for that is all there is to you."

Digging Deep

July 8, 2015

Happy Month of our Independence! My recent travels have left me inspired. Last week, I was part of the support team for my two sons who were Ironman competitors in Coeur D Alene, Idaho. When the starting cannon sounded, my eyes filled with tears, as over 2000 very fit men and women dived into the lake to begin one of the most grueling physical contests in the world. The 2.5-mile swim began at 5:30 in the morning, with the 112 mile bike ride up next, and finished up with a 26.4 mile marathon, closing 17.5 hours later. The racers knew they faced 108-degree record breaking temperatures and yet they were digging down deep into who they were, racing undaunted.

As I cheered on my sons, a blind veteran leashed to his trainer ran by me. I was seized by emotion imagining what the event would be for one who could not see. I wondered where do we get such people; fearless humans putting themselves on the line? We have a country full of them. I thought of our mighty volunteer military as my mind scanned to World War II and the effect of those deadly bombs dropped on Pearl Harbor in 1941; their impact on our American psyche. They awoke our "sleeping giant." As America's arsenal for democracy became activated, our factories poured out an unequaled volume of planes, Jeeps, mortar and artillery. With our able-bodied men at war, our women stepped up; hundreds of thousands, taking over in the factories, keeping the war machine going. I thought, this is what Americans do.

With that in my head, I was particularly interested in the 4th of July piece by my friends, doctors Pedro and Priscilla Partridge de Garcia, who documented just what the signers of the Declaration of Independence endured to ensure our freedom. They wrote that of the 56 signers: "five were captured by the British as traitors and tortured before they died. Twelve had their homes ransacked and burned. Two lost their sons serving in the Revolutionary Army; another had two sons captured. Nine of the 56 fought and died from wounds or hardships of the Revolutionary War. They signed and they pledged their lives, their fortunes and their sacred honor." The article went on to explain that they were gentlemen; lawyers, merchants, farmers and plantation owners. They were educated men knowing that the penalty for their acts, if captured, was death. This proved to be true, yet they signed.

This is our heritage, a story of bravery and commitment. During my 45 years in the college classroom I was continually reminded of our American story as the Viet Nam vets rolled into my classroom on gurneys and wheelchairs, eager to finish their educations so they could support their families. Then later the Desert Storm vets, men and women warriors who taught us about sacrifice and desert warfare, and then the Iraq War vets who shared about IED's and canvas doors on their Humvees. They all demonstrated a bravery and a commitment to our freedom that I will never forget. As many of you know I have traveled the corners of our globe, and almost everywhere I visit, I learn the people of other places can only dream of the freedoms we enjoy every day. How blessed we are to live in the "home of the brave."

Our Indomitable Human Spirit

January 13, 2015

Recent events prove the indomitable nature of the human spirit, from million person solidarity marches to hosting an elite athletic event. In the wake of the Paris attacks last Friday, my three adult children and I felt the burden of those barbarous terror attacks lifting from our hearts as we crossed the Catalina Channel toward Avalon for their big 50-mile Avalon foot race. As the knots clicked by we searched for grey whales; before long blow spouts splashed on the horizon. My son, Dan, quickly maneuvered the boat toward the blows. Smooth whale trails led to the majesty of watching a long sleek whale as it rose out of the sea. I gasped in delight! More blows. Before long another whale sighting. We were in that thrilled state of mind when we entered Avalon harbor. Suddenly seeing the flags at half mast, we were jolted back to reality. The truth of the wicked nor'easter, the week before, and the havoc it wreaked on the small island became evident, resulting in the death of two island residents.

As we moored, I caught sight of a giant orange tractor on the beach, clearing the remains of two crushed boats, victims of unrelenting twelve-foot waves. As a lifetime visitor to the island my heart was heavy. In all my years of boating I have never witnessed such destruction; ruined boats, fields of debris, and evidences of broken dreams.

On shore my three companions checked in for the race. They posed under the "Catalina Benefit 50 Mile Run" banner that hung between two palm trees next to the demolished hull of an enormous boat. On the walk to our hotel we studied the impromptu memorial to the two fallen Avalon boaters killed in the tumult of the storm, one of the worst to ever ravage the small island.

At every turn, residents of Avalon, seemed to need to share about the murderous storm. We learned that "Pretty Boy" or "P.B.," the dog, came shivering into the Marlin Club where his owner spent time. The dog's owner, Bruce Ryder, and the boat they lived on, Ocean Ryder, had been lost. We listened to details about Tim Mitchell, the first harbor patrolman killed in the line of duty in one hundred years. He had been trying to save the 65' dive boat, King Neptune, when it crushed him. His successful effort in moving it out of the trajectory of the several boats moored in the harbor, boats with people aboard, likely spared lives.

On Saturday, race day, the memorial for Bruce Ryder was underway fifteen feet from the race headquarters. I felt a mix of emotions as I observed the miserable faces of the mourners juxtaposed against the triumph of the early finishers. I thought more about the events of recent days, how bravely the residents of the island were trying to move forward by hosting the event, even though they were still very clearly in the middle of their own tragedy. Some twelve hours later, my wet but jubilant runners crossed the finish line; strength in the midst of adversity. Today's headlines are filled with reports of the millions marching across the world in demonstrations of solidarity against terror attacks. These events once again highlight for me our indomitable human spirit. We don't stop and we are not giving up.

Maya Angelou: A Hero

May 30, 2014

As my daughter Julina and I boarded the airbus to fly home from our trip to Paris, the news of our nation's foremost poet, Maya Angelou's passing came to us. Tears filled my eyes as I realized how fortunate I was to have had the honor of hosting and being befriended by Dr. Angelou two years in a row when she was the guest speaker at my college, during her College Circuit years in the 1970's. I can still visualize her taking the stage, dressed in her colorful orange printed African caftan and empress head wrap. The head wrap added to her already statuesque six-foot height.

As a young college teacher, I was impressed with everything about her from her strong voice to her commanding message. She told the audience of college students about visiting campuses across the country, and finding the audiences thin, going out on campus to recruit audience members. She made things happen. It was as if she grabbed life by the shirt front and demanded that it listen.

I had read her 1969 *I Know Why The Caged Bird Sings* which resonated with me, even though at that time I had not dared to share my own secret of childhood violation. She modeled bravery for me.

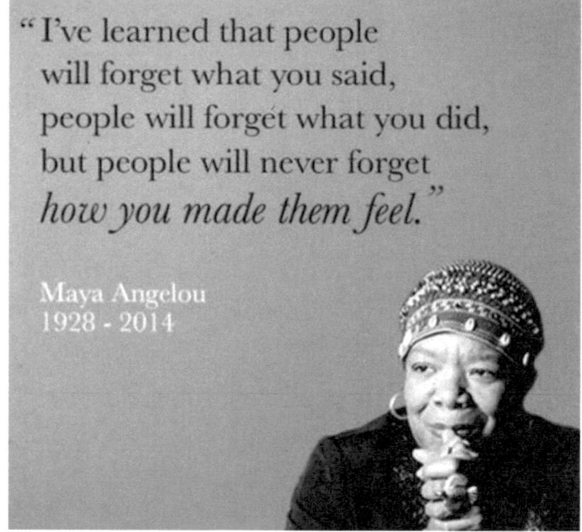

After her first event, as I drove her back to her hotel, safely cocooned in the darkness of the interior of my car, she looked over at me and said, "Nothing (meaning Civil Rights) will get better until people like you understand." She was referring to my blonde Anglo-Saxon self. Perhaps I only understood part of the concept in those early years, but across the next decades, I did get it. Equality for all of us is deeply embedded in my soul. I doubt that I would have had the courage to share my truth in Cry the Darkness had it not been for the inspiration of Maya Angelou when she looked me directly in the eye, and beseech me to understand.

I do understand, I understand that America lost a true hero on Wednesday May 28th, our poet laureate, a prolific writer, an actress, a professor, a singer, and an inspiration to the Civil Rights Movement. She will be missed, but her legacy of making things happen will remain. She was a fighter and a doer. It is hard to imagine that the amazing and impressive Maya Angelou ever had to walk a campus to recruit students to listen to her poetry and her wisdom. The force of her character was life-changing for me. Hers was a life fully lived!

Let's "live out loud!"

April 3, 2013

"Let's live out loud!" Last night that sentence practically jumped off the page of the book I was reading as I recalled the spectacle of the week before when 11,000 of us lined the streets for the biggest, noisiest non-motorized parade in the whole of the United States! We thrilled to 400 prancing horses as we celebrated spring and the return of the swallows to San Juan Capistrano. Spell bound by the pageantry of 200 entrants, we cheered dancing horses, admired the nutty clowns, enjoyed the spinning tee pees, the 11 marching bands, troops of acrobatic girls, and energetic old-time cowboys. Costumes, music, and rowdy antics; it was a festival of noise and fun. It was Americana living out loud!

I thought about living out loud in terms of my new coaching clients who have challenged me to help them to grow their self-confidence and happiness. Life can squash down the resilient part of our personalities leaving us feeling bereft. I think it is important that those with wounded hearts take back their power and find the courage to transform themselves into strong "warrior's hearts." A "warrior heart" is one which once broken mends stronger than ever.

Certainly we cannot always control what happens to us but we can control our attitude toward it. A first step is to adopt an attitude of gratitude, to cherish precious moments. It is up to us to nourish our tender inner child. Our American culture celebrates hard work, but many get stuck overdoing the work aspect of life, while others become frozen in despair. Studies show that at the end of life few people wish that they had worked more, but many do regret that they did not stop and further enjoy life; many wish they had been fully present in their own lives.

There is no time to waste. Living out loud is about living life in vivid Technicolor. You can become conscious of the moods and messages you allow yourself to have. You can stop the negative narrative that our brains seem to automatically run. It is up to us to nurture and care for the tender child within. We need to make time to have fun and to develop an action plan to become "unstuck." Let us make the conscious choice to live the best we can. Let's more fully control our brains by seeing the positive all around us. This is YOUR TIME NOW! What specifically did you do this week that was enjoyable? How did you live out loud? I would like to hear about it.

Gone Fishin'

March 19, 2013

As you might recall I have committed to training for my first full marathon (26 miles!) thus giving me more time than ever to reflect as I trek through the long miles readying my body for such a challenge. Earlier this month, my husband and I lost a dear friend to cancer. My mind keeps returning to thoughts of her, on how well she lived her life; in joy and productivity as she modeled excellence for her two daughters. I think her life was her lesson. I keep coming back to how important it is that we be present in our own lives, not on automatic pilot. In a way, how we live could be seen as our ultimate art project. Is your life rich and vibrant, valuable, and enjoyable? Is it full of color and adventure?

Last week I was training along the shoreline at Crystal Cove and several surf fishermen were casting their lines in the gentle waves and it reminded of another such scene I once encountered. Ken and I were on the way home from one of my presentations when we decided to stop at Carpinteria State Beach, in California. We delighted in being together on a sunny fall afternoon and removed our shoes to wander hand-in-hand along the wet sand. Far down the beach we came upon a barefooted woman standing in the surf throwing out her fishing line. Curious as to what she had caught, I raced up the beach to peer into her bucket. It was empty.

As I walked back down to her we exchanged smiles. I noticed her wide straw hat, her radiant face and the fact that she was well into her eighties. Remarking on her activity, I asked, "Are you enjoying your life?" That question might have startled her a little, but immediately her face broke into a wide grin as she heartily explained, "Why this is fun!"

"So did you catch anything?" I continued.

"Why I caught a rather nice perch a few minutes ago though I put it back." Conspiratorially, she whispered, "We don't like to eat them!"

In that moment I saw her key to happiness. She was doing what brought her joy. She was fishing in the warm November sunshine for fish she did not need nor want, just for fun. That simple incident highlighted for me a secret to a satisfying life. I think we need to find things to do which fill us up. This may require some changes on our part. By making the best choices available, happiness and taking care of ourselves can become a habit. As the authors of our own lives, I like these words of Ralph Waldo Emerson: "It is not length of life, but depth of life," and I take solace in the fact that my wonderful friend lived a rich, deep and joyful life. I'd love to hear about how you are taking steps to ensure yours is too.

Beyond!

February 19, 2013

Having arrived at the doorstep of my 7th decade, I cannot help but consider time and how to best use it. I believe that one's life is the result of past decisions and I weigh that thought as I plan ahead. Yesterday I committed to completing my first ever full marathon. I have started my training regime and that got me thinking about another first I experienced last fall and I want to share it with you.

As I clamored into the rickety old motorized rickshaw called a "tuk tuk" at 4:40 a.m. on a pitch dark October morning in Luang Prabang, Laos, I was about to realize a dream that had dwelled in my heart for a very long time. Inhaling the fragrant perfumes of the tropical night, a smile played across my face. I recalled the hunger I felt across my teaching decades as I studied the world map mounted in my college classroom; I would imagine a time when I would be free to experience the planet. I hung on tighter as the tuk tuk bounced me along the rough road toward the day's adventure. One of many I planned to have in my life after 45 years in academia.

I felt fluttery with nervous butterflies as I readied myself to participate in an ancient tradition of giving alms to the town's Buddhist monks. Our little group disembarked the rickshaws at curbside where embroidered mats were lined up with pots of steaming sticky rice provided by our group's support. We were instructed about the seriousness of this religious tradition of giving alms in the hopes of earning good Karma. We were told it was imperative that we be properly draped in our silk scarves and exhibit the appropriate solemn demeanor. We were warned not to raise our heads higher than the monks' (we are mostly taller than they, so this required a lot of bending forward) and we were admonished not to look at, nor touch the monks as we presented our food.

I was not sure what to expect as I peered into the murky darkness hoping for a sighting, I had only read about this; I knew they would be coming with their collection pots. The streets were alive with excitement as others were vying for good wishes through giving to the hundred or more who would pass our way. Finally, after much anticipation I spotted a flash of orange color way up the street. They were coming! Suddenly out of the humid night, a single-file line of men was in front of us. They were moving silently and very rapidly. I scrambled to get my portions of rice into their waiting buckets. There were mere seconds between buckets to manage the rice delivery. I felt pressure to do it right and I had to learn fast, focusing completely on the task before me. I could hear my fellow travelers' worried whispers as they missed their targets and rice servings fell to the ground.

After the first group went through, I began to relax a bit. With the next band I found a millisecond to look into the open pots to see fruits and candy bars donated along the route. My bravery was increasing as each cluster came. With head bent down I studied their bare feet, and eventually sneaking a peek, I noticed a wide range in ages from a few men over sixty years old down to boys as young as six. The area's dozens of monasteries offer the best chance for an education for the boys of rural Laos. The monks venture out each day, all year, to collect the meals. For many this is their only food.

As dawn broke and the processionals dwindled, I could see the gatherings of colorful monks along the streets as they returned to their sanctuaries. I took a deep breath. It had been such a thrill. Then I took in another longer breath and slowly exhaled, lingering in the amazing images of the morning. I could only think "Wow, Really?" It is my turn to see the world; to explore what I only dreamed was out there waiting. Participating in that ancient rite had been awe-inspiring. I marveled that in my decision to travel alone to Southeast Asia, I was opening a personal door to a new world. I had been anxious about traveling by myself, as it was out of my comfort zone, but my time had come. Often the window of opportunity between the responsibilities of career and family and the ability to travel is small. As I headed back to the tuk tuk, I thought about the words of Emerson when he wrote "Unless you try to do something beyond what you have already mastered, you will never grow." There is some truth in that, as well as a whole lot of adventure! I would love to hear how you have gone "beyond."

Journey to the Center of the World

September 5, 2013

Hi there, it seems like I have been sort of missing in action. I have been finishing my book, Cherish the Light, and traveling. Now with school back in session life is getting back to normal. You might know that one of my dreams for my eleven grandchildren is to help them to feel comfortable as citizens of the world. To that aim I have been taking them, often two at a time, on adventures.

A week and a half ago we returned from a marvelous journey to the center of the world. I took my two 16-year-old grand girls and it was joyous for me to watch them as they discovered more about our planet. At the Center of the World, which is the equator monument in a tourist village, not too far from Quito, Ecuador, they delighted in having one foot in the Southern Hemisphere and the other in the Northern.

My daughter's girl, Jaycelin, has an app on her phone which allows for truly tricky photography. She and her cousin Megan entertained themselves with this app for some time. The result showed their full bodies in both hemispheres at once! They were entertained by the photo trick and I was gratified watching them discovering all that they were learning in the middle of the Earth.

Ecuador has 250 volcanoes, some active, and we spent a good deal of our time at high elevations, both admiring their splendor and hiking below them. The headwaters of the Amazon River are also in Ecuador and we enjoyed three days on the river exploring the rain forest. I admired the way the girls climbed like gazelles up wet and steep mountains in the jungle with never a complaint. They were enthusiastic participants when it was time to float down river on the balsa wood raft, or to practice on the poison blowguns of the indigenous people, or even to carry on a conversation in Spanish. A big hit for them was taking photos of the monkeys leaping through the trees overhead, and of the various loose dogs we constantly encountered. Perhaps the biggest reward I took away from the eight days was being reminded again of what delightful fun young people can provide.

Sometimes when we are out of our usual comfort zones new opportunities are presented. This tour was such a case. There were 28 of us on the trip, Americans of all ages from all over the country. We were together for all of the activities including three meals a day, for eight days. That was a lot of togetherness! My true delight was to observe my girls interacting with the others, sharing thoughtful opinions and political ideas. I got to learn firsthand their world views.

In the weeks leading up to the trip, I had perhaps a dozen people ask me to please put them in my suitcase to take them on the journey. I always smiled as I replied, "Of course."

I sometimes sensed that others do not see themselves taking advantage of the precious opportunities that are out there. It seems to me that we can have the life of our dreams if we can imagine it. Certainly it does not have to be a trip down the Amazon, it could be a camp-out in the backyard, but everyday creativity and imagination simply mean breaking out of our usual patterns and trying on something new; perhaps even rounding up some young people. They can be a hoot.

Finding Courage

July 11, 2013

Hi there, Happy Summer. You know that when I write to you I like to keep it light, about special moments, but yesterday I saw a feature story in the Los Angeles Times (7/10) and it reminded me of one of the scariest and hardest things I ever had to do. The article was about the 39-year anniversary of the Stuart House in Santa Monica, a program through UCLA'S Rape Treatment Program.

The House is what saved our family when we had to fight a horrendous legal battle to stop my father from abusing his 4-year-old granddaughter, my niece. The Stuart House provides a safe environment where victims can dare to reveal their secret and get help. The case in the article was against a stepfather for hurting his 7 and 8-year-old girls. Those little girls were terrified to tell what had happened to them. The verdict was a maximum sentence of 65 years in prison.

You may know that my work these past decades has been to strengthen the laws to protect the children. I am glad to see serious consequences for such heinous behavior, but it reminds me that we must all stand together to protect the children. Reliable research shows about 1 in 3 girls and 1 in 7 boys will be abused in this way before puberty.

I am spending my summer writing the sequel to *Cry the Darkness*, which is *Cherish the Light: Breaking Free of the Dark* (which will be available this year). I have just released an expanded edition of my *Cry the Darkness: One Woman's Triumph Over The Tragedy of Incest* which is now available as an Ebook through Amazon.com's Kindle and will soon be on Barnes and Noble's Nook. It can also be ordered in printed book format through Amazon or through my website.

That Stuart House story reinforces to me that you and I must be more vigilant than ever to protect the children in our sphere. Life often presents terrifying situations and serious challenges; our job is to somehow find the strength to face those fears and move forward making the best life we can. I like when Mark Twain said, "Courage is the mastery of fear, not the absence of it." Our family finally had the courage to face what we had to and we have moved forward, but it was not easy. I wish you the most strength and tenacity to deal with whatever life presents.

On the Power of Cooking!

October 8, 2013

Last week, I was sharing with my daughter that I was working on coming up with a precious moment theme for the next article. She said, 'Mom, why don't you write about our family gatherings? You don't get it. What you have is what all of us parents want..."

"Huh?" Was my highly intellectual response.....

"Mom, take Sunday dinner. You invited us and we all came: your kids and their kids. It is what we parents are all hoping for, that our kids will want to come home. Mom, you do this all the time and do not even think about it. What could be more precious than all of us wanting to come home and you being surrounded by your loved ones? Plus it just means so much to us. You make that happen!"

"Oh," I answered softly. I guess I have taken it for granted. I invite, I cook, and viola there it is: a big family get together. I have often thought to myself, "ah the power of cooking!" but I know better. I remember a line under a poster when I was a young mom. It

was something like a graphic of an open palm and it said, "Set them free and they will return." I know that I took that to heart. I have always avoided using guilt, there was never the "command appearance" request some families employ. They all knew that they were free to accept or decline, no consequences. Maybe that is why they are happy to come over, even if it is just pizza. They seem to love to be in each other's company. Yes I have taken that for granted, but Julie was not finished with me.

Mom, I have only two friends I can think of who enjoy this constant flow of family interaction and frequent family dinners. You should be proud that you have created something where we all want to come home."

"Oh."

That conversation got me to thinking how easy it is to take things for granted, to not really notice what is timeless and wonderful right under our noses. I cherish this family time. Take last Sunday, they arrived before 4 and left after 8. It was a magical few hours as the children played Marco Polo in the pool and the teens and adults talked non-stop. We all sat around enjoying dinner as we marinated ourselves in each other's company. As the queen of being "in the moment" I think I was so in it, clearly, I did not even stop to reflect on it...

I thank my daughter for that reminder. Sometimes the best is right there in front of us. Perhaps Art Buchwald was right when he said, "The best things in life aren't things!"

Section III

Mindfulness: The Art of Being Present and Living in Gratitude and Awe

"Only we can take care of Ourselves"

~Vera May Lewis, Donna's Grandmother

Finding the Magic in the Season

December 19, 2016

Perhaps this is a good time of year for marinating ourselves in the many wonders that abound in everyday living. One of the most powerful action steps we can take toward happiness is living in gratitude. Why not take up the challenge in these days leading up to the holidays to search out what is precious in your daily rhythms and celebrate them?

Our twenty-two-year-old grandson returned last week from a six-month study abroad program in Australia. As our wonderful Jake returned to the family fold, with longer hair than we'd ever seen and a hairier face it called up an old, sweet memory for me. I want to share it with you as a holiday "feel good."

As I recall it was a dampish winter afternoon ten years ago, when I had the pleasure of accompanying my daughter as she picked her three children up from elementary school in San Diego County. The energetic enthusiasm of the children freed after seven hours in the classroom was contagious. A huge smile was stuck on my face as the children raced past us, some playfully pushing and poking at one another, glad to be free. We gathered up two of our kids but after some time, the oldest, Jake, still had not come out of his room. We went in search of him.

Upon arriving at his classroom an electric wave of excitement spilled over us as we crossed the threshold. I blinked my eyes. I was stunned to find that the room was still full of sixth graders who were happily working at their desks! By now about 20 minutes had elapsed since the dismissal bell and yet the students were not leaving. The culture of the classroom engulfed me in its warm embrace. It seemed almost magical. Soon Jake introduced me to a key element of the class: Tank, a big yellow service dog that the students supported and loved. I thought, why would the children want to leave?

Tank was their philanthropic project. They supported him and one other service dog, Foster, through their non-profit business. The students made and sold dog biscuits and dog houses. All of this was to help support the service dogs which assisted in their reading-buddy project with the younger children. Clearly the opportunity to know Tank and Foster, to support them, to have a business and a business plan had brought out the imagination and enthusiasm of the children as it was teaching them life skills. I recall how proudly Jake showed me the cubby area where the service dogs, the 2nd graders and the 6th graders worked on their reading. The young children read to the dog under the supervision of the older student. Jake explained to me that research evidence showed a gain in confidence on the part of the young reader when the child reads to the dog. I could see that confidence was gained by the 6th grader as well. As a lifelong classroom teacher myself, I was simply overwhelmed with excitement at what was going on in Jake's educational world!! I wanted to share this with you, to celebrate the everyday heroes, like his teacher Mrs. Benowitz, who are making a difference out in the world, quietly, with no fuss, just accomplishing amazing things.

There are examples like this all around us, regular folks adding magic to life. My son and his girls joined a dozen or more volunteers at the Boys and Girls Club last weekend for Operation Homework. The volunteers created an assembly line, wrapping donated gifts so that the children can "buy" presents for their families through the points they earned doing their homework. It was a noisy and fun workday of helping a few hundred children to do their "shopping!" I hope you look for these little acts of magic and celebrate them.

Opening our Eyes to Awe

October 14, 2016

Last Sunday *Parade Magazine* had a most provocative article by Paula S. Scott science of Awe. The Project Awe labs at UC Berkeley are studying this powerful phenomenon; the experience of feeling something huge beyond our selves. As my dogs and I clicked off our miles this morning, my brain flashed to some of my most memorable moments when I was so awestruck that tears pierced my eyes. A few years ago my friend Suzanne and I were touring the Van Gogh museum in Amsterdam when I came upon his famous sun flowers painting. Standing in that gallery, as I interpreted what I was seeing, I was overwhelmed. My heart rate accelerated and those darned tears fell down my cheeks. I was held hostage by awe.

After a bit, Suzanne came over to check on what was holding me up. She immediately understood as I had shared with her that during my apprentice years as an artist, while my babies played at my feet, I sat in my kitchen painting those Van Gogh flowers, perhaps a few hundred times. My desire to become an artist had burned so intensely that I wanted to learn through the master. Seeing them in person brought anew that intense drive I felt decades earlier, and then the realization came that I had somehow become a competent painter. Well, all together, it was just too much. I was both awed and humbled.

This Project Awe headed by Dacher Kelmer describes awe as "the feeling of being in the presence of something vast or beyond human scale, that transcends our current understanding of things or experiencing an electrifying emotion." The article cites gazing at the Milky Way, seeing the Grand Canyon, or something simpler like receiving an act of extreme kindness. The project teaches that awe helps us see things in a new way, binding us together, allowing us a fresh point of view. I know that when I was at my worst time, having to hold my father legally accountable for deplorable acts against our four-year-old niece, the most comforting place for me was at Mammoth Mountain, where I could sit in the shadow of the majestic peaks taking in their ageless enormity. It helped put my small self and those smaller problems into perspective. It was healing for me.

Scientists are learning that Awe experiences seem to help overcome depression, that there may be a healing potential to awe. Awe is a positive emotion reducing levels of cytokines, a marker of inflammation linked to depression. Considering the research, maybe we can begin to open our eyes and collect our own awe moments. Many of my Facebook friends frequently post beautiful sunsets, funny videos of their pets' crazy antics, the beauty of their child's face. I now realize they are sharing "awes"with us. Perhaps we can look at awe in a new way, with new respect. As I recall the birth of my only daughter, the nurse saying, "you have a baby girl!" I was overcome. When I first saw my husband, Ken, at age 14, through our friends' glass-paned door, I could not eat nor sleep for a week. I was overcome. When I was baptized in the Jordan River the emotion I felt was so intense I have never forgotten it.

I think that when we are able to surrender to the wonder of such powerful emotion it transports us.

We Stand on their Shoulders

March 21, 2023

On Monday March 13, 2023 twelve term congresswoman and persuasive feminist, Pat Schroeder, died. Her passing coincides with National Women's History Month. Her loss has caused me to reflect on the impact to the generations of American women coming behind me who are benefitting from Schroeder's important legislation. Many of us today stand on her shoulders and those of other Americans who have worked toward equal rights for women.

When I was hired in 1966 as a full time tenure-track college teacher there was no such thing as family or maternity leave. I was hired at age 23 as a married mother of one small child. It was not a problem. The issue was that Ken and I wanted a larger family and we did not want to sacrifice my career, the alternative, to growing our family.

Ken and I worked the problem. We became strategic. We figured out that if our child's birth coincided with my summers off, my career could prevail. Beyond our strategy, we were fortunate. Our second child was born July 30, 1968. When classes began the day after Labor Day, we secured childcare for our tiny five week old daughter, Julina. I will never forget my drive to work that first day of school; I sobbed the entire way as leaving my newborn was against every fiber of my maternal being. I sucked it up and kept going, knowing that for the rest of my life, leaving her would be one of the hardest things I would ever have to do.

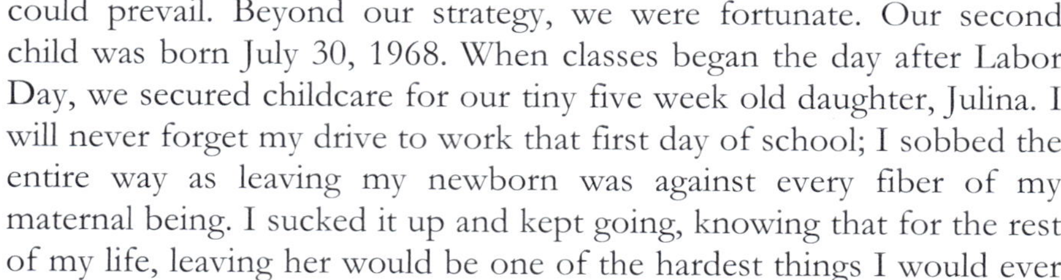

A few years later, once again strategizing toward summer break, luck was again on our side. Baby number three was scheduled to arrive in July of 1971. My voluminous dresses did their best to cover my girth. "Don't Ask Don't Tell!" was the rule of the day for expectant teachers. In May that semester, I had a meeting with the district chancellor. He held eye contact with me during the entire appointment, never acknowledging my huge mid-section. I lumbered through the June graduation in my oversized academic robes. Baby Dan was born the next week. There was never a mention of Donna or a baby boy, nothing, by anyone, not in a faculty newsletter, nowhere. My students understood and threw me a big in-class baby shower. Otherwise, mum was the word on campus except in the faculty lounge where the sentiment was in keeping with Paul Erlich's Population Bomb which called for a limitation in family size. Certain faculty members enraptured with that idea, were wrapping his explosive books in black paper and delivering them to local maternity wards. My girth and I stayed away from the faculty lounge.

When Colorado woman Pat Schroeder decided to run for congress in 1972 the newspapers described her as only a "housewife." She drew so little credibility from the media that her name was NOT even mentioned in the articles. Mind you she was a Harvard trained attorney, and an accomplished pilot. In fact, after her election to congress she was chosen as the first woman to ever sit on the Armed Services Committee. Her aviation skills were of value in that forum. Two of her most important accomplishments in the U.S. Congress were to benefit the American family. In 1978 she championed the Pregnancy Discrimination Act which barred employers from denying maternity benefits. In 1993 she helped get the Family Medical Leave Act passed which permitted workers to take up to 12 weeks of unpaid leave to bond with their newborn child, to care for the health of a seriously ill family member or tend to their own serious health issues without concern for losing their job. Being allowed a leave back in 1968 would have helped my broken heart. My daughter was 25 years old when this important legislation was passed.

Recently, the Ancestry.com website sent me a notice that my 2nd great grandmother, Mary Jane Swan Lewis (my grandfather's grandmother), at age 82 fought across heavy rain and snow on November 2, 1920 in Altoona Kansas to stand in voting lines so that she could finally legally cast her vote for president. The 19th Amendment had been ratified and nationwide women were permitted to vote. Prohibition was the big issue; she could have voted for James Cox or Warren Harding. Her stand on prohibition is lost to me, however, the majority of Americans overwhelmingly voted for the popular Harding whose slogan was "Return to Normalcy." It warms my heart to think of that lady wrapping herself up in layers of clothing against the snow to stand in a long line to have her say. I stand on her shoulders.

I also stand on the shoulders of my great grandmother Lydia Cram Lewis who was a pharmacist in the family's R.W. Lewis Drug Company which had nine drug and cigar stores in early 1900's Los Angeles. I stand on the shoulders of Vera May Lewis, my grandmother who was a pioneer in children's television. She hosted the first local TV show for kids in Southern California. It was The Playcrafters Club on Channel 5, KTLA, Thursdays at 5, from 1950-1953.

We American women benefit from and stand upon so

many shoulders of strong women and men. Some of our influencers have been more outspoken than others. Ruth Bader Ginsberg, for instance, was a fearless advocate against gender discrimination. She was also the first Jewish woman and only the second woman to serve on the United States Supreme Court. Reflecting further upon gender discrimination in the workplace, I think about my Aunt Margie. In the 1930's during the Great Depression when she applied for an adult night school teaching job, she was forced to hide the fact that she was married; jobs were reserved for men who had families to support.

This month, National Women's History Month, provides us with an opportunity to pause and appreciate the strides taken forward toward gender equality such as the passing of Title IX in 1972. Title IX legislation gave women the right to equal opportunity in sports and in educational institutions which receive federal funds. There is still a lot of work to be done. We can slide into complacency or we can be inspired. Perhaps Pat Schroeder, Ruth Bader Ginsberg, the women behind the passage of Title IX, and thousands of others who have been banging away at the glass ceiling, can embolden us to continue to actively teach our children and grandchildren the importance of gender equality. As the grandmother to nine young women and two future fathers, it has been an urgent matter to me that they have every opportunity available, that they see themselves as equal and believe in their hearts that they have what it takes, and most importantly that they understand the battles that must continue to be won to move to gender equality.

Observing the independent nature of my grown grandchildren, I interviewed them and their parents asking if they could articulate their thoughts on gender equality. It's a hard question. Not everyone got back to me, but what answers I learned are compelling. My oldest son, no doubt thinking of the arduous Saturday before in which he and four of his daughters endured competing on the muddy, watery trails of the Catalina Marathon, immediately offered up his family's tireless marathon participation as a metaphor. The marathon participation as vehicle to illustrate that he and the girls' mother have inspired their girls to believe in themselves, to understand that they can accomplish significant goals, regardless of gender, through determination and practice, even a horrific nine-hour trek through mud so thick that it pulled their shoes off!

Marathons, half marathons, 5 and 10 K races have been a family affair of ours for decades now, with almost all of us participating at one time or another. I continued to think about that difficult course and the fact that our daughter and her youngest son, James, also took up the same brutal challenge. The twenty-six plus mile dirt course is exceedingly challenging even when it is dry, imagine wading through knee high lakes and deep gullies! The torrential rains had only stopped two hours before race time!

Our youngest son, Dan, decided to run the steep 10K as a buddy to his 13 year-old daughter, Caroline, as it was her first time to compete. Laughing he admits, "Caroline was so fast that I almost struggled to keep up with her!" Caroline came in first for her age group winning a nice trophy.

This is not to say that the entire family is populated with natural athletes. It is not but it reflects the belief my children have taught their children that they have personal power and can achieve whatever they set their minds to. Statistics show that only .05% of Americans, and only .01% of the world's population ever complete an arduous 26-mile foot race! The "Can Do" messages we teach the generations behind us are critical to moving forward in human rights. When I asked my 25-year-old granddaughter, Jaycelin, what thoughts about this were in her head as she completed her own 10K run, she responded, "I believe I can do anything I set my mind to."

Who are the strong advocates both men and women who have helped shape the independent person you are today? What have you taught the younger people in your sphere? Who influenced you to be all that you could be? I would love to know upon whose shoulders you stand.

There are Still Lemonade Stands!

August 26, 2023

The other day I was leaving a local event when I encountered three young children on the corner of a quiet neighborhood selling lemonade from their homemade stand. I smiled to myself. I continued my short journey home and upon entering my own area, I drove by yet another such lemonade stand. This time my eyes filled with tears for the innocence of it. For the next few days my mind kept steering back to the image of those sweet little kids and their entrepreneurial zeal. I basked in the vision of them.

Later that week the real horror of the destruction that consumed Lahaina on Maui became apparent. Lives destroyed. I thought of the ongoing devastation to Ukraine, other horrifying issues which the 24/7 news cycles blasts our way. It can feel overwhelming; the power of the bad news headlines insistent upon grabbing our attention. Oftentimes I even worry about our country's ability to sustain our democracy. When I let those thoughts run away in my head, Ken manages to talk me down. Anyway, the purity of the lemonade stands moved me so much that I began telling my friends about them. Invariably they'd grin and exclaim, "Well there's still lemonade stands!" Meaning that in the face of all the negativity in the world there is still purity. I believe that!!

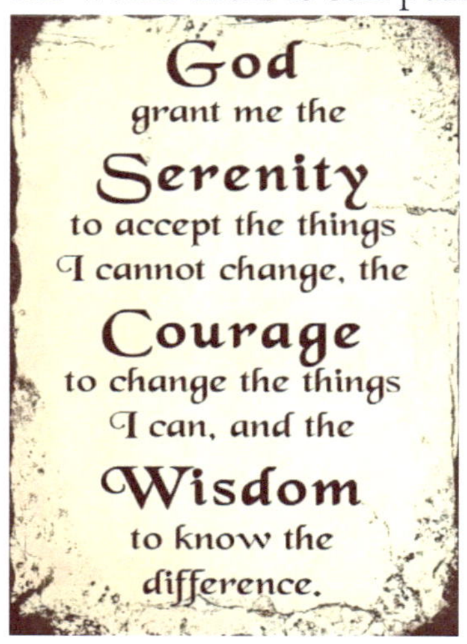

If you too find yourself feeling anxious I think a trick is to practice getting our "calm" on; managing our thoughts and being mindful of where we allow our thoughts to stray. One of my all-time heroes is author David Rock in his book Your Brain at Work. He writes: "The human brain likes to wander; it is like a sniffing puppy!"

Ever since my husband, Ken, received his diagnosis of advanced heart failure and the changes it brings to him, he has become proficient at practicing mindfulness to stop himself from over thinking it. He favors reciting the Serenity Prayer to himself, especially the line "God, grant me the serenity to accept the things I cannot change." He challenges himself to concentrate his energy on the life paths still open to him.

Mindfulness is the practice of being present in the moment and becoming aware of where our thoughts have meandered. It requires that we are conscious and aware — that we learn to choose our response instead of simply reacting.

When we feel our thoughts escalating out of control we can work to contain them by purposefully bringing to mind something positive; we can exercise; we can celebrate being alive; and we can focus on what is right with the world. Years ago, in my Interpersonal Relationship class I had a very stressed-out middle-aged woman who had endured decades of therapy regarding her serious "mommy issues." When my assignment required the students to write on "What is Right with Your Life," she had an epiphany! She confided to me that she had spent the last thirty years focusing on what was wrong with her life. At the end of the semester she whispered to me in private that that assignment helped her more than all the therapy she ever had put together! Whew! That was a lot to say to me, but it speaks to the power of positive thinking and how important it is to take control of our thoughts.

I think we humans are brave. Fight or Flee is built into our brains. We are absolutely wired to action: but who do we fight? Where do we flee? Really, there's often nowhere to flee nor anyone to fight, so many of us feel plagued by anxiety. It is normal to have some anxiety. Change and stepping out of our comfort zones can sometimes elicit some profound discomfort, but it can also bring growth. Meeting the new situation head-on can oftentimes dispel that uncomfortable reaction. It is human to experience all this. Maybe we can do better by working to control our wayward, perhaps catastrophic thoughts. We can find realistic ways to manage and live with our anxiety.

So tell me, what is right with you? In what ways are you thriving? How do you get a handle on your own anxiety? I would love to hear what you are thinking. In the meantime keep your eyes peeled for those corner lemonade stands.

Lunar Events Promise Awesome Opening to 2018

January 2, 2018

Happy New Year! I feel a little thrill writing this first post of a new year knowing all the possibilities that are out there waiting for us. This morning after a particularly lovely two-hour horse ride in the hills of San Juan Capistrano with my pal, Christine, I settled down to think about this coming year and to refine my goals list for 2018. In comparing it to my 2017 list, I did even better than I had hoped. Globally, 2017 was a hard year, offering many anxiety producing events. Though our US economy strengthened, and we thrilled to a solar eclipse, the year was still hard. However, a celestial extravaganza projected for 2018 offers us a fine chance for reflection and hope.

On January 1-2, we get to enjoy a Wolf Moon (the first full moon of the New Year) and then later in the month, a Blue Moon (the second full moon in a month). That's not all! We'll also see a full lunar eclipse! It's a bit amazing to get two full moons in one month, and our Wolf Moon will also be a Super Moon, appearing to be 14-30% larger than it usually does!

Since the heavens are lining up for us, I think we should celebrate this symbolic nod from above. Folklore has it that the Native American tribes in the northeast noticed that during the first full moon, around what we call January, when the days are the shortest, that the hungry wolves were howling at the moon more than usual. Thus, the name, "Wolf Moon." It was considered an omen directing humans to listen to their soft internal signals; a chance to improve oneself, and to strengthen one's relationships.

For me the New Year is always an opportunity to plan. (I am a lover of lists!) In recent years, I've been trying to be a bit easier on myself. As one who thrives on work, my new list has "rest more," "work less," repeated a few times. One of my goals is to keep writing my book Capistrano Trails, but in an attempt to not pressure myself, I am keeping the completion date flexible. A new trend for me. What goals do you want to set? Are there projects that you want to complete? Are there trips you want to take? Are there people you need to boundary against who are not good to you? Do you want to make a new friend? Do you want to feel happier?

Being in sync with ourselves, listening to our internal messages, and noticing our moods, can allow us the ability to stop negative thoughts. The problem with negative thoughts is that they rob us of our peace of mind, of our hope. They help produce the hormone cortisol, the primal survival hormone that breeds anxiety. We can stop that nasty stuff, but it requires we pay attention to what is going on inside our heads. Recently, former Vice President Joe Biden has been talking about the essential importance of having hope. Hope gives us the will to achieve our goals, to have the personal agency, the grit, and determination to reach those goals. Hope is the engine that takes us toward positive outcomes. It is the foundation that allows us to approach life with a mindset for good results.

As we ring in this New Year, with the Wolf Moon and the Blue Moon watching over us, let's have the awareness to live with the best choices possible. Let's more fully manage our emotional responses and aim to train ourselves to see the positive in situations, to be hopeful for a good tomorrow. A Pinterest line I liked is: "In the end all that matters is that we loved..."

I send you my love and my very best wishes for a wonderful New Year. This is your one life. This is your time.

On Growing Happiness

May 4, 2023

Recently, I have admitted to you how chaotic parts of my life have felt as I have dealt with loss and serious medical conditions with those whom I love. I've been struggling to keep balance in my life, to feel happy. The other day my brother, Chuck, emailed a Time Magazine January 5, 2023 article "The Daily Habits of Happiness Experts." Eager for more answers, I studied the article. It pointed out that "we must do the work every single day of deciding to be happy." It is a different twist than I had ever thought of: Putting in the Work. It got me to thinking about what exactly is the "Work" necessary to grow happiness?

"YOU ARE ENTIRELY UP TO YOU."

The article listed the experts' daily habits: a healthful diet, getting at least 7 hours of sleep each night, regular exercise, practicing a hobby, and spending significant amounts of time with friends outside of the work environment. Certainly those habits are part of the Work. They agreed that having a sense of purpose and living in gratitude are also core habits. My own studies have also taught me that a certain level of complexity in one's daily life can yield a sense of excitement about feeling alive.

All this got me pondering. I woke up in the middle of last night thinking that life is sort of a balancing act, like being on a teeter totter. I shared that idea with Ken about happiness coming from being in balance. He could not have disagreed with me more! He said, "Balance is boring! It is the rush of pushing upward to the top of the teeter totter that yields that kick to one's heel, that zesty thrill of being in the world." I responded, "But too much downward push can leave us feeling stressed out, or sadly, bored or lonely." I know America

is suffering an epidemic of loneliness and anxiety and that youth and seniors are hit the hardest; we also have a generation of workers stuck at home working through Zoom and the computer. What is that isolation doing to them? It can't be a positive condition.

With that in mind, how exactly do we pull in enough adventure, new situations, and new people to bring us joy without stressing ourselves out? The evening news just had an intriguing segment. It was about a high school teacher who dared to have his students put their work and phones away. He then directed them to talk to one another for the last ten minutes of the class. They were bewildered as the teacher usually required quiet. That made the news! The teacher is concerned that we are forgetting how to talk to one another face to face. Could it be that our instant capabilities to silently communicate are messing with our heads? Could these new technologies be cutting us off and weighing us down toward isolation? Is our tech driven world of email and texting making it too easy to isolate?

Last week three different people approached me for help. They were hoping for ideas about how to get back in their lives, how to feel some of the old joy from their youth, how to feel happier. Their drive to feel happier forced me to think more fully about doing "the work" to create more happiness. Our conversations kept coming back to daring to step out of our comfort zones, having enough courage to push the teeter totter up, and exalting in the trip down. I thought about my husband Ken's high school girls' wrestling team, how he frequently has to coach them not just about strategic moves but about stepping out into the unknown onto the mat in front of others, being bold enough to go for it. Some of them, unfortunately, cannot face that risk and leave wrestling, others suck it up, anxious and scared, and become accomplished wrestlers enjoying the benefits of trying something new; participating in fresh activities, belonging to a team, making more friends.

0Across my life I have had to force myself out of various comfortable cocoons. I've never shared with you that one of the reasons I taught for so long, 45 years, was that I was more terrified of trying to create a new life outside of teaching, than continuing in my same known routine. My mind imagined me at home sitting alone at my computer in the fog of a Fall day. I hated that mental picture. Eventually the 70 miles a day commute, and being well past retirement age, was beginning to look silly. I had to become brave and figure out a new life. One year I made up my mind, I would retire! However, I could not go

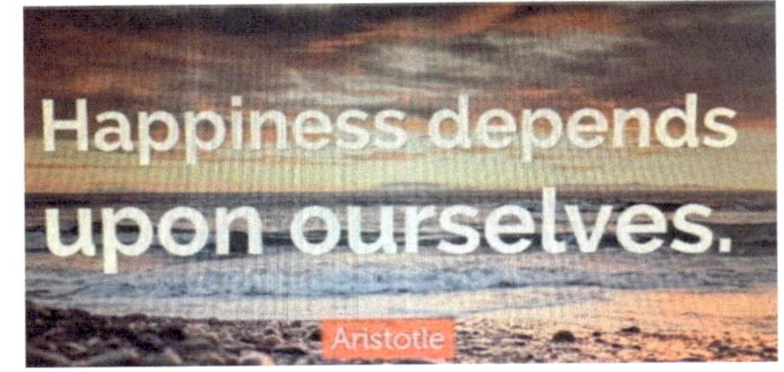

through with it. I told myself that I would miss my students too much. I taught for several more years. Translation: I was afraid of the unknown. You are probably laughing at me right now. What a ninny? It does, however, speak to the emotion involved in keeping the upswing of the teeter totter.

Once I made the move and stepped into retirement I discovered a wonderful new set of risks and challenges. I began getting better at putting my angst aside and going for it even though it is scary. I think you know that Ken recently gifted me a 2014 Corvette for my 80th birthday. Within a few days I was loading groceries into the back of it at Von's when a stranger rolled by me, asked about the car, and invited me to join his Corvette club. I thought it over for a few days. I looked it up online, filled out a form, and received a call inviting me to the meeting. I was going.

So on January 5, 2023, I put my arms around myself, took a big breath, got into my car by myself and drove into the great unknown. I was pretty nervous. I arrived at the meeting place, a restaurant, with my stomach full of butterflies. I checked in with my contact, sat with him and his wife. That was the beginning of what is turning out to be one of the most unique and joyful experiences of my life. This generous and friendly couple metaphorically wrapped me up in their welcoming embrace and introduced me to others. I was a stranger in a strange place but they made me feel at home. I decided to join. A month later I found myself taking part in something I had never in my wildest imagination dreamed of doing. I was showing my car at the San Juan Capistrano Rotary Car Show along with 400 other car enthusiasts!

What I have learned is that if We DARE TO STEP INTO THE UNKNOWN, sometimes magical things can happen. I had forgotten how much I love cars, that I was actually a lifelong car enthusiast, that there were new friends waiting for me, that new activities would present themselves. I had NO idea. That is the thrill of the unknown, of the upswing of the teeter totter, we don't know until we try, and the down swing can be enjoyed as an interesting change as well.So I am interested in you. What have you been contemplating doing? Are you secretly thinking about taking up something new? Going on an adventure? Joining a new group? You might need to step out of your usual routine. It's possible something marvelous is waiting for you.

If This Tub Could Talk!

February 4, 2024

Friday my friend, Anne, asked if I wanted to tag along to a designer furniture warehouse sale. Eyeing the rainy day, I replied, “Sure.” Strolling through the haphazard pieces of decorative items, I soon stumbled upon a distressed 19th century portable bathtub with peeling paint. It was 75% off. I grew a bit excited imagining its gardening possibilities.

It is light weight, made of tin, probably from the mid 1800’s. It is not of much monetary value, but as a representative of a bygone era where hot water was heated on a wood burning stove and poured into the 40” long x 20” wide tub, it was catnip for my imagination.

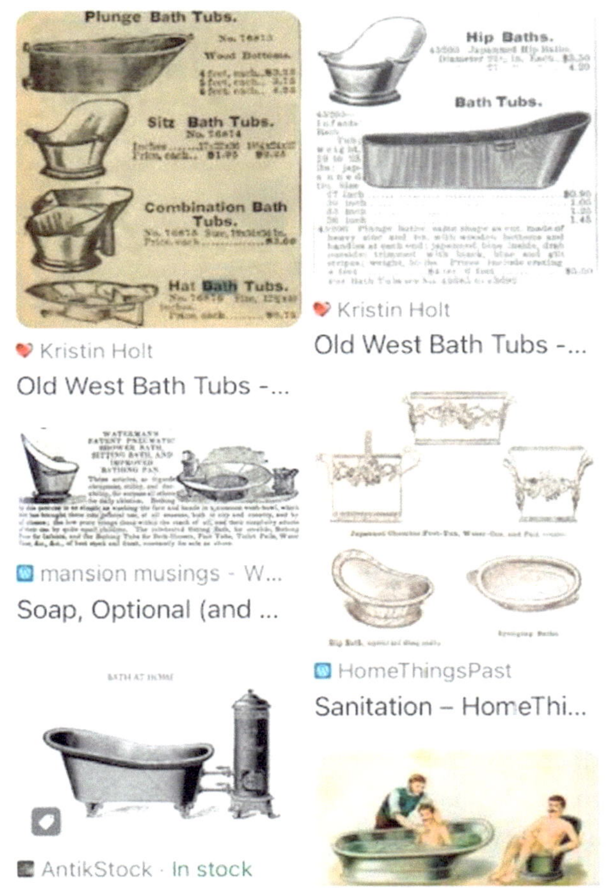

I pictured a youngish mother dressed in a long calico skirt, heating a kettle of water over her big black stove. I could almost hear her yelling for her three kids, “Its bath day. Come on you all!” In my mind I could see two little boys whining. “Aww mom, do we have to?” While their little sister grinned from the corner of the kitchen, knowing she could splash to her heart’s content. The tub is big enough for two children or an adult to squeeze into. Smiling to myself, I could not help but wonder what kind of lives its bathers had lived; where had they lived? If only it could talk.

Back in the early centuries of our country, bathing was not the daily custom we enjoy today. Washing up in one’s bedroom at the washstand, using a pitcher of water, a large washbasin, and a sponge was sufficient. Ladies might add a drop of perfume to the water.

Immersive bathing became more frequent and popular as urban homes were constructed with indoor plumbing. Prior to 1900 that was not the norm. In fact, across our history until the 1900’s, bathing was viewed by many with suspicion as it was thought to remove the protective layer of oil and dirt on the skin, thus exposing the skin to the “miasma” of diseased air. Indoor bathrooms, even in 1910, were seen as a luxury. A 1950

Gallup poll revealed that fewer than 30% of Americans took a daily bath or shower during the winter with low income families reporting that children bathed once a week or less.

This morning I planted my friend Janet's great grandmother Anna Launer's swamp lily offspring in the tub and placed it on my patio. The two flourishing lilies seem fitting dwellers for the tub as they have a story of their own. In 1898 their "mother" swamp lily, the original plant, was traveling on a rail freight car from Illinois to Los Angeles packed in with the stock for the Launer's new La Habra ranch: horses, chickens, and assorted plantings. During the long cross country trip there was a rail accident and the freight car with the stock was demolished. The horses and chickens scattered, while the original mother swamp lily lay quietly waiting to be turned right-side up. After a long chase the horses were rounded up, while the swamp lily enjoyed a prosperous life, growing many off shoot lily bulbs that were transplanted. The hallmark of the beautiful pink lily plant is that it can grow for many decades unattended. The plant is treasured by gardeners. One of this lily offshoot plants decorates the entry to the La Habra Historical Museum. There is an inscribed plaque describing the lily's origins and tumultuous journey to California.

I often reflect on the past, lounging in images of prior times. It seems to me that when we appreciate the past, we better understand the present. I am so grateful that those who had custody of this little tin tub during the last 150 or so years, chose not to toss it in the recycling bin. Maybe it cannot talk but we can imagine what it might want to say, and how happy it is to house the beautiful pink swamp lilies.

Enchanted Day

October 17, 2023

Across our sixty year long marriage, when Ken and I find a break in our schedules we often head out for what we refer to as one of our "adventures." We have some favorite spots. This past Saturday was such an occasion. With purpose, we turned off the agony of the devastation in the Middle East reported on the news, focusing our thoughts inwardly. On this day we were heading to Balboa Island, our first home as newlyweds and to which we brought our first new-born baby; It is a place that holds a lot of magic for us.

It was a bright Indian summer day as we began our walk around the perimeter of the island. I felt a wave of peace wash over me as we ambled along, admiring the glistening water and the boats lolling against their moorings. The elaborate Halloween decorations adorning the homes and docks added to the joy. Before long, we came upon a five foot tall sand sculpture declaring "Larbear's" love for her guy. We grinned. How cute. About 100 yards further up the beach we encountered the actual sand sculptor at work. He was filling two tall plastic forms with wet sand while four little kids, probably under age six, were trying to help him, armed with their own little shovels. The parents seated nearby, nervously called out to the artist, "Are you okay? We can call them in!"

Smiling, he looked over to them. "It's fine."

Ken and I enjoyed watching his flock of helpers; one little girl was holding a very full shovel of wet sand toward the top of the form. The form was taller than she. As she struggled to drop her load into the form, it looked for a minute like she might miss. We held our breath, worried for her. But she succeeded! We smiled and walked on, reveling in the warm sunshine, hopeful to see a finished creation on our return.

Taking in the sights of the sunbathers, street artists, and passers-by, we boarded the ferry for the short trip across the Newport Bay channel. Suddenly the ferry's horn sounded! Things got a bit too exciting as the captain of our ferry issued a second loud blasting warning! A youth a few feet off our bow in a sailing dinghy was on a collision course with us! At the last second, the young sailor was able to make a quick turn and missed crashing into us! Whew!

We arrived for lunch at the historic 1906 Pavilion Restaurant. It was the terminus point for the Red Car trolley of old that traveled from Los Angeles to Newport Beach during the early 1900's. As the hostess seated us we remarked on the hubbub of people in the dining room. She explained that a 100th birthday celebration was just breaking up at the other end of the large room. Seated, we took in the huge balloon bouquet boasting its shiny silver inflated 100th sign. We couldn't help but admire the crowd of forty or so people as they dispersed, from babies, to toddlers, to the elderly; smiles on everyone's face. The day before, my sister, Jackie, our mother, and I had a lengthy planning session for our mother's 100th coming up in January. I was mentally taking notes.

Ken and I lingered over lunch, entertained by the 100th- year celebrants as well as the spectacular scenes of boats passing outside the window. Our waiter was engaging and we three enjoyed chatting about high school wrestling and his son, a soon-to-be wrestler.

Eventually we paid our bill and left the dining room. On the way out we studied the old photos on display. There was an historic line-up of beauty queens in their long, old-fashioned bathing costumes. Whispering to Ken, I pointed them out, "They enjoyed their days in the sun… and here they are memorialized." He nodded as he replied, "Indeed we have our time." He was quiet for a long pause and then he observed, "Donna we are seeing both ends of the spectrum today, a 100th birthday marking a milestone near the end of a very long life, while those little sandcastle builders back there are experimenting and learning as they begin their life journeys. It's remarkable."

I knew what he meant, that this is our time now and it is precious. He took my hand and we walked on. On the way back we stopped to admire the progress the sand artist had made. We could see that Casper the Friendly Ghost was emerging out of the sand while the gaggle of excited children had swelled significantly. There must have been about nine of them, all of whom, by now, were busily at work on their own elaborate creations. One little girl called breathlessly to the sand artist, "Richard, is this good. Is this enough sand?"

I laughed. "Ken there is a real-life Pied Piper! He is not only creating a delight for we who stroll by, but he is graciously entertaining all those little kids in a very unique way." My phone camera was in my pocket, but it did not feel right to insert myself into the scene by taking a photo. Honestly, it was just too precious. I needed to let it be what it was.

Of course when I got home I realized I wanted to share with you what an enchanting "adventure" we had on Saturday, and how important it is that we be mindful of all the beauty and joy that is surrounding us. There is so much pain in our world, I think it is important that we do what we can to alleviate it while seeking to strike a balance so that it does not pull us all the way down. It is still our time now and it is precious.

He replied with a grin. "It's perfect." As he went back to smoothing out his ghost.

In retrospect I have considered the others with whom we interacted on our brief adventure. I thought how so many of them were making a difference, making the world a bit better. There was a young woman with a seven-month-old Golden Retriever, Nash, a twin to our Ginger. We exchanged a heartwarming talk about our dogs with her; that waiter made our day better by sharing of his love for his son. We met Gary, a working artist with a paint brush in hand, who shared a photo of one of the 18 full length knitted coats his wife had created for him, his most prized possessions. Lastly, bearing witness to a real-life Pied Piper at work, a man taking time to inspire children, all has to add up to the fact that each of us in our own way can help to make the world better, one little kindness at a time.

As I sign off, I'm including a few photos collected in my phone from other sandcastle, beach visits to Balboa Island and some of my own castle builders when they were young.

An Extraordinary Encounter

April 27, 2022

I've been aware for a while now of the incredible power of serendipity, placing ourselves in the path of opportunity, where remarkable things often occur. I had such an encounter Sunday at Mission San Juan Capistrano.

Eight weeks earlier, I had signed up as a volunteer to lead a tour for the Wounded Warriors Project. I looked forward to it. That morning, as I donned my docent attire I was aware of a shimmer of excitement charging through my body. I knew the day would be a challenge, that it could rattle my emotions in ways I did not yet know, as I would be touring a small group consisting of veterans who might be wheelchair bound and or blind. I mentally prepared myself. I might need to become the eyes.

I arrived at the mission early on a warm April morning and waited patiently for my guests. I was told that today only one Wounded Warrior would be joining the tour. Soon a tall woman, near my age, with one leg encased in a heavy metal brace, using a white cane, slowly ambled through the gatehouse door on the arm of a young woman guide. I greeted them and introduced myself. I learned their first names.

"Do you hug?" the veteran asked hopefully.

"I do, of course." I responded as I leaned in. She dodged my big Spanish hat and proceeded to kiss me on one cheek and then the other. Later I realized she was using her remaining senses of smell and touch to get an idea of who I was. That embrace alone was astonishing. She next asked her aide to take our photograph together.

Feeling a bit rattled, and to ensure that I had their names straight, I repeated my name and she offered, "I am Angela Longboat." I was startled by her intriguing last name. She elaborated, "I am Mohawk. My DNA says I am 93% Mohawk. I am descended from longboat builders, you know, the big canoes which carried ten to twenty men, hence the last name "Longboat." I grew up on the Rez in upstate New York. When I went to Indian school the authorities changed my tribal first name to Angela."

Flabbergasted, I shared that I had seen photos of the big canoes the Tongva people built in the Los Angeles basin, I explained how they had extensive trading with the inhabitants of the Channel Islands. I could see that I had Angela's full attention and she certainly had mine. We proceeded to the grinding stone where my explanations continued. I handed acorns to her and described the pockets in the grinding rock. Narrating, as we slowly walked through the gardens, I described the colorful red hollyhocks, the abundant yellow and pink roses, and the physical structure and texture of the mission. Angela's recreation therapist joined our group.

Arriving at the museum room dedicated to the local Acjachemen people, I described the display items; the decoy duck, the handmade fishing nets, the beautiful baskets exemplifying the many skills of the indigenous people of the West Coast. Angela said that she had earned a doctoral degree in Native Studies and began telling me of the life and skills of the native people of the East Coast. I was spellbound. I could not imagine that I had a Native American sharing all this with me!

The tour continued. We wandered into the wine making room and I told them that my fourth grade students loved to mash imaginary grapes. I offered that they could go down the three steep steps to the bottom of the vat if they wished. I was thinking it was too much. I was wrong! Angela was up for anything! The three of them slowly descended the stairs, I continued talking about the wine making. At the bottom of the vat, Angela held onto the rail and using her strong left foot, we all began delightedly stomping imaginary grapes. Angela's face was beaming with joy! As she stomped she exclaimed, "My people placed skins on top of the fermenting vats to enhance the process!"

The tour continued like that, she would ponder what she was hearing and then share her own knowledge. The narration had become a conversation. Understanding she was from out-of-state, I was not sure how much she knew about California geography as I elaborated on the mission's vast land holdings.

She explained, "I attended Cal Poly at San Luis Obispo, and then I transferred to USC." Having Cal-Poly grandsons, I am particularly interested in San Luis Obispo. I told her that the Mission at San Luis Obispo was an "accidental mission." Father Serra had not planned on it, but during the early days of the Spanish arriving in Alta California, the soldiers and missionaries were starving until they discovered bears in the San Luis Obispo area. The bears provided a rich food source which got them through a cruel winter. Father Serra decided then to build a mission in that area to ensure the food supply. Angela knew of the area's bears, "Los Osos", the bears. She then told me a lot more about those bears, and what kind they were [black bears], than I had known before!

To say that my 90-minute encounter was exhilarating would be an understatement. I would have never imagined sharing one of my favorite subjects with a person so deeply engaged with it, who had lived it. I could tell that I was in the presence of a great intellect, an intellect both humble and fascinated by history, an intellect eager to exchange ideas.

As the day unfolded I learned that the injuries she had sustained were so devastating that she was not expected to ever walk nor talk again, but there she was walking, stomping "grapes," and offering me a view into the indigenous Native American experience that I could not possibly ever achieve on my own. I was inspired by the who of her; an injured warrior defeating all odds and walking and talking, enjoying life and sharing her knowledge. I mentioned about being inspired to write about her. She handed me her card.

At home I did an Internet search to discover that she had sustained massive injuries during an explosion while serving in Iraq, that she served 25 years in the military and retired as a Colonel. I put myself in the path of possibility and came away being inspired by a true heroine, a warrior, a patriot, and a great intellect. I feel blessed.

The Thrill of the Unexpected

February 18, 2022

Do you recall a TV show back in the day, People are Funny? It was hosted by Art Linkletter. A theme from that show became a very popular book, also by Linkletter, Kids Say the Darndest Things," and the phrase became a part of our national lexicon. Other such humorous shows have delighted us across the years. The fact is that people are funny and when one has the sublime pleasure of encountering such a person in such a rare moment, it is something to marvel at, perhaps even to cherish. Last week, I had such an encounter. I am still smiling about it.

It all started when my bestie from the fourth grade, Leanne, learned that her out-of-state twenty-five-year-old granddaughter, Raven, was coming from Colorado to stay for a few days, to be accompanied by her friend Lauren. Lee and I had been prone to laughter as girls and teens and pretty much giggled our way to adulthood. Anyway, as Lee got to planning their stay, she discussed possible itineraries with me. Recalling our sun-kissed growing up years, I enthusiastically volunteered to be "Uber" driver and tour guide, as I knew four of us gals together would have an enjoyable time.

SoCal put on its best show for the out-of-staters, gifting us with 80-degree Santa Ana days, the kind of days which Easterners only dream about as they dig out their snow covered cars. The first day was filled with browsing the boutiques at Balboa, ferry rides and feasting at the historic Pavilion restaurant. The second day was a tour of Ole` Hanson's Casa Romantica on the cliffs above San Clemente Beach Pier. All of it was as much fun as we had hoped. On the pier, overlooking the surf, our visitors marveled at the California beaches and wet-suited surfers. We stuffed ourselves with delicious seafood at the Fishman Restaurant overlooking the water.

Sated, we strolled along the rough planks of the pier, admiring the day when we came upon a strikingly beautiful seagull. We stopped and stared at the elegant bird. He did not blink. He stood like a sentry, feathers gleaming in the midday sun. Lee commented on the beautiful spots on his tail feathers. I noted the red mark on his beak. Raven considered its relationship to albatross. We stared. The bird continued to stand erect. We four studied him in awe. We were transfixed.

Suddenly, from across the width of the pier a fisherman appeared, speaking in a falsetto to mimic the seabird, he declared, "Five dolla to look!"

A bit startled, all of us glanced across to the ventriloquist's grinning face. We, all four, are experienced international travelers and understood at once his joke. In many parts of the underdeveloped world, it is common practice for visitors to ask to take a photograph and to tip for such an opportunity. It is considered a great faux pas to simply take a photo without seeking permission, nor sharing a small payment. Knowing all this, we grinned back at the beaming fisherman, as we began to chuckle.

Soon we moved off a bit from the bird. The fisherman understanding that his audience got his jest persisted, louder this time, still in the bird's high voice, "You wanna picture? You pay ten dolla!"

That cinched it! It was too funny and we nearly doubled over in giggles as he had hit a nerve of common experience. Between gasps of hilarity, Lauren offered a memory. She explained that as a student in Ghana, she was the first white woman many villagers had ever seen and people often stared openly. Smiling at us and recalling her own joke, she would grin at those gathered around her, and say, "That is five cedi." We laughed some more.

We had a golden visit, perhaps all the more enchanting for enduring the endless months of mask wearing and fighting to avoid the ubiquitous coronavirus. In any event, the next day the young women made their way to Venice and the sights of Los Angeles. We had luxuriated in their energy, laughter, and in seeing our own corner of the continent through new eyes. My favorite take-away, however, was our delight in the unexpected. Imagine a chance meeting with a fisherman ventriloquist! Maybe the thing about joy, is that it can pop up anywhere, proving once again that people are funny.

Angels Among Us

November 29, 2021

As I adventure through my life my radar is always on, scanning for unique moments. The other day I went birthday shopping with my granddaughter Kate, who is turning seventeen. We were strolling through the mall after an indulgence at the Cheesecake Factory when Kate encountered a school friend, Angelina. After hugging their greetings, Kate bent down on her knee to meet Angelina's five brothers, two of whom were toddler ages. The greeting became extended to the point that the children's dad, Scott, and I introduced ourselves and began to chat as he stood sentinel over the mighty stroller where the two jumpy three year olds were contained.

"Hey, what a beautiful big family you have!" I admired.

"We adopted them all out of foster care."

With that proclamation my heart did a little skipping thing. Here we were on the eve of the season for giving thanks and appreciating family life, and I got to meet a big, strapping dad who described himself as a stay-at-home-dad while his wife held down a job. Joking, he offered, "She's the one who has it easy!" We laughed.

Our conversation continued and he shared their personal story of wanting a big family. This was the boisterous result. I told him that long ago, my husband, Ken, and I had fostered a teen for a few years and how well her life had turned out. After learning the names of all the smiling boys and their ages, we parted. Continuing down the mall, Kate filled me in about Angelina and how in the fifth grade she was formally adopted, and how jubilant she had been telling Kate all about it on the school bus.

Later that day when I could really think about this husband and wife growing a lively family of five boys and one girl out of the foster system, my heart swelled to comprehend the colossal commitment this couple has made to change the lives of these very fortunate children. I could feel Scott's steadfast strength, pride and commitment. Poems and TV profiles are offered up about our unassuming neighbors, people of valor and pluck quietly making the world a better place, but you do not necessarily encounter them at the mall!

The next day I was able to have a conversation with the mother, Aubrey, of this beautiful brood and she reported that she was moved to tears by my "take" on her family. She described how humorous and what a "rock star" her Scott is. She said that she remembered looking in the rear-view mirror of their van about a year ago, seeing laughing and screaming children running amuck, and saying to Scott, "How did this happen?" In his wry way he answered, "It escalated quickly!"

She further explained that they had six adoptions in a five-and-a-half-year period and that as the mother she feels incredibly blessed, and that having such a husband who would adopt even more and loves them all abundantly is huge.

So often we hear naysayers complaining about the hopelessness in the world, the problems with our youth and more. To me this couple proves that individuals can have a positive impact. Their loving influence on these six children will magnify into the future. We must not believe others when someone decrees that individual efforts make no difference.

Do you recall that Starfish story? The one where the cynical old man is walking along the beach at dawn when he spies a youth far ahead, bending and reaching his arms near the shoreline. He had thought the person was doing Pilates poses. When he neared he saw a youth who was bending down, sifting through the debris from the previous night's storm and grasping a starfish which had washed ashore.

The critical man demands, "What are you doing?"

The young man replies, "When the sun rises the starfish will die. They cannot get back to the sea!"

"Ha. You could never save all the starfish washed up here on the sand. Look, the debris goes on for miles. You cannot possibly make a difference!" The man concluded.

Bending, the youth smiled and flailed a starfish out to sea. "Well I made a difference to that one!"

Indeed there are angels walking around among us. My heart is full as I think of this robust family quietly changing lives and making a positive impact on the world. I wish you a beautiful holiday season. I would love to hear what you have been thinking about, about what angels have been walking nearby.

Let the Ordinary Become the Extraordinary

December 16, 2020

This morning on my dog walk along the oceanfront, I encountered this remarkable rock art left by an anonymous stranger for anyone who is paying attention to enjoy. I could not believe what I was seeing; a small flock of birds created on the edge of the beach parking lot. A shiver ran through me as I pondered the simple beauty and magnificence of the tiny flock.

As the dogs and I strolled along, I reflected on the sentiments expressed in the Christmas letters my friends have been sending. The dominant theme is: "Out with 2020," "I haven't done much this year," "A terrible year." Such sentiments are part of our collective experience, perhaps exacerbated by California's most recent shut-down, again limiting our freedom.

Together we have endured the worst national health crisis in a century and witnessed an unprecedented political polarization. To say the least, it has been distressing. However, as 2020 comes to a close, it affords a perfect opportunity to take a personal step toward healing. We can begin to have hope as the Covid-19 vaccine is administered, and the national political hotbed cools down for a while. Perhaps we can work on where we allow our thoughts to carry us.

Where go our thoughts, so follow our feelings. Even though another mandatory lockdown leaves us more isolated than ever, there are certain actions we can take to redirect our outlook toward the positive. Ten years ago this week, I packed up my office at Cypress College and loaded the boxes of books and papers into my car. I said my goodbyes, and as in many retirements, I was physically escorted to my car. Adios! After 44 years of appearing on campus every school day, the uncertainty of my future plagued me. Could life possibly hold as much meaning without my students? Truly, I had no idea.

Those who have followed my posts have witnessed the fact that I have, indeed, found some interesting places to focus my attention. I have long adopted the HABIT of looking for Precious Moments. Historically this is a good time for all of us to do just that, mindfully adopt the HABIT of focusing our attention on the small delights lurking around many corners, like the impromptu flock of stone birds this morning, or another rock sculpture I saw yesterday. My daughter, Julina, has the habit of photographing the sunrise many mornings and sharing the extraordinary colorful photos with me. My friend, Sioux, discovered a beautiful hand-painted rock in the shape of a heart the other day, and has gleefully posted it on social media.

If one has their eyes peeled there are unique forms of public art hidden in small corners. Several cities around SoCal have invested in public art. At the corner of Coast Highway and Palisades Drive in Dana Point there is a beautiful portrait of famous author, Richard Henry Dana, Jr. adorning the electrical transformer box. That painting is sponsored by the City of Dana Point. Another city with awe-inspiring public art is Venice, California, where whole buildings are adorned with gorgeous murals. Our pets offer moments of delight as well. My granddaughter, Caroline, often shares photos of her cat, Stella, doing hilarious things.

The habit of keeping our eyes open for little delights can be our challenge for this holiday season. The universe has even seen fit to help guide us toward a positive outlook for the coming year. It has aligned the planets Jupiter and Saturn so close to Earth that on December 21st they will appear as one glorious bright star. Imagine that, a huge bright "star" visible to the naked eye. The last time this "Great Conjunction" occurred was in 1623, and before that in 1226. This bright "star" is most often referred to as the "Christmas Star." Developing the habit of looking for "surprises" is a valuable tool for making the negatives in our lives to seem to be a little less important. More than ever, this year I wish you a safe holiday season with a heart full of promise for a better year to come. I cherish the words you send me and look forward to reading what you are thinking about.

Hello from Rainbow Land

March 23, 2020

Hello my friends! Wow are we challenged or what? This sequestering is more grueling than the calamities in a bad Hollywood Sci-Fi film. So we are mostly all sheltered in place, unable to go about much semblance of our normal lives. We are only in the middle of Week One, and some of us are already chafing at it, while others ignore the threat completely. ABC News this morning showed thousands of partying youth crowding the warm sands of South Beach, Florida. The on-camera quote by a grinning young man, "If I get Corona, I get Corona. We planned for this vacation for months."

As the world shuts down in an unprecedented way, something unseen in our lifetimes, we cope with not just the threat of this deadly and invisible virus, but a very real and serious economic reality as well. In addition, we face the risk presented by those who are cavalier about the seriousness of it.

I am certain that the attitude we choose to take toward this crisis, toward our freedom being curtailed, will determine how well we get through it. My hero, Austrian psychologist Dr. Victor Frankl, Man's Search for Meaning, was locked up in a Nazi concentration camp. He was horrified to see men literally fighting over a scrap of grizzle lying on the prison floor. After his release, he wrote that in that moment, he decided to turn his incarceration into a sort of real-time laboratory study, to determine what it was within the psychology of the prisoners which determined who survived and who died. What he learned was that those who survived had a larger goal than survival. They focused on something to accomplish or do once they were free. He saw that they had a purpose that kept them going against the worst odds. The survivors had a WHY to live. For Victor, he wanted to find his family. During his long life he wrote many books about what he learned regarding finding one's purpose and about pursuing happiness. His thinking has been a cornerstone to my own philosophy of life.

Somehow I managed to survive the worst abuse a young girl can suffer at the hands of her father. My incarceration sentence was my entire childhood. The secret to my survival with my sanity intact was to have a get-away plan. My purpose was to create a life where I was "normal," once I was free. I knew that adulthood would bring freedom. It was an overriding vision which somehow guided me through the horror. You know me well enough to know that I have succeeded, against heavy odds. This explains why I live in gratitude. I am so grateful to be free.

Our challenge is to accept our current reality and do as we are instructed by the authorities. The societal goal is to get the virus infection curve to flatten so that the lowest numbers of us become ill and our medical facilities will be able to cope. I am fascinated to begin to study the reactions from those around me to this mandate. Hundreds of missives are coming my way each day via the news, posts on social media, telephone calls and emails.

Certainly for many Americans, our sense of humor is firmly intact. My friends are sending and posting truly hilarious bits. The toilet paper hoarding has struck a funny bone for many. I cracked up at the photo of a huge sandcastle created on Balboa Island made of toilet paper rolls crafted of sand. I saw a poker game pic where they were betting toilet paper rolls, and innumerable messages about the crazy role reversal where 50-somethings are forced to admonish their Baby Boomer parents Not to Go Out!

On Monday, the first day of our California "quarantine," my ten-year-old granddaughter, Caroline, sent me a long video called Rainbow Land. Caroline had already created a miniature theme park down the hall in her home and into the living room. Many rainbows were in evidence. There was an "art museum" taped to one wall, a fun zone with a ball pit, then a "pin the gold on the rainbow" attraction, water rides and so much more!! Seriously, how clever to invent a Pin the Gold on the Rainbow game!!!

So this is our challenge. We can bitterly bemoan the state of affairs, huff and puff about the governmental "overreaction," or figure out a game plan for the foreseeable weeks, perhaps months, to keep ourselves on an even keel. Maybe we figure out how to pin the gold on the rainbow?

The moms around me are creating plans to help their shut-in children to cope. My daughter is sending challenges to the other young people in the family. The other night the challenge was to hold a plastic cup of water on your forehead as you contort into a sitting position, and ultimately to a position where you can set the cup of water on the floor without spilling it. The videos of my daughter and her daughter accomplishing this feat created the challenge for the cousins. Other moms have a schedule of family game time, family walking time, free time, chores time and so on. The moms are gearing up! It is still okay to go outside in the fresh air. We just need to keep our distance from those not in our family.

Clearly our attitude is up to each of us. I am journaling each day, because when we come out the other side, it will be hard to remember exactly what it felt like to have our freedom of movement taken away from us, our jobs, good hugs, and our human face-to-face interactions. I think we will forget, like we might the pain of childbirth. Anyway, I'm writing it down.

I loved this post. "When this is over: may we never again take for granted a handshake, full shelves at the store, conversations with neighbors, a crowded theater, Friday night out, the taste of communication, coffee with a friend, a boring Tuesday, or life itself! " Or toilet paper! That's my addition. So for now. Our challenge is to take the best care we can of ourselves. To adjust our attitude and soldier on.

Burning Man 2019: A Social Phenomenon

September 9, 2019

My fascination with culture building has kept me a devoted fan of the popular reality TV show, Survivor. When I learned that my wonderful 24-year-old grandson, Jake, had managed to purchase a ticket to the famous Burning Man event this year I was enthralled. I could hardly wait to hear all about it. Three days after his return, we met for lunch. Seated comfortably in a corner booth at The Sun Dried Tomato, I plied him with questions about his recent nine-day-long sojourn into that world held at "Black Rock City, Nevada."

As a social scientist and world traveler, I have been blessed to have visited and studied the Wonders of the World as well as many of humanities' great works of art. I have been fortunate to create a life where this is possible, however my travels have shown me little comparable to Jake's adventure.

I can barely visualize a "city" of 70,000 inhabitants which rises up from nothing in the bleakest of deserts only to be burned down or physically removed nine days later. Truly, I can't imagine. In my world we would preserve the art and turn it into a World Heritage Site.

I had done my homework before I met with Jake. I understood that Larry Harvey had founded this phenomenon thirty years ago when he gathered his friends for a bonfire at the beach near San Francisco, burned an effigy, and celebrated the Summer Solstice while trying to get over a bad break-up. As the event grew and was moved from the beach to the desert, Harvey had a vision. He saw the event as a "shared intention to restore community and creative expression."

I knew that Burning Man had grown to become a world-wide social phenomenon attracting "Burners" to play and create in the arid, dust blown Playa and Black Rock Desert, one hundred miles north of Reno each year. As Jake opened the photos on his phone and began to describe the many roving "art cars" and the "light art," and the massive temporary art exhibits, I felt lightheaded from the thrill of it all. Even the "Burners" themselves are part of the scene with their costumes and makeup. His photos showed me lots of fur, jewelry, tutus, masks, and goggles. I knew there was nudity. (My grandson did not have such photos in his collection, however he knew that I had come to my majority during the turbulent 60's, The Age of Aquarius, and was pretty immune to certain aspects of communal living). He described a party he attended on a big 747 airplane which was rolled onto the sandy desert and gutted. It became a dance hall with portions of the top of the plane removed so participants could enjoy the view of the "city" which follows an organized grid pattern with the camps erected along designated blocks.

A favorite photo was of an art car which was a lit-up sailing ship with three masts, mounted upon a truck chassis. I could image how majestic it must have appeared "sailing" across the dark desert at night. I loved the photos of the "Folly" which is a life-sized multi story "town" made of wood. An important piece was a giant wooden birthday cake upon which stood the 40 foot tall Burning Man effigy. Further reading taught me that the "soul of Black Rock City has always resided within the structures, the artists and the builders." Fifty years ago, Woodstock was built on its music. Twenty years later, Burning Man, which has persevered for thirty years, is built on its art. The burning of the "man" marks the culmination of the celebration.

The communication teacher in me is interested in the development of cultures. I got a kick out of the event's tribal greeting. Instead of a handshake, there is a hug; instead of hello, during the first days of the gathering, it was "Welcome Home." As Jake recited the tenets of the gathering, I could not help but flash back on recent television accounts of the 1969 crowd of a half million at Woodstock. Woodstock was a cultural flashpoint. I thought of its ethos of peace, and love against the protests of the Viet Nam War; I also recalled the massive mounds of debris left in its wake.

This is the Burning Man Code:

- Radical Inclusion - anyone may be a part of Burning Man
- Gifting - Burning Man is devoted to acts of gift giving
- Decommodification - (Immunity from market dependency)
- Radical Self Reliance
- Radical Self-expression

- Communal Effort
- Civic Responsibility
- Leaving No Trace

The "city" is guided by its own laws and mores. Jake explained that safety and consent are of key importance and there was a visible police presence. Money is not allowed, only gift giving. (Cash is only allowed for the purchase of ice and coffee). Brand names are taped over or marked out. One of Jake's favorite activities was riding his bike on the open desert and stumbling upon pieces of art. Another interesting moment was walking into a boutique and finding a piece of clothing he liked and being invited to take it. No charge, gift giving being the cultural norm.

Jake smiled as he explained the feeling of strolling into the playa (the sandy dry lake bed a bit away from the city) in the middle of the night to think; to appreciate the beauty and darkness of the desert, and the enormity of living in a social experiment where one is free from ordinary social constraints. Always careful, he assured me that he was safe in the dark. He wore lights on his clothing as mobile art pieces were often moving past as well as bicycles.

My guess is that Burning Man will continue to grow, but as the rich and famous want in on the action, hiring folk to set up and tear down their camps, rolling-in expensive RV's and personal chefs, it will change. For now, much of the community building, art installations, and personal expressions remain somewhat true to Larry Harvey's vision.

A quick Instagram review showed video snippets of the scenes. I encourage you to explore the event online. I know from studying world history that in ancient times there were similar communal rituals such as those centered at the Winter Solstice. Events, like Stonehenge, where humans gathered eons ago to celebrate life are not new, but we know so little about them, while this event is alive and growing during our time. I find it magical and exciting!

As we finished up our lunch and Jake prepared to go back to the "real" world of work, I knew that I would not be attending Burning Man for many reasons including the heat and sand, however, through the luxury of narrative and photos, I am able to glean a sense of the adventure without the dust storms or high temperatures. I've had a vicarious thrill through my grandson's special experience. Surely this wild city is in a class of its own, far different from my adventures around the world, but most importantly, this has given me something precious which my young man can eagerly share with his very fascinated grandmother. I feel lucky.

Gateway to the Past

August 28, 2019

Happy Labor Day! This holiday signals the end of summer for many of us; time to put our boogey boards and sun hats away and begin the routines of Fall. As Fall is a time of change, I had decided to move some of the wall art in my home, and had begun thinking about what to do. I considered taking some pieces to our home in the mountains. Last night, however, I awoke in the middle of the night out of sorts. The mere thought of moving a certain piece distressed me. It is an oversized canvas, painted by my son, Rick, when he was five years. I realized in the dark of night, that the painting has comforted me since 1970! It has captured a moment in time for me. It reminds me of a long ago past when my little kindergartner son, Rick, passed his time flying his kite while his two-and-a-half-year-old sister rode her plastic Big Wheel nearby, a time before my last child was born. I realized that I cannot bear to move it.

That got me thinking about art and its ability to freeze time. Perhaps that is the most heady aspect of art, including film and photography; its ability to stop time. My thoughts raced ahead of me to my docent training at the Mission San Juan Capistrano. That, too, has been an adventure in stopping time; in sifting through history, as we tell the mission's 250-year story.

A while back, I was in a training session where the Mission's plein air exhibit was being curated for us docents. During the lecture, my eyes wandered to the eastern wall of the adobe room. I gasped as my eyes landed on the lovely oil painting of silent film star Mary Pickford's wedding done by renowned impressionist Charles Percy Austin over a hundred years ago. As I gazed at the charming work, my brain took me back to a sleepy San Juan of a century past. I knew about silent film star Mary Pickford. I could not help but smile at the temerity it must have taken for her to ask the resident priest, Father O'Sullivan, to perform the renewal of her

wedding vows!!

The setting for the painting is at the Mission between the colonnades. The portrait captures the couple as they emerge from the Sala after the ceremony. Flowers and musicians embellish the scene. It is a lovely piece gifted to Father O'Sullivan by the artist.

This painting, too, offers a gateway to the past. It reminds me of when tempers were running hot in the tiny village of San Juan. Mary Pickford, a darling of the silent movie era, arrived in San Juan in 1910 as a part of the entourage of pioneer filmmaker G. W. Griffith's big movie making crew. I could imagine the scene in town when Griffith pulled up to the depot with three rail cars full of actors and equipment prepared to film the first every movie made in Orange County. The film, Two Brothers, was a period piece where the outlaw scenes were to be filmed in the local foothills. That portion of the filming came off without any problems, but trouble started when the locals observed the filming on the downtown streets. As the actors moved in a mock processional toward the Mission a crowd gathered to watch. Before very long, however, some of the townsfolk got the idea that Griffith was belittling a funeral procession that had taken place the day before. The observers became hostile to the point of throwing rocks at the actors!

The situation was growing uglier by the minute. It was only after some cajoling and quick negotiations by the town's hotel proprietor that the angry crowd settled down. Griffith suggested a peace offering of holding a rodeo and roping show to be performed by the cowboys in his troupe. That did the trick and the filming was allowed to continue. Whew!

Across her life, the Canadian born actress made 40 movies for Griffith's company, plus some 160 films for others. Her contribution to the art of film is undisputed. She co-founded United Artists Studio with Charlie Chaplin and her second husband, Douglas Fairbanks. She was also a founder of the famous Academy of Motion Picture Arts and Sciences, known today as The Academy. She was known as "America's Sweetheart" decades before Shirley Temple usurped the title.

To think that something as simple as a painting or photograph has the power to transport a person backward in time is awe inspiring. Recalling Rick (who was Ricky back in 1970) as he flies his kite and his baby sister wheels by on her plastic trike, somehow takes me to a different world. Thinking of Miss Pickford and her love for the mission allows me to appreciate history in a different way. What power these items can have! Clearly, I have learned a lesson. I will not be moving my son's painting!

Life Itself

April 10, 2019

This morning, the dogs and I hiked down the steep hill at Salt Creek. As the ocean came into view, I was pleased to see crowds of surfers and onlookers lining the shore, scrutinizing the dozen surfers paddling frantically into the next breaker. Trucks with WSA logos were parked all along the beach road. As we continued, a woman stopped me to meet my dogs. I asked about the event. "It is a Western Surfing Association competition. I'm taking a break."

"What's your role?" I asked.

"I'm a judge."

"Oh how nice." Offering a connection, I replied, "I only know Kevin Skavarna in the surfing world."

"Oh I know Kevin. He's wonderful."

We smiled at each other enjoying the common ground of world surfing champion Kevin. I felt proud to have known him since he was a little boy, and to be able to share about him. We exchanged our names and smiled our goodbyes.

As I walked away I passed a trio of wet-suited adolescent boys deeply engaged in an animated discussion. They were wet and shimmering. I admired their slim forms and how heavily engrossed they seemed in what they were doing. They were so in the moment. I thought they personified life itself.

Life itself. I thought about that for a moment as I continued on. A beautifully perceptive participant in my loss support group two days earlier had described her recently deceased husband as being "life itself." That description resonated with me. What a powerful testament to the man he had been; what a beautiful compliment.

After a while I found a picnic table next to the water's edge and sat down. The dogs settled in the shade under the table, while I gazed at the scenes unfolding around me. A couple walked by arm in arm. The young man tickled the girl. She giggled, leaning into him and smiling. I thought how sweet that simple gesture was. A teen came by with his dog and caught my eye. He was sporting the tallest Mohawk hair-do I had seen in some time! The surfers continued to master the waves as the photographers snapped photos. Life was all around me.

Somehow it provided a fresh counterpoint to my last two weeks. I had just completed long nine days supporting my husband at Mission Hospital. Ken had undergone a very serious, life threatening heart surgery. Those days were new proof to me of the preciousness of human life and the extent we go to protect it. During the eight days he was in the ICU, I witnessed a number of "Code Trauma" emergencies. I watched as the medical staff rushed to the rescue. One night after there had just been another "Code Trauma," it was time for me to leave Ken's room. As I walked down the hall, I passed by the patient who was the subject of the emergency. I was awed to witness an entire room full of professionals tending to her. The next day I was relieved to see that she was still in her room.

During those difficult days, I grew used to the wailing of ambulances and fire engines as they rushed to the ER department; first responders fighting to keep people alive. I had the opportunity to witness our modern medicine in action, to see up close the dedication the doctors, nurses, paramedics, and hospital staff have as they do everything within their power to support life. It was a lesson in living.

I understand that it is easy to be affected by the negativity around us. I was recently in New Zealand, only missing the massacre in Christchurch by 15 hours. Bad things happen. The news is full of emphatic stories detailing the worst in humanity.

My time at Salt Creek today, and my nine days at Mission Hospital, have provided me with a renewed commitment to the importance of celebrating the beauty of life, in cherishing our loved ones, in reveling the fact of our breathing and beating hearts, the magnificence of the Super Bloom adorning our hillsides, and the idea that we, right now, have the luxury of being alive in the world. So that is my renewed perspective. I am grateful that Ken is now home and recovering.

Good Luck Charm

February 8, 2019

I ventured into the unknown on Wednesday February 6, unsure of exactly what was going on, but determined to honor my commitment. It started two weeks ago while I was having my regular nail appointment at the Vietnamese salon where I go. As the ladies were putting the finishing touches on my fingers and toes, they commanded, "You come back for Vietnamese New year. You come back. Come at 10 am. The shop will be closed. It is the first day of the New Year. You come back. The owner will be here. You come back."

Not certain what I had to do with the Vietnamese New Year, nor with the shop being closed, I negotiated that I could come at 11:00, allowing time for my morning activities. I put it in my phone calendar.

I protected the time slot for them, still unsure of what this was about. Across the decades, teaching at Cypress College, my Vietnamese speech students would regal my classes with colorful stories of Tet, the Lunar New Year on the Chinese calendar. They told about the exchanging of tiny red envelopes filled with money for the children, to bring luck. They shared about boisterous parades and family feasts. They had taught me that the Vietnamese New Year is a very big deal.

On the day in question, I called the shop at 10 am. to confirm my appointment. No answer. I called at 10:30. No answer. Not one to fail to honor an obligation, I dragged myself away from the research project I was doing and drove to the shop. It was dark. I walked up to the door and tried it. It was open. I walked in and all three technicians were waiting for me.

Excitedly, they greeted me with big smiles as they directed me to sit down. I sat. Instantly, all three began to work on me.

As my treatments began, they shared that in their culture it is important to bring good luck for the coming year. They needed me in the shop because, as they explained, "You are the happiest client we have. You will bring us happiness and luck across the year."

What? I thought to myself. I asked, "You mean to tell me that of your hundreds of clients I am the happiest?"

"You are. There is one other lady who also laughs but she is traveling in Israel. You are our good luck charm. You are good omen."

I wasn't too sure what to make of this so I relaxed back in the leather spa chair as they continued working on me.

That evening my daughter, Julina, called and I described the odd experience I had at the nail salon. She jumped on it. "Mom, that wasn't odd. Those ladies chose you across their entire business because you live what you say. Mom, your mantra is Happiness is a Choice. You are living proof of that."

Feeling the need to say something, I responded, "Oh, well okay."

She continued. "Had you grown up in a Leave it to Beaver childhood their choice of you might not have meant anything too much, but your growing up was horrendous, and yet you have chosen happiness. It proves that it is possible to be mindful and choose one's way of being. Mom that was really cool what they did. Mom, you have to write about that. It is possible to choose one's attitude."

A bit stunned, I thanked her and we went on to other topics. Later on as I prepared dinner, I was thinking about what she said. I thought about my Loss of a Loved One support group participants. They are working on their mission statements, their guiding purpose for the next chapters of their lives as they struggle to move forward through grief. My mind fast forwarded to the years of coaching women in transition, how miserable they seemed in the beginning of our classes and how joyful they became as they learned that they could choose their responses to life events. I thought about my response to my own devastation. One of my guiding goals as a young teen was that I was not going to let my father destroy my happiness. It was important to me. I was determined.

I succeeded.

I have invested a considerable amount of energy studying human happiness. My hero, Dr. Csikszentmihalyi, in his famous bestseller, Flow: The Psychology of Optimal Experience, teaches that joy comes in the midst of the flow experience, that is while we are engaged in doing something we find meaningful. We can find happiness in doing! I know that sometimes good feelings simply come from having something to look forward to; that is important to take regular daily exercise, to eat properly, to be around uplifting people, and to celebrate one's blessings. It is up to us to take care of ourselves.

Time is short. If we are not careful it can simply slip through our fingers like grains of sand. Right now, this moment, is our time and I think we need to make the most of it. While

I am not so convinced that I am a good luck charm, I do know that I respect the traditions and beliefs of those around me and feel honored to think that the ladies at the salon feel that I will bring them luck and happiness in this New Year.

Toot! Toot! Here Comes the Helm's Man!

July 20, 2020

Hi there! I hope this note finds you well. Back in April, when we learned that our Covid-19 isolation orders would continue for some time, I woke up one morning with a new idea. We had been tackling the attic, and I'd been going through old photos and papers belonging to my great grandparents and grandparents. They were intriguing, depicting rare views of old Venice Beach, California, when it was known as Venice-of-America. How sweet it was to see my great grandparents smiling out from their perch on the sand at the end of Venice Boulevard in 1900! My family arrived in Los Angeles around 1887 when the train came through from the Mid-West and spent a great deal of their time in the coastal area of Los Angeles.

It got me thinking. I, too, had lived some remarkable aspects of lost Los Angeles history. The look backward inspired me to write the story of my growing up years in Venice, California during a period when it was an industrial zone, the fourth most productive oil field in the state. I know it sounds crazy to tell you that my next door neighbor was a gigantic oil-well derrick attached to a working pump house, whooshing up and down during all the days and nights of my growing years. We lived in a 400 square foot bungalow built out of war surplus materials. It was located right on the beach but surrounded by these steel monoliths.

Energized, I began writing, while Ken kept offering to drive me on research field trips up to Venice. The trips were fun and easy because the traffic during lockdown was non-existent. The book Growing Up Venice: Parallel Universes will be available soon. For now I want to share a particularly charming result I encountered.

About a week ago, Ken and I drove up to the old Helms Bakery Building on Venice Boulevard in Culver City. The trip was prompted by a picture of a Helms truck and childhood memories we both have of its visits to our neighborhoods. It is a design center now, boasting a pedestrian walk with restaurants and places to meet up. We took photos, bought chocolate éclairs, and took an outdoor seat looking across the street toward Paramount Studios. Of course, it was something of a walk down Memory Lane for me. My third-grade field trip had been to this famous bakery. I could almost see the huge metal machines mixing thick dough and could smell the sweet aroma of baking cookies. The friendly "toot toot" of the Helms Man's yellow and blue truck was clear in my memory.

My most beloved remembrance is during visits to our grandparents. They lived near the Farmer's Market at Fairfax and Third Street in Hollywood. My sister and I would hear the Helms whistle and race around the house looking for our grandpa. He would smile at us as he escorted us out to the waiting truck. The Helms Man would grin as he opened the double doors at the back of his truck, and slowly guide the smooth wooden drawers out, revealing row upon row of pastries. There was never a rush. I could take my time and choose the perfect treat. I mostly went for the cream puff in the top drawer. The Helms Man would hand it down to me, wrapped in a paper. My grandfather would pay, and I would run to the porch, sit down, and slowly enjoy the creamy sweet. The memory for me is more than the Helms Man, it's wound up in the idyllic days with our grandfather. He was wonderful, a storyteller and one who took the time to teach me. The Helms Man sparked something old and cherished in my life.

Our Helms trip made a wonderful day, and I posted a few of the Helm's photos on social media. The result I received was staggering!! Many of my social media friends enthusiastically shared their experiences. They told me the Helms Man went all the way to

Fresno, to Laguna Beach, to San Diego. It was so much fun to read what they had to say. One friend, Karen, told me about how her mom put the big blue H letter in the window so that the Helms Man would stop by others told me about getting candied apples, sugar cookies, cream puffs. They recalled the metal change maker around his waist; that sometimes he would let them place the coins in it. I learned about how as kids they would hear the whistle and come racing. One friend, Royce, said he and his brother would beg for a coin from their grandma and go running. One time his brother tripped and lost the coin! Oh No! They missed the Helms Man as they searched for that coin. He invited us to look for that missing coin from 50 some years ago at his corner in Long Beach!

The Helms Man whistling through our neighborhoods was a daily ritual for thousands of us children in Southern California between 1932 and 1968. When the 1932 Summer Olympics in Los Angeles struggled financially due to the Depression, retired banker turned baker, Paul Helms, with his newly opened bakery, stepped up. He helped out and tied his bakeries to the Olympic athletes. His was the "Choice of Champions." The Olympians continued to ask for Helms bread across the next twenty years. Helms also participated in the Rose Parade, sponsored television shows, and provided the bread for the Apollo missions, becoming the "first bread on the moon." Even though his products were never sold in markets, he was remarkably successful. When he died in the late 1950's the family operated the bakery for another ten years. Today it is commemorated as an historic building and the area is noted as The Historic Helms Bakery District. I would recommend a visit. Perhaps you could enjoy a cream puff as you sit and take a little side tour to your past.

When I wrote the Helms Bakery post, I had no clue that my friends would be so overjoyed by recalling their own precious memories. The Helms Man was commonplace to us, perhaps that is part of it; the innocence of us as children running for our jelly donut. I know that writing my new book, remembering what it was like to range free across the sand through all the days of my childhood, has helped me get through this trying moment in history. It has reminded me how grateful I am for being alive; what a gift life is. We are going through one of the most complex, frightening times in our lives. Our world has been turned upside down and many of us are reeling trying to remain upright. Maybe that's what we all need to do, search our memories for precious moments, and notice other such events in real time. Perhaps we can remind ourselves each day, what a gift it is to be alive.

Ripe with Possibilities

April 25, 2016

"A Lost Daughter Speaks Out and All of China Listens!" (March 30, 2016, FP News) is the touching story of recent Yale graduate, Jenna Cook. She is a former abandoned infant, left on the streets of Wuhan, China, who went looking for her birth family. Having long been interested in the "One Child Policy" of China, I recall being seated next to an American couple back in 2005 as we made our way to Beijing. They were on their way to adopt their new daughter. The flight was long and they were far too excited to sleep. I provided an eager audience. I learned about the hundreds of abandoned babies, the orphanages, and that some families in China needed a son over a daughter. The couple explained that the baby girl they were getting had been left under a tree in a park. I listened with rapt attention. As an American, it was difficult for me to imagine a socio/economic climate that could force people to abandon their children.

As our family toured Beijing, we rode on rickshaws through the tiny streets of an ancient hutong, a very old neighborhood of tiny homes and narrow alleys. As we wheeled by we could not help but notice that only boy children were out playing. A few days later, we were visiting the Great Wall and, much to our surprise, we discovered an entire "class" of adoptive couples who happened to be there as well. They were gathered with their new little daughters in bright shiny strollers. I struck up a few casual conversations with the beaming mothers and was even allowed to hold one of the babies. It made an impression on me. On the trip back home I was again seated with an adoptive family. Their new 11-month-old daughter crawled from one of our laps to another. As the airplane grew quiet and the baby fell asleep, I thought of the opportunity that lay ahead for her. I knew about the success my friend had some years before with her two adopted Chinese babies. Those girls were thriving. I leaned back in my seat and scanned across my teaching career to the hundreds upon hundreds of students who were given the opportunity and achieved remarkable success. My thoughts paused on one young Hispanic man I had in my public speaking class. He had regaled us with stories of his life in one of the more infamous Southland gangs. He confessed that when he had stared down the muzzle of an opposing gang member's gun in a dark Los Angeles alley, he knew he would soon be dead if he did not get out. In order to accomplish that, he had to withstand the ordeal of being "jumped out" which meant he had to endure a horrific beating. I followed his progress through college. He was a magnificent student and when he graduated from UCLA Law School he came back to share his triumph with me.

From gang banger to lawyer, from abandoned infant to Yale graduate; it interests me to note that often when people are offered the opportunity for a different kind of life, they grab hold and soar. I hope as we stare at the nightly news and see the animosity and dirty fighting of the current presidential primary campaign, that we do not become so disgusted and disillusioned by what we are hearing that we lose sight of what it is we have here America. We have freedom and opportunity. My travels from the heights of the Himalayas, to the plains of the Serengeti, to the meager dried mud huts along the Nile, to the volcanic mountains of Ecuador, have taught me that what we could all too easily take for granted in the U.S., is just a pipe dream to most of the people of the world. For all of our public blemishes what we have achieved here in our amazing country ultimately works. I think it takes all of us working together to ensure it.

On Not Taking One Breath for Granted

November 20, 2018

The lyrics: "Don't take one breath for granted....it could all go away.... if you have a dream, chase it...if you feel hope, don't waste it..."

In the peacefulness of the dawning morning, my brain played a kaleidoscope of recent headlines: synagogue massacre, cowboy bar shoot up, historic death toll in California wildfires juxtaposed against the sudden onslaught of holiday television commercials pressing us to buy buy buy for the festive season. It would be easy to succumb to the pressure of all that.

Then Groban's "Never take a single breath for granted" again resonated through my ear buds, quite literally helping me to reframe my thoughts. The grim mental pictures began to recede. I became aware of the calls of the crows overhead, the rhythmic breathing of my dogs, and the vista of Saddleback Mountain shrouded in purple in front of me. I realized anew that we have the power to control our thoughts without diminishing the need to honor the memories of the victims. We have the power to continue to celebrate all that is right with the world.

1. We can focus on the positive
2. We can celebrate being alive
3. We can collect precious moments
4. We can take control of our thoughts

Years ago I found a book in a used bookstore in Bellingham, Washington, called Chasing Daylight. It was the true story of an extremely successful international businessman, Eugene O'Kelly, who was given just six weeks to live. The book was written during those final days. He stopped chasing dollars and began to spend time with his wife and young daughter. His story reveals a secret; he found more joy in those last six weeks, collecting precious moments, than in the forty years leading up to then.

I took his message to heart and began collecting any precious moments I could. Recently my friend Mary shared one with me. It seems she started her docent tour at the mission and a little fourth grader announced that she was starving. Mary explained that lunch would be after the tour in an hour or so. As she guided her group around the mission sharing about the wine vat, the Catalan furnaces, and the padre's kitchen which boasts soot from two hundred years ago, suddenly the little girl turned to Mary and said, "I'm not hungry anymore, I am full of knowledge!" Everyone within ear shot smiled. Mary knew to collect that sweet moment and even shared it with me.

I think we humans are brave in the face of adversity, and that it is important NOT to take for granted the plenty we enjoy even when the news is filled with agony. I hope through the holiday season we can reflect on what is right within our own lives and with the world. Perhaps by example we can show those around us how to appreciate the fact of being alive and to honor the riches we often take for granted as Americans. Perhaps we can reach out to others in need during this beautiful season as we consider the thought that it is possible to celebrate each breath as a blessing and not take life for granted.

They Came Before Us: Trail Blazers

March 12, 2021

I recall how nervous I felt the day in 1951 when my eight-year-old self reluctantly appeared on my grandmother's weekly children's TV show!! Today I realize that she, Vera May Lewis, was a pioneer in television! This month, National Women's History Month, allows us to celebrate the pioneering women on whose shoulders we stand.

Our sagging family album revealed her photo on the set of The Playcrafters Club. It aired on Channel 5, KTLA, Thursdays at 5, from 1950 through 1955. According to the Los Angeles Mirror, Playcrafters Club was the oldest educational children's program on the West Coast. My grandmother was breaking new ground. Today there are hundreds of programs for youth, but back in the early days of TV, in the late 40's and early 1950's, the pickings were slim, relying heavily on regional programming. Hers was a local show sponsored by Los Angeles County. As a Senior Recreation Director, she was assigned as host. It was a 30 minute-long craft program where local children created art projects for those at home.

Today our devices allow us to watch anything at any time, nearly anywhere!! Ninety-eight percent of Americans have televisions. Back in the beginning things were far different. There was one national children's program, The Howdy Doody Show on NBC which aired from December 1947 until 1960, and by 1956 The Mickey Mouse Club, and soon others, but hers was an important early step.

I am proud of my grandmother, Vera May Cooper Lewis, born in Los Angeles in 1901. After marriage and becoming a mom, she went on to graduate from the University of

Southern California in 1929, majoring in Speech. Her career modeled possibilities for me.

What about your own fore bearers on whose shoulders you stand? What family member pioneered for you? I'd love to hear about them.

Still pondering the trail blazers, I examined a few more pages in our decrepit album and came upon my father's grandmother. A pioneering woman; she raised her two small children while working full time in the family store. She was Lydia Cram Lewis, born in Minnesota in 1859. She, with her pharmacist husband, Charles H.V. Lewis, arrived via rail to the City of Angels in the late 1880's leaving the civilized comforts of Des Moines, Iowa, for the rugged frontier of the rough "out west," where gun fights on Saturday night were the norm, and the population was about 15,000 people.

In my mind's eye, I can see them lumbering off the train, their hands heavily laden with bags, struggling to hold on to their two small children. Their children, daughter, Fayetta, was six and their son, my grandfather, was two. The trunks and cases would have held their worldly household possessions as well as the starting stock for their intended pharmacy. This 1894 photo is of Lydia behind the counter of the Lewis Drug Company at 4th and Broadway in Los Angeles.

They would ultimately become a family of druggists, owning nine pharmacies and cigar shores in Los Angeles. Lydia would earn her California State Board of Pharmacy certification in 1901; as would both of her children. Fayetta, after owning and operating her own pharmacy, would go on to manage the pharmaceutical department of the Hollywood Hospital, while her younger brother, Ray, would also own his own businesses.

My memory skipped to my favorite of his stores, at Sunset and Gardner in Hollywood. I loved the sparkling medicine ball hanging over the front door. Upon arrival at the store, my little sister and I would spring from the car and dash, giggling, through the front door heading straight for the candy counter!

Lydia and my grandfather were very close, hence my childhood was filled with his fond narratives about her life. One of my treasures is a collection of his 1903 letters to her. For several months at age 19, for health, he needed to live in the Mojave area, a long, dusty, and bumpy 66 miles in a stage coach from Los Angeles. The penciled, handwritten pages describe tasks of everyday life like his packing his trunk for the stagecoach and oiling his gun. Like teens today might do, he asked his mom for clean socks! These stories allow us a peek into lives lived in Southern California almost 120 years ago, and the pioneers who settled our land, making possible the lives we live today. I realize that through my grandfather's stories, Lydia Lewis has influenced the woman I have become.

Not a Journey But a Musical Concerto

October 12, 2017

I was a little worried this week when I invited my friends, Mary and Leanne, to see the art film Loving Vincent (Van Gogh). I read the reviews including the one that said, "a lunatic effort in adoring Van Gogh." That had me more worried. My friends insisted they were "game" even if the movie turned out to be a stinker. Well, we were in for an incredible surprise, the creative genius behind the film left us breathless. Filmmakers Dorothy Kobiela and Hugh Welchman took seven years and 125 artists painting in the style of Van Gogh to create the world's first fully painted animated film. A masterpiece in my way of thinking. As the closing credits rolled and the words to the musical theme repeated, "I hope you understand what is in my heart through my work," I dabbed at my eyes. The experience moved me profoundly, on many levels. The dominant takeaway for me, was how important it is that we choose our life path and not live on auto-pilot. I have long seen that our everyday behaviors are in many ways, brush strokes on the canvas of our lives. In these posts over the years, I am often encouraging you to live in your own best interests, to live joyfully, to live purposefully.

Anyway, when I arrived home after a two-hour bumper-to-bumper five-mile drive made impossible by the many fires closing the accesses to the inland cities, my husband was waiting for me. He was eager to share something new he had discovered. It was an Alan Watt YouTube video clip which reinforced what the film had said to me - that life is not about getting somewhere. It is about being in the present as we live it. Van Gogh painted ferociously for just eight years, but I know, as an artist myself, that he was in the moment. If he had a destination, it was to communicate what was in his heart. His paintings are now valued at something like $82 million dollars but that was not his goal, he was in the present, painting what was in his soul.

Alan Watt's (a writer-philosopher from the 1960'-70's) message is that somehow in our go-get-'em culture, many folks have the notion that we are on a journey, struggling to get to some final destination . Retirement? I once read that a huge percent of retired American males watch in excess of 40 hours per week of television! Watt explains that the universe, for example, is not going anywhere, it just is. He argues that our lives are not about getting somewhere, but about the actual act of living which he compares to a dance or a concert. We do not go to the concert to get to the end. If that were the case, we would buy our ticket and the orchestra would play the last booming chord and we would leave. The goal of the music is the music. He says a dance is about the dance, not about getting to the edge of the dance floor. He believes we are missing the point when we live every day like we are going somewhere. Where are we going? Are we aiming for the place called "success?" Where exactly is that? Maybe Watt is correct to see life as something musical, that we are supposed to sing or dance while the music is being played. Perhaps life itself is the music. Surely Vincent Van Gogh was at his best with the paint brush in hand painting for life. Certainly, we need a plan, goals, but it is important to cherish the experiences that come with reaching them; so that when one is completed, we are excited to start again with something new.

Gathering Up More Precious Moments

June 13, 2017

Greetings! Summer is nearly upon us. My Mission tour this morning of thirty fairly rowdy nine and ten-year-olds who will soon be free from the confines of school was a daunting challenge!! I really had to up my game to keep those wriggly students focused!

Last week during my granddaughter's eighth grade graduation from the small Christian school, where she has been enrolled since kindergarten, I observed something I want to share with you. It was one of those precious moments. The graduation was a formal affair with caps, gowns and valedictory speeches. Afterward, the school hosted a reception in the gymnasium. I approached my granddaughter and hugged my congratulations. She hung on as long as she could greeting all of us, but then the enormity of leaving all of her friends and moving on to a big public high school overtook her. She was overwhelmed with emotion, and burst into tears, nestling her face into the safety of her mother's waiting shoulder. I watched as her mother quietly engulfed the bereft child into a private sanctuary of long hair and kindness.

I saw. I reflected. It was just a moment in parenting of a thousand such moments across a child's growing up, but it said so much. It showed that my daughter-in-law has created a safe haven for her girl, that it is she who is dependable to draw closer when one's world has turned up-side-down. Certainly, not a moment of drum rolls and trumpets, but a silent illustration of just how instrumental moms, dads, grandparents, and siblings can be to a child's wellbeing. I knew I had witnessed something important.

I began collecting such moments a few years back after reading *Chasing Daylight* by Eugene O'Kelly. It is the story of his last six weeks of life. Too late, he discovered that his fast-paced international work life had precluded him from being present in his own life. With a catastrophic medical diagnosis he determined to make his last six weeks on earth the most compelling possible of all. He did that by, as he said, "collecting more precious moments than he had in the entire preceding fifty-two years!" Inspired by O'Kelly, I have been keenly aware of such special moments. One of my strongest life goals has been to see the world. I have dedicated myself to that end in recent years. Joyfully; I have now trekked the Himalayas, explored the temples of Ankor Wat, thrilled to the majestic sight of thousands of wildebeests, elephants, and rhinos in their migration across the great Serengeti Plain, jumped with the Masaii, all the while savoring the enormity of meeting new people and thrilling to other ways of living life. I am out-the-door this week to see where Nelson Mandela was held for 27 years fighting against Apartheid in South Africa, and to endeavor to understand that part of the world more fully. My eyes and heart will be open.

I am hoping that you will reflect on the special happenings that are occurring around you every day, and that you will take them in. I think precious moments help to make our lives richer and more full. I for one have a profound respect for the loving ways of my adult children who are parenting their many offspring. As always, I would love to hear about a precious moment you have encountered of late.

I'm Experiencing Deja Vu

April 13, 2017

You haven't been hearing much from me lately as I am practicing what I preach and seizing the day. My days have been jammed with fun new endeavors, but I have been thinking about you and hoping that your Happiness Tank is heading toward the "full" mark . Yesterday was especially noteworthy and I had to share with you.

So last Saturday, perhaps having lost my mind once again, I drove to pick up my new eight-week-old golden retriever puppy, our dog Lacey's sister, from my friend Linda. I've spent the last few days getting used to having baby gates all over the house and my new routine. It's been going well, however yesterday morning while she was napping, I grabbed my minutes off to use the garden blower on the garage. Clean garage, right? About fifteen minutes later she woke up and we went out on the lawn. It was all good, until she sauntered into the garage to have a look around and came out racing with something dangling out of her mouth! Oh no! I gave chase. I don't think you have seen a puppy race so fast in your life! All the while I was yelling, "No Dixie, No!" That just caused her to run faster!! Around the patio, the yard, and the garden we raced. Finally she backed herself against a tall planter and I managed to grab the still warm dead gopher out of her mouth with my bare hands! Yuck! Clearly my cats are very serious about clearing the yard of critters and their pride in their achievements has them delivering the bounty to my back door.

When I picked Dixie up from Linda, she shared her recent rapid-fire pursuit of one of the male puppies all over her yard, as he had somehow found a rat. Oh my! This is the side of raising a puppy that is often overlooked in the dazzling joy of their fluffy cuteness. Linda laughed as she shared that moment with me as she knew I had had a similar scene with Lacey four years ago, when Lacey found something awful the cats dragged in as well. Of course I had forgotten all about that! For sure I was now experiencing Déjà vu! I recalled that episode. Lacey had been older and even faster than Dixie! I was so thankful then and now that the World's Funniest Videos producers were not in my back yard watching these crazy chasing scenes!

As a diligent puppy mom, I am on guard against the dangers lurking around my big yard for a baby small enough to slip through the wrought iron fence, but I had completely forgotten about what joys Dixie would find in the cats' hunting activities!! Perhaps in the future I would do well the scan to the yard for any hidden cameras--- or dead gophers!

It is lively around here and a permanent smile is etched on my face as I watch the dogs in their wrestling matches, and running around the yard with Dixie's new toys.

If your Happiness Tank is not on "full," I think this could be a good time to entertain something new that has been swirling around in the back of your mind. Spring is good for planting flowers and vegetables, signing up for a new class, planning a trip, or perhaps taking on something new (ahh, I am not recommending a puppy unless you are feeling very energetic!). It's possible that you can imagine something altogether new to stimulate your mind. This is our precious time on the planet and it just seems urgent to me that each and every day offers us something soul enriching. I want that for you. This is YOUR time and there's not a minute to waste. Let's ensure that our Happiness Tanks are all the way to the top.

Oh, How Precious is our Time!

January 30, 2017

Two things happened today that got me thinking about the unknown limits of our time on Earth and how we carve out our place here. This morning my beautiful sister-in-law, Kassie, missed being killed as a giant Eucalyptus tree fell inches from her car at a stop sign near her home. Late I took myself to see a provocative film about a single mother struggling to raise her teenage son. The film, 20th Century Women, starring Annette Bening, depicts a significant conflict between the mother and the son. She yearns to "know" him, to grasp the inner workings of his heart, all the while remaining closed off to him. In a telling scene she complains to another woman, "I will never see him (the son) as he is in the world, as you do."

The film addresses the teen's heartfelt attempts to engage his emotionally sterile mother in meaningful dialogue. In one failed try he reads to her from Sisterhood is Powerful, a feminist anthology, a quote about older women becoming invisible. The mother reacts, "You think I'm invisible?" then stubbornly turns and walks out of the room.

I don't think we have time to waste. Kassie's near brush with catastrophe and the frustration of the characters in the film point out to me that our time on the planet is brief. It is precious. My husband often reminds me that "we are going to be gone from this world for a very long time." In Kassie's case I cannot think of anyone I know who is living her life more fully. In the conflict of the characters in the film (which the critics say is personal to the director) their unwillingness to be knowable to each other seems like a big waste.

For many of us time is quickly escaping, slipping through our fingers like warm sand. For twenty-two years my cars' license plates have boasted my glee in being a grandmother. But times have changed. The children are mostly grown up now, taller than I. The Mimi plates came off this month, as did the eleven plaster-of-Paris baby handprints from the walls. Our grands have grown. Time is accelerating by. I think it's essential that we make each day

count and find new ways in which to do so.

I've listened to women lamenting the fact that they no longer turn heads when they walk into a room, or about feeling invisible after a certain age. It seems to me that if we live a life of meaningful engagement with others, our lives will be fuller and we will remain visible. I still don't quite get why the mother in the film believed she'd never really see her son as he was, perhaps she suffered tunnel vision. I'm not sure. But I do know that when we interact with others in a meaningful way, magic can happen. When we ask others about their lives, and then actively listen, the most interesting phenomenon often occurs, we see them and they see us! It can become a rich reciprocal experience. People are honored when we show our interest in them and they often return the attention.

When I was a little girl, the book, How to Win Friends and Influence People, by Dale Carnegie came into my grandfather's pharmacy to be sold. One of my jobs was to put the incoming books and magazines in the racks. I read that book, and even though I was just a little girl, I began to understand that humans have a hunger to connect; that when others see and acknowledge us, we will open like flowers. Dale Carnegie told his readers to ask questions of others and then to really listen. It is the key to meaningful conversations, the antidote to shyness, a way to make friends, and a way out of loneliness. Today psychologists are teaching about emotional intelligence, pointing out the value of practicing empathy and drawing others out. One of the most powerful and priceless things we can share with those in our sphere is the gift of our attention; listening to them, giving our time. I think we humans hunger to be seen and acknowledged. Perhaps the riddle in the film about the mother being unable to "see" her son, is the fact that she was unwilling to be seen herself. Remember the old adage, "See and be seen?" If we are unknowable, then how can we know another? Time is too precious to waste like that.

Beauty in the Ordinary

January 6, 2015

Yesterday the man standing behind me in line at Costco was talking on his cell phone saying, "The holidays aren't what they're cracked up to be. They were okay, but I'm glad they're over." That got me to thinking how easily we can take for granted time spent with family and friends. I believe that what we pay attention to and how we pay that attention determine the content and quality of our lives.

A new year is upon us, and a new opportunity to refocus our thoughts. Perhaps we can train ourselves to find beauty in the most ordinary of everyday life. Lately I have had a heightened awareness of the mundane. Sunday, for example, my husband and I packed up the last of the holiday decorations. As we labeled the plastic bins and tucked them into the attic, I thought how profoundly confident I am that I will be around to open them next year. Even the simple packing up, a routine, ordinary detail in our busy lives, can be seen to hold layers of meaning. The ornaments themselves hold value for many are handmade treasures from decades ago when our children were little. Others are inherited antique glass bulbs. As I wrapped them, I could almost see my child self-standing next to my little sister lovingly decorating our aunt's tree. Ordinary, but yet layered with meaning.

Last week my Golden Retriever, Tessie had a sore foot. I had to leave her home while I took the other two walking along the beach trail. Many passers-by asked after my missing dog. I smiled and explained. A few days later, this time with my usual three, I encountered more walkers and bikers who noted that Tessie was back. As I passed one man on a bicycle he cheered, "Ah they're all here. Have a Golden day!" We both laughed at his little play on words, but it got me to thinking how easily we can take for granted the richness of our most ordinary everyday experiences. Clearly many of the same folks enjoy the routine of our exercise course. Sometimes we stop and chat, but mostly we are simply aware of one another, content to merely smile or say hello as we trek along next to the seashore. The walks are everyday ordinary but I see richness and meaning in them.

For the new year let's take notice of these commonplace moments and perhaps celebrate them and in so doing enrich our lives.

Life Should Not Be Lived, but Celebrated!

December 12, 2014

On Saturday I was honored to be among the five hundred or more celebrants at a friend's memorial. His time was cut short, but the many eulogies reflected the rich way in which he approached life, deeply touching all who knew him. By the end of the beautiful celebration, I could not help but smile and think, "A life well lived! Bravo!"

I continued to think about him and about the many indigenous people I encountered on my eleven-day adventure to Peru last month. I came away from both experiences with a new perspective and appreciation for what it is to be human. I am impressed that we humans, no matter how hard it is, just seem to continue to move forward. Our friend fought bravely, never losing his love of life, for a very long time against the cancer that gripped him.

High in the Andes, I was awed by the fact that people have so little but yet seem content and cheerful while they work very hard. At 14,000 feet native women sit hunched at their blankets of wares far into the freezing dark of early nightfall, hoping to earn a few dollars by selling their mittens and curios. In Machu Picchu, our guide, Sonia, endures a three-hour train ride from Cusco, a half hour bus ride through the jungle, to arrive at the park gates in hopes of a chance to guide someone. She earned $45 for taking us around for two hours, then she repeats her trip back home. Seven hours in transportation for a chance to earn $45. Yes, the Peruvian economy is different from ours, but still, a big effort for the rewards, and she is happy to do it!

Two thoughts keep running through my head, how brave humans can be in the face of adversity, and how important it is NOT to take for granted the plenty which we enjoy. I hope through the holiday shopping and wrapping that perhaps we can teach the children in our sphere to appreciate the fact of being alive in the world and to honor the riches we might almost take for granted as Americans. Perhaps we can reach out to others in need during this beautiful season as we consider the thought that Life should not be lived but celebrated!

Way Up the Hill!

July 2, 2014

As a collector of precious moments, I have to share with you the scene I observed from my living room last evening. Our youngest son and his family live across the street, but up a hill, above our home. Monday was trash pick-up day. I was cooking dinner, when suddenly, my husband, Ken, called to me, "Come quickly!"

I rushed to our living room window. What a sight! There was turning-eleven, granddaughter, Ashley, pulling the big recycle trash can up the incline, while her four-and-a-half-year-old sister was pushing it! They both seemed quite cheerful about this relatively big job. They were obviously completing their "chores" and it impresses me that my son and his wife are teaching responsibility to their girls. But what an exquisite image, seeing the big sister pulling, and the baby sister pushing, and with all her might. I will never forget the huge grin on my face every time my mind's eye recalls those two little girls and that very big trash can as they ever-so-slowly made their way up the grade!!

So far this summer I have collected so many of those special little sightings that I have been too busy to jot them down. Last Friday, for example, I was boogey boarding with my daughter and her son in the 70-degree California surf. What delightful fun to catch a wave and look over at your exuberant grandson who has caught the same wave!

Last weekend, Ken and I traveled to Yosemite with our family to renew our vows for our 50th wedding anniversary. It was lovely. Our eldest son was the officiate, and our daughter and daughter in-law saw to the details of flowers, table decorations, bird seed thrown at us as we walked back down the impromptu "aisle" consisting of our children and grandchildren, near a pond in the forest. That was an experience I shall cherish for many years to come.

Everywhere we have been recently, people ask, regarding our 50th, "So what is the secret?" We smile and say, "Have an attitude of gratitude." It sounds simplistic, because of course life is not easy. We all have bumps in the road, health issues and more, but, if we can celebrate the blessings that we do have, it helps us live more joyfully and gives us courage to face the hard stuff.

Planting Happiness

March 7, 2014

Yesterday, as I headed to meet up with my power walking pals, I noticed that my favorite Red Bud tree was showing its vibrant colors. Ah spring is in the air, I thought contentedly. As I drove along, my eyes fell upon the row of sunflowers that someone has whimsically planted in the vacant field by the elementary school. I smiled to myself as I admired their open faces. I could not get the "I-love-the-world" smile off my face!

Soon my friends and I were consumed with our fast-paced strides and catching-up chat. We proceeded along for a few miles when suddenly, our friend, Diane, exclaimed, "Donna you are always on the look-out for precious moments. Here's one for you. Look. There!" she said pointing toward the neglected, wild open space by the trail. With that I looked more carefully to discover the source of her intrigue. There it was, something magical and serendipitous: about a dozen brightly colored bird houses and feeders planted all around, like a garden, in a forgotten patch by the pathway.

All evening, I could not stop thinking about it. I told Ken and he shared that as he was driving to work he looked over and a young mother with a car full of kids, was singing her heart out as she waited at the signal. Happiness was abounding, it seemed contagious. We laughed about it.

Today I went back to that bird house garden to take some photos. I examined the blue one labeled, "The Swallows Inn," the bright yellow one said, "by Cash Vargas age 7," another had a crazy skull and crossbones on it, while another was adorned with pink hearts. The garden was alive with color and whimsy. I was in heaven delighting in each little work-of-art house.

A lady with two small poodles was crossing the street as I went back to the car. I asked her about the bird houses. "Oh, the neighbor down the street, the pastor, thought it was such a shame that in a beautiful town we have such neglected areas. A few years ago he began with the stone wall, then he added some bird houses, then the rock pond. People have added the plantings, more bird houses and feeders. It is growing. You should talk to him," she concluded, smiling at me.

"So it has a spiritual element with the pastor and all?" I asked.

"Of course," she responded knowingly.

"Well it certainly called to me. I am very excited about it. I think it is a celebration of life. Thank you." And I hopped back into my car, loaded with my three huge Golden Retrievers.

So, I am inspired! I am going to plant myself a bird house garden and I know just where to begin, the grand kids have gifted me some of their crafty houses, perhaps I can show them off! Maybe I could embellish the garden with some wind chimes. . . What fun. With the California drought upon us it is a perfect time to take out some of the water hungry plants and try something new. The more I think about this, the more excited I am becoming. But there is something else here, the lesson could be about imagination and taking action. The man behind this has started something precious. His random act may not be for any huge, important reason other than to bring joy. My guess is that he is happy for no reason, and cherishes the thrill of being alive in the world. I hope you are singing your heart out in the car and finding precious moments in the strangest places. I would love to hear about it.

Six Degrees of Separation

November 13, 2013

It takes my breath away to remember how scary the music was leading into the drama on the old-time radio show The Whistler. Excitement oozed out of our Philco radio as my little sister and I sat spellbound waiting to hear what would happen next. Being a kid in the era before television offered thrills of the imagination. Those old shows, such as The Shadow, tantalized us with their scary, creaking, suspense!

Simultaneously, many of us were also the lucky recipients of the oral tradition of storytelling. My sister and I would wile away long hours at our grandparents' knees, captivated by their adventures. Our grandfather owned a pharmacy in the horse and buggy days of Los Angeles, and we would delight in hearing how he foiled a robber by pretending that the over-sized candy bar in his coat pocket was a gun. We were often told about his amazing teacher Miss Mary Foy, an early suffragette who helped to bring the vote to women in Los Angeles in 1911, that was almost ten years before the rest of the country. Our grandmother (who was 20 years junior to our grandfather) would intrigue us with stories of how she would ride the Red Car to the amusement pier at the end of Venice Boulevard where she would romp in the fun houses and whirligigs. Another of her favorite topics was about the best teacher she ever had; also Los Angeles High School's Miss Mary Foy. We learned that as a young woman, Mary was the first female librarian for the big public library on Temple Street. As frequent visitors to that library, my sister and I could hardly believe that when it opened in the latter part of the 1800's women were not allowed to use it!

Those enchanting memories of old Los Angeles came rushing back as I opened my invitation to the annual luncheon of the First Century Families of Los Angeles and Mary Foy's photo adorned the front of it! The luncheon last week was in her honor. I was delighted! It is one thing growing up hearing old stories, and quite another to hold a photo of one of the main characters in your hand. The First Century Families consists of the descendants of the founding families in Los Angeles who lived there between 1781 and 1881. As I scanned the program I saw that

Alice O'Neill Avery, her son, Tony Moiso, and granddaughter Trina Moiso were speakers. I closed my eyes and marveled that the generations from so long ago were able to come together each year and that the ties were so much deeper than a mere luncheon. I am fascinated that so many early Los Angeles families have developed interconnecting roots in Orange County. My husband Ken, for example, who worked with community members to build the Capistrano Valley Boys and Girls Club credits Tony Moiso and his family with substantive financial support and leadership in allowing the club to be born. I knew that my son Dan worked with members of the O'Neill family as well, in his construction business.

On luncheon day, as the attendees gathered in the reception area of the California Club in downtown Los Angeles, I made small talk with a woman and shared my relationship to Mary Foy. The lady responded, "I wore her graduation dress from Los Angeles High School at my own graduation from there!" I smiled as I thought about my grandfather's 1904 "Los Angeles City School" diploma hanging on my wall, of my own mother's graduation from Los Angeles High School. I thought of her classmate Mike Marienthal who was my husband's high school boys' vice principal and personal hero.

As the program got underway, I was captivated by the history being shared; especially the daily shootings, in what was a wild outpost of civilization in those early days. I recalled that my grandmother's grandmother, Mary Berry Mathews, climbed off the Southern Pacific Rail car the day she arrived in downtown from Virginia, only to witness a gun fight and deadly shooting at her very feet. Her many children crowded behind her skirts. We learned that 5% of the population was killed in one year due to lawlessness and shootings! The program was a history buff's banquet. As the facts unfurled, I was flabbergasted to learn that Mary Foy had founded this organization. No wonder my grandmother attended so many luncheons. I also learned that Alice O'Neill Avery was the last living member of the first gathering of these descendants.

As I drove home and passed Avery Parkway in south Orange County, and the communities of Ladera Ranch and Mission Viejo, I thought of how they were all part of properties owned by the O'Neills and other early families, and that all of the vastness of beautiful Southern California was once part of Spanish land grants. I thought of our good friend Tony Forster and the fact that his great grandfather had once owned Mission San Juan Capistrano, the icon of our city. I am fascinated by the degree of closeness we share. My grandchildren attend Marco Forster Middle School, Tony barbecued at my daughter's wedding. My sons are in Indian Princesses with an Irvine family grandson. My grandchildren are friends with his children. History and our links to others fascinate me. I relish the fact that as a country we are still so relatively young compared to other parts of the world that we can name our touch points. I cherish the fact that we are so marvelously interconnected, held together by mere degrees of separation. I leaned back into the headrest of my seat as I thought that perhaps history could be more compelling than even the most powerful episode of The Whistler. I could only imagine what more I could discover with an opportunity to exchange more family stories. There is always next year!

A Sense of Community

October 28, 2013

Delighted to be included in "family weekend" we joined our daughter's family to visit our first grandson, newly settled in his new university life. Husband Ken and I turned the occasion into a bit of a holiday. On the way north from Orange County, California, we stopped at our old favorite, Carpinteria State Beach, where we happily walked along the wet seashore in our bare feet. There were children playing and people surf fishing; the park seemed full of campers and RVers. This was odd as it was a non-holiday Friday in October, just after lunch.

"Ken, look at all those people. How can there be so many families here during school hours?"

Ken just shook his head. He had no idea either. After a bit we came upon a fisherman and I queried, "Hi! Why is the park so full? What is going on?"

Smiling at me as he cast his line, he explained, "Why, it is Halloween Haunt in the park!"

With that explanation Ken and I continued our walk along the seashell strewn sand delighting in the afternoon sunshine of the beautiful Fall day. On the way back we decided to walk through the park, past all the campsites. We were surprised to see the big RVs decked out in colorful pumpkin lanterns, tents sporting scary witches, and truck campers with goblins and spider webbing. My imagination could visualize it after dark. The weekend vacationers were turning the park into their own Haunt! No wonder it was quickly filling up with families. Who would want to miss this?

This was amazing to me because throughout all my years as a youth in this very park, we kids made our own amusements with "kick the can" or hide and seek. Nothing was organized.

At that point we approached a truck with a camper on it. Ken pointed out a huge Golden Retriever jumping into the back before I could get a good look at him. Oh darn it! I missed him.

"Donna, why don't you ask the owners if you can meet him?"

That was all the coaxing I needed. Walking toward them I asked, "Oh I saw your beautiful dog. Could I meet him?"

"Well, he will bark at you!" Replied the grinning man.

"I can take barking, as long as he doesn't bite me. Will he bite?"

Chucking, "Oh no. He is just full of a lot of noise."

With that a beautiful 100 plus pound male dog bounded to the camper door, and sure enough, he was barking. He jumped down, followed by a friendly lady. As I admired him, he sniffed my hand and allowed me to rub his downy fur.

"His name is Bodie and he's five." They said.

"Bodie. I had a Golden named Bodie." I offered. "I had her for fifteen years and believe it or not, she too greeted people with a lot of noise. Hers was a big 'woo woo' greeting! This is such fun!"

We chatted another minute while Ken waited for me on a nearby bench. As I left, the lady looked at me and smiled. "We will be here all weekend. "Come back."

"Oh, thank you. We are just passing through. Off to see our grandson at college!"

I saw a flash of disappointment cross her face. She no doubt thought I was a fellow camper.

Rejoining Ken, I shared about the big yellow dog, Bodie and his barking greeting. We continued our stroll reminiscing about our own Bodie of years ago and how she would let the grandkids hold on to her tail as she pulled them around the pool.

As we walked past the various camp sites, we were met with friendly hellos and smiles. I could feel a powerful sense of community among the campers. I reflected on the idea of community, from "communare" meaning coming together. I often hear people complain that they feel isolated, they don't even know their neighbors, yet here at the water's edge, I was amazed to see how artfully these folks were making a beautiful celebration out of a something as simple as a campground and Halloween. They were all in, maybe that's what it takes to create such a culture, the desire to participate. I felt proud of my fellow humans!

As we cleaned the sand off our feet, Ken commented, "Donna, I think we have collected another of those Precious Moments you are always talking about!"

"Why, I think you are right." The friendliness of the dog owners, the decorations and excitement in the campground and the beauty of what it is to be human. I grinned as we got into the car to continue our adventure. Yes, we had collected another precious moment.

Look, a unicorn!

May 23, 2013

Yesterday my three grand girls who live across the street came swimming at our pool. Ashley, age 9, shared with me her Sunday afternoon petting zoo adventure with her daddy. It seems that upon their arrival, my son Dan, their dad, spotted a goat with a single horn. In a delighted tone he called his girls' attention to it saying, "Girls look, a unicorn!"

"No Daddy," corrected Ashley in gleeful tones, "A unihorn!"

I am sure that they all laughed at Ashley's clever turn of phrase, I know that I have been mentally replaying her line and each time a smile and chuckle bubbles up inside me. "No Daddy a unihorn!" Ha Ha.

Earlier in the day yesterday I presented a training session for the staff of a county agency devoted to preventing child abuse in the community, a difficult and stressful job. The training was aimed at helping the participants to decompress after stressful cases. Toward the end of the workshop each member was asked to share his or her most effective stress reduction strategy. They had good ones: exercise, yoga, meditation, prayer, working with the preschoolers at church, listening to music, zumba dancing, blogging, playing with their grandchildren, or visiting with nieces and nephews. All of these were effective coping methods, but I noticed how many were in touch with the power of children. I recalled the statistic that children laugh about 425 times a day compared to 10-15 times a day for adults. Clearly as we take on the burdens of adult life we lose something. Perhaps silence grows within the humorous jokester inside of us.

As Ashley related her "unihorn" story to me she was strapping on her new lavender swim fins and matching mask and snorkel. Soon she slipped into the pool and began cruising the length of it, back and forth, no doubt imagining some treasure lurking at the bottom. As she swam away, I remained in the spa with her 3-year-old sister, Caroline, who now had me to herself.

"Mimi, will you play with me?"

"Sure, Caroline. What should I do?"

"Well I am going to be the evil queen Maleficent from Sleeping Beauty and I am going to......." And with that she outlined a very elaborate plan which somehow paralled the Sleeping Beauty story. "So Mimi, when I say all that, you say, 'Okay', alright?"

With that, Caroline donned her mask and repeated the rather complicated story line. I was getting the idea that somehow we were actors in a play. When her words came to an ending, I dutifully repeated, "Okay", as I had been directed. A huge smile beamed across her face and she dived into the water. Clearly I had said my line correctly! I was very pleased with myself.

As she merrily swam away I grinned. At that precise moment, 12-year-old Elizabeth did a running double flip off the diving board, sending a wave of splashing water cascading across the pool deck, much to the delight of 12 week-old Lacey the Puppy who had been standing nearby taking in all the excitement that shadows these three exciting girls.

Neuroscientists know that the mirroring neurons in our brains act like wi-fi, picking up signals from those around us; that depression and joy are in some ways "contagious." Science also knows that the mere act of creating a smile lets us feel happier. There is evidence that 40 smiles a day can actually allow endorphins to dump into our blood stream, that it is possible to "trick" our brain into thinking we are happy even with a fake set of smiles, and then we actually feel better! Why wouldn't we want to feel happier? Perhaps we should give ourselves permission to fall into the magical world of the children around us? If we would just stop for a while and really enter into their imaginative and creative worlds, I think we would laugh and smile a whole lot more. So have you orbited with the kids lately? I would love to hear about it.

Start Horn Blasts in the Early Morning Dark!

May 9, 2013

Hi there, Happy Mother's Day. You might recall that I have been adventuring in Croatia and some of the Balkan Republics. I have found myself hitting the ground running, literally! I arrived home a little over a week ago and collected my new puppy the next day. At the same time my son, Rick, invited me to participate in the Orange County Marathon last Sunday. Since my granddaughter Jill was going to run it, her first such event, I jumped at the chance to spend time with them.

Sunday morning in the dark, we three adventurers met up at 4:30 a.m. with our running shoes securely fastened to our feet for no reason other than a chance to challenge ourselves. We arrived at the start line along with some 12,000 other like-minded enthusiasts. The air was charged with excited energy. Jill and I saw Rick off for his full marathon at 5:45 and before long the starting horn sounded for our half marathon. We were off! Jill and I smiled our best wishes and headed south toward Corona Del Mar. She soon pulled ahead, intent on running, while I stayed focused on my passion for power walking. As I found my stride, I could feel the smile covering my face. As the thousands of us wound through the early morning streets, the residents cheered us on. My grin grew wider. Dawn was breaking and the Pacific Ocean glimmered in the background. What a great delight!

As the mile markers clicked by, I was alone in my thoughts. I took in the sayings on each. One of them said, "I celebrate our armed forces who give me the freedom to run." I thought about that and the fact that my nephew had just made the rank of sergeant in the Army. A wave of pride washed over me and a pang of gratefulness as I thought of all our young men and women risking their lives so we can be free. I lingered in the idea of what a privilege it is to be able to run. Another mile marker proclaimed, "I run for those who cannot." I thought of my friend who passed away six weeks ago. I imagined how much she would have loved to be out here celebrating the sheer pleasure of life.

A young woman speeded ahead of me and the back of her shirt said, "I am a survivor" and I flashed to the devastation that was my childhood and mentally paused to think about what it had taken to wade out of the murkiness of my father's pathology. For a long minute, with a few tears on my cheeks, I allowed myself to reflect on the little Donna inside of me who never gave up. Her deepest desire was to get free of her father and to live a normal life. I let myself feel a pang of respect for that brave little girl. I continued onward contemplating my thoughts. Soon another mile marker, "I run because I can!" By this time I had come upon some age-mates, grey hair, more my speed than the youths who literally raced past me. I raced up to one handsome couple, "Hey, there you are, my age-mates!" They laughed and greeted me back. "We race for longevity don't we?" I heartily agreed. "Motion is lotion!" I replied as I slipped ahead of them. They smiled.

Later at mile marker 13 they came upon me, "Hey your age-mates are here!" We all laughed again, and because I was in no real hurry I let them get ahead of me, after all, I was just there to have fun. That smile was still plastered on my face. I powered into the finish line with 600 people behind me having thoroughly enjoyed it. I was presented with my medal and met up with my family. Later, my husband, Ken, went online and discovered that I was one minute and thirteen seconds from taking 3rd place in my age category. So now I am thinking perhaps I could have steamed ahead. I actually had no idea that I was anything like competitive in my age group, I was just trying not to come in last! Now there is a new idea in my head. Hummmm......... Competitive power walker! That sounds like even more fun. June 2nd we are all signed up for the San Diego Rock n Roll Marathon....

I just love the fact that there is so much opportunity out there in life if you just imagine it. An 80-year-old man won the half marathon in his age group by doing it in 2 hours and 8 minutes!!! . I admire the 67 participants in the events of Sunday who are age 70 and over. It goes to show that it is not over until it is over. One single idea can set off a life-changing chain of events. Here I wanted to spend time with Rick and Jill and now I am imagining being competitive in San Diego. What a crazy and exciting idea! What crazy new adventure have you been thinking of? I would love to hear about it. I have my shoes on; I am out the door to train for San Diego!

On Puppy Love

January 22, 2013

Sometimes they come out of nowhere, those amazing little episodes. It happened again today on my morning dog walk. My two golden retrievers were leashed up as we ambled down the lane by our home, when suddenly out of nowhere a fluffy long haired black and white dog raced up to us. Zoe, my older dog, was on instant alert. However, as the furry ball rubbed against us, clearly oblivious to any canine confrontation, she must have realized that the wagging little thing was just a puppy. I tied up my dogs and bent down to properly meet him. He jumped into my arms, all wriggling energy and softness. He nuzzled me. Time stopped as I was enveloped in his sweetness. I buried my face in his long silky coat. After a while his owner came to collect him. It was not easy as he and I were locked into a puppy love. Stalling for more time with him, I asked his name, his breed, his age - and if I could have him. Of course, I knew I was kidding (NOT!) His firm little body felt so yummy leaning into me. Finally, I had to surrender him and continue on my walk.

I could not wipe the grin off my face. I realized that it had happened again!! Many of you know that I work with women in transition and those suffering grief through loss. You might know I facilitate a Loss of a Loved One support group through the City of San Juan Capistrano. In that work, I help others to steady themselves and come to terms with their loss or new status in life. I teach that happiness is living through one's purpose and collecting "precious moments." I understood that I had just gleaned another one. What could be more precious than a 6-month-old puppy racing to greet you and sharing his enthusiastic little self with you? All it takes to gather these moments is to notice them.

Last week driving to a meeting in Costa Mesa, I culled another as I drove north on the 405 Freeway. The sun was setting, it was dusk when I looked ahead and in the distance saw two huge birds flying low over the freeway. I thought, "Are they pelicans, sea gulls? They are too big...huge wingspan." As I drew closer I could see that it was a pair of huge Snowy Egrets heading toward the ocean. I laughed out loud! I thought, "Where but in Southern California in the middle of a cold winter, could you see giant waterbirds flying over the freeway?" In utter delight, I laughed again. How lucky we are to be alive. Part of the joy is being present enough to round up these precious moments.

Ah, Sweet Serendipity!

January 13, 2019

The recent storms have wreaked havoc on my favorite dog walking spot just south of Doheny Beach. Waves hitting the parking lot have been devastating; as a result that area has been shut down. This has forced me out of my comfort zone. I have been hunting for new walking spots near the edge of the water (within the confines of the dog law) for a few weeks now. The other day I hit the jackpot! My new adventure spot confirms that: "LIFE STARTS OUTSIDE YOUR COMFORT ZONE"

Recently the dogs and I visited Salt Creek County Beach situated next to the Ritz Carlton Hotel. We walked down the steep hill and headed north on the trail. After a few miles we turned back south. Hugging the cliffs and walking near the waterline, we encountered a serendipitous spectacle I had not seen for nearly 60 years from back when my husband and I used to pay a dollar to drive on this very beach. The waves were humongous!

A group of elite surfers, clearly having heard that some of the biggest waves of the year would be brewing at Salt Creek came en masse with their boards. Dozens of wet-suit clad surfers were straddling their boards, lined up in the water waiting in the waves for the next 6–8-footer. To my delight, there was an occasional gigantic ten foot wave which climbed up above the smaller ones. The huge surf alone was a show, but that was not all. I was privileged to witness the best of the best surfers traversing the waves, often in the barrel for great distances. I observed them swooping up and completing "air-revs" (360's) on the lip of the waves, and then gracefully returning to ride the face to the shore. I was awestruck!

I took a seat on a nearby bench, securing the dogs in the shade of the picnic table, and sat spellbound for the next two hours. About ten professional photographers with their 18-inch-long lenses began to take spots nearby to film the show! It was high tide. Before long, a wave cracked close enough to us spectators that one photographer yelled as his equipment was sprayed by the salty water. The gaggle of photographers moved back. I stayed fixed on the bench.

As the athletes staged more and bigger tricks, those of us on the sidelines couldn't help but shout out our delight at the spectacle. There was a lot of cheering as the show was so out-of-this world. Also, the water-soaked photographer was really complaining loudly about his $5000 lens being wet and adding to the volume.

It was one of the most incredible days I have enjoyed on my beach dog walks. What is interesting to me is that the surfers were not the only aspect of the adventure that day; the spectators were also noteworthy.

With my fluffy and friendly Golden Retrievers at my feet, I guess I was approachable. Anyway, one man with a giant camera lens to his eye, sat down next to me. Before too long he introduced himself. He taught me something of surfing photography, and I discovered that he is a famous photographer with thousands of followers! A bit later a tattooed young man came up to meet my dogs. We visited comfortably, as he shared more about what I was witnessing in the waves.

I learned that he is Ryan Rustan and he and his dog Sugar are National Big Dog Surfing Champions. He opened the photos on his phone and introduced me to Sugar. He sent me a few still photos of her.

Eventually I tore myself away from the surf show and headed up the hill to the car. As I drove home, I could not believe the remarkably good time I had had, and was unable to wipe the grin off my face. It was a golden day that might stand out in any year. It wasn't just the surfers; it was also about the friendliness of those random strangers. I had put myself in the path of opportunity by sitting down on the bench. I had also wandered outside of my usual comfort zone.When I got home I Googled Sugar the Surfing Champ and was delighted by the many national news videos in which Ryan and Sugar starred. I'm still smiling about that day. Maybe this is something for all of us to think about for this new year of 2019, maybe it's time we wandered outside of our comfort zones and put ourselves in the path of new opportunities. This is our precious time on the planet and it just seems like we should make the most of it.

Grab the Brass Ring!

Apr il 17, 2015

Have you grabbed hold of the brass ring lately? If you are old enough you recall that back in the day the merry-go-round offered a tray full of rings for the merrymakers to grasp as they twirled by. The luckiest of the lucky caught the brass one which was worth a free ride! Heady rewards indeed!! Do you still feel that way? Last night I was presenting to the teens at the Boys and Girls Club about what it takes to live a winning hand. We contrasted that with non-winners and losers. The teens immediately recognized that winners try new things, risk, follow through on what they say they are going to do, and exude a sense of zest for life as they delight in their own victories and those of others.

It seemed like big ideas for young people who were attending the 6 pm program after an already long day at school, but young as they are they get it. Earlier in the afternoon I was a panelist on a Sexual Assault Awareness panel at Cypress College. It was particularly poignant for me as the very fact of the program was a dream of mine to come true...to get sexual misconduct out in the open. The campus worked hard to that end including flash mobs and meetings to help students protect themselves. As an advocate for women and children, my dreams are coming true. What are some of your dreams? Maybe it is time to accelerate forward.

For spring break last week my husband and I took four of our granddaughters to Hawaii. I had a stunning experience last Friday. My eyes filled with tears as the baby dolphin swam over to me, squirted water at me, and then came into my open arms for an embrace! I was awestruck by the encounter. The world is a big place with opportunity for all of us to squeeze the most joy out of it possible, to grab the brass ring. I think we can be happy for no reason and cherish our time of being alive in the world. If you've had a brass ring moment lately, I'd love to hear it!

Section IV

Adapting to Change: The Art of Reinventing Ourselves

"The only constant in life is change."

~Heraclitus , Greek Philosopher 6th century BCE.

Treasure?

May 2, 2022

I don't know about you, but I have a habit of "saving" bits and pieces of memories. This morning I got in the mood to clear what I refer to as "my debris field"; the growing stack of thank you cards, invitations and clippings evolving near the phone in the corner of the kitchen desk. I dug into my task, out! Out! out! The thrill of tossing things carried over to my dressing room catchall travel drawer. I got so into my task that I dragged the big kitchen trash can into the room to have at it; sorting through the saved "treasures;" complimentary airline eye masks, combs, tiny packets of extra buttons, cards, receipts, and foreign coins. As I got closer to the bottom of the drawer, I came upon a small stack of blank hotel stationery from my travels. I scolded myself, "Come on Donna, you've got to stop saving these sorts of things. People no longer even write letters." I heard that critical voice in my head.

I stopped what I was doing and stared out the window. Possibly a bit lost in thought, I wandered around the house with the small bundle until I found my husband. "Ken, Ugh! I have been saving blank hotel stationery. How silly I am."

"I'm not so sure it's so weird. " He said, smiling as he drew me into a hug. "You are my revered, possibly strange wife."

We both laughed. I tried going back to my sorting but the past pulled me into it. When I was a little girl my grandparents, who lived across the street from Farmer's Market in Hollywood, were my frequent babysitters. Both my grandfather, Big Ray, and my grandmother, Maymie, had a profound influence on the woman I would someday grow up to be.

In 1929 as a young mother, my grandmother traveled, by herself, around the world, on a six month tour. Her habit was to take a sheet or two of the hotel stationery from every exotic hotel in which she stayed. Across her life, she doled those pieces out in long and friendly letters. She treasured those pieces of paper and taught me to do so.

My grandmother modeled so much for me. When I was 18 years-old she took me as her companion on a six week cruise of the South Pacific on the Matson Line ship, the Mariposa. It was time-dividing for me as it was six weeks of being treated as a real adult. She modeled high values, the importance of independence, and taught me about investments. In 1963, before I married, she drove me around the Venice, California peninsula (now Marina Peninsula) and showed me lots for sale filled with oil wells. She explained that I could purchase such a lot, a block from the beach, for $10,000 and that she would help me. I decided not to do that, but the fact that she took me real estate looking at age 20 was an important lesson.

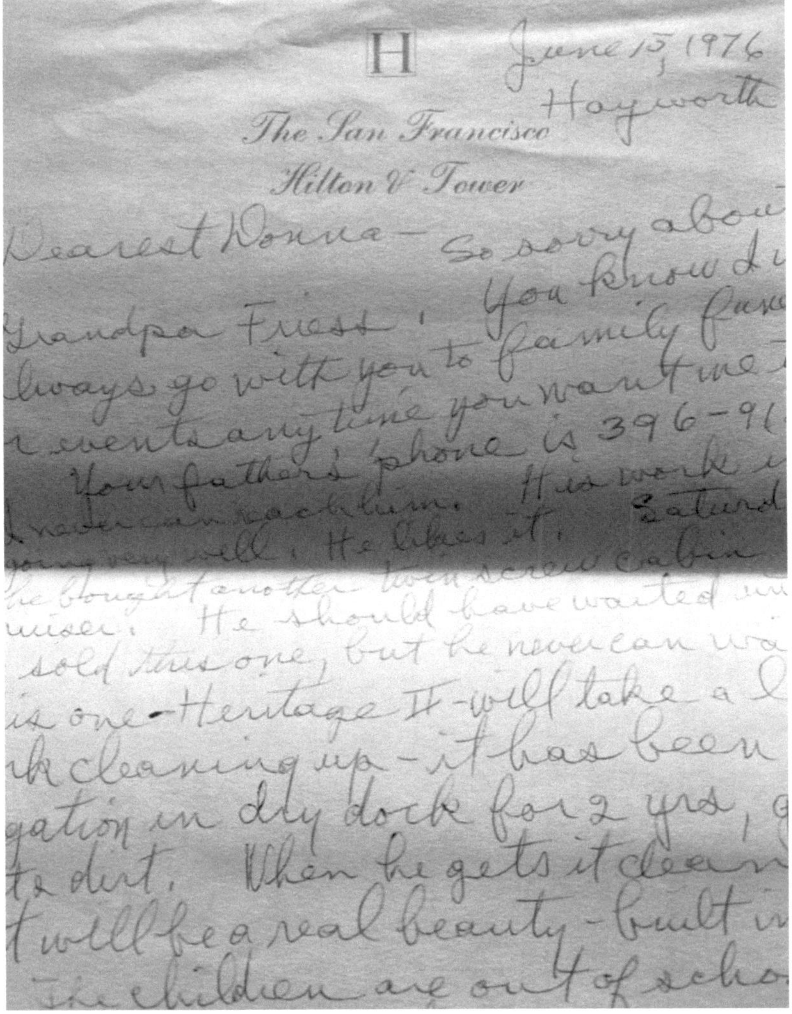
H
June 15, 1976
Hayworth
The San Francisco
Hilton & Tower
Dearest Donna— So sorry abou
Grandpa Friest! You know
lways go with you to family
events any time you want me
Your father's phone is 396-9
Your father's phone is 396-91
His work
Satur
very well. He likes it.
bought another twin screw cabin
He should have waited
sold this one, but he never can wa
one - Heritage II - will take a
cleaning up - it has been
gation in dry dock for 2 yrs,
dirt. When he gets it clean
t will be a real beauty - built in
The children are out of scho

She taught the value of world travel and having a heart for other cultures and people. It was she to whom I ran as a ten-year-old in the Woolworth's ten cent store in Little Rock, Arkansas. I was eager to show her that I had found a drinking fountain that served mineral water, surely that's what "Colored Water" must have meant?

She taught me to have compassion, to treasure the past, and to have an appreciation for the family collection of hand painted porcelain. Only recently did I realize that my living room looks an awfully lot like the living room in her house during my growing up years, complete with her small Chinese nut bowl on the coffee table. Certainly, without her guidance during my impressionable years, being a port of calm in my chaotic childhood, I would not have come to be who I am, to appreciate the past, or to love history, or art. In rethinking about my stash of blank hotel stationery from the 2017 Japan trip, staying at the Keio Plaza Hotel, Tokyo, I am realizing it is emblematic of my grandmother's great influence.

Maybe I need to relax a little. If saving some sheets of stationery for letters I will never write is some small act which connects me to my heritage, maybe it's something for me to celebrate rather than to criticize. Surely Maymie helped to mold the anxious girl I once was into the woman I became. Perhaps those little blank pages are in many ways a bit of buried treasure. I shared this with my youngest sister, Diana, who came along 27 years after me. [I have 4 sisters and 3 brothers]. Diana says she too has the same stationery habit! We both laughed and understood that this is one more lovely connection that further binds us to our past. So "treasure?" I think so.

What quirky little habits do you have which draw you closer to some moments in your past?

1961 Maymie and Donna aboard The Mariposa

Savoring Watershed Moments

July 18, 2022

Hello, it seems I have been missing in action these past months since I last reached out to you. I have had a lot going on, including a ten-day escorted tour of Canada's Maritime provinces for which I hosted my daughter Julina and her only daughter Jaycelin. We had planned the trip many months prior and were excited about spending time exploring a part of the world together where we had never before ventured.

I've been back a week or so returning with Covid and am finally over my covid isolation. Our claims are in to the airline for the three cancelled flights, the lost luggage and the nights spent in the airport. So, finally I can mentally focus on the experience of the adventure itself with two of my loved ones. We learned so much; about the Acadians, the French Canadians who settled in Eastern Canada and suffered consequences in the 18th century due to their Catholicism; the story of the 80,000-100,000 Loyalists to King George III who fled to safety in Eastern Canada during the American Revolution; the intricacies of the oyster farming industry; the immensity of the 110 million pound haul of lobsters harvested annually out the deep Canadian waters; and so much more. All of what we learned was fascinating including meeting the generous, friendly Canadians themselves. However, it pales when put up against the experience of time spent as roommates with my daughter and granddaughter.

As I continue to mull this over, the mental picture projects of Jaycelin jumping up on my queen-sized bed and tucking herself under my left arm as I sipped my morning coffee in Nova Scotia. The image fills my heart with joy. She snuggled in just as she did twenty years ago as a five-year old girl. Another mental vision that makes me grin is being on the top deck of the ferry as it crossed from Prince Edward Island to Nova Scotia, and looking down through the pouring rain to a lower deck where my daughter and granddaughter were delighting in the raw weather. I called to them for a photo and they smiled up at me and spontaneously slipped into dancing an energetic jig right there on the deck of the huge ship! It is all the sweeter for my awareness that Jaycelin's life in the future will probably not allow the luxury of so many days traveling with her grandmother.

Exploring these magical trip experiences has provided a channel down which I can see other such long ago precious watershed moments in life. I can look back through a nearly sixty-year lens to the last day of my undergraduate education. I was the last roommate to vacate the Lavender Room in the Alpha Gamma Delta house on 28th Street in Los Angeles. It was 1964 and I can vividly see my younger self sitting on my roommate's stripped down bed, staring out the front window as other students on the Row moved packed boxes back and forth to their cars. I was then keenly aware that my life was about to change drastically, for I would be married the following Saturday. I knew then that I was having a watershed moment; I contemplated what living in the sorority house had meant to me for those two years, and how my life would be very different as I moved into my future. I was right. I did move into my future but not before I took it all in, savoring it.

I shared the idea about these watershed experiences with my husband, Ken, and he too pulled up some exquisite time dividing moments he has savored with his girls' wrestling team, a journey he began 15 years ago when many of his peers headed for retirement. Perhaps as we move further and further through life, these mindful pauses where we take it all in become more and more valuable.

The agony of our lost luggage and cancelled flights is fading and I am left with some treasures of memory that I will enjoy far into the future. Another such experience was with our tour of the Alexander Graham Bell Museum in Nova Scotia. Bell, the inventor, was fascinated by flight, inventing flying machines, based upon his study of kites. The museum offers up kites for the patrons. Julina, Jaycelin and I spent a delightful few hours laughing, running, and flying those kites, catching the strong wind off the world's largest salt water lake, and being somewhat shocked that we had mad kite flying skills!

Travel has many advantages, in that it can allow us to be in the path of opportunities that might not exist in our daily lives. Our trip offered such experiences. I would not ordinarily spend an afternoon successfully flying a kite.

So my take-away from this trip is not just the time spent with my daughter and granddaughter but the value of being mindful of these precious opportunities when they present themselves. They are rare and worth everything. What watershed, time diving moments, have you enjoyed which you can take out and think about in your own life?

Change is Inevitable

October 27, 2022

I recently heard this stunning quote by the Buddha: *The biggest mistake in life we can make is to think we have time.* Time is free but it's priceless, you cannot own it, but you can use it; you can't keep it but you can spend it. Once it's lost you can never get it back.

Monday morning, fortified with Buddha's reminder of how truly precious each day is, I knew that I had to pull myself together after the passing of my beloved golden retriever, Lacey, over the weekend. A life change was being forced upon me. I braced myself. After some 3000 morning walks with my beautiful Lacey, and her kennel mates, today was going to be difficult; the first day in many years when my morning walk did not include at least three dogs wagging their way down the trail. Awhile back I had come to the decision that in the future I needed to simplify, by limiting myself to just two dogs. Sadly, I found myself at that juncture far sooner than I had expected.

I tied my shoes on, ushered River and Dixie into the car, and prepared for the first day with just two pups. I grimly thought of a new beginning. I headed to the ocean determined that today was to be a celebration of all Lacey had meant to us, and that I did not want to lose another day to being so sad.

My grief work has taught me some

fundamentals of moving forward in the face of loss. I knew that I had to try to feel better, that allowing what seemed like a concrete brick in my stomach to remain was not the best. I knew I had to reframe the loss and take physical action. It seemed that it was time to practice what I knew.

I decided to change things up. I drove much farther than usual, to a beach trail along the coast of San Clemente starting at the pier. The dogs had never been there before. I parked, leashed them up, and we were off.

Goodness! The moment they were out of the car they became ecstatic over all that was new. There was much excited sniffing as we headed down the hill from the parking lot. I held on, as it felt like I had hold of a team of racing dogs. They were in overdrive, eager to get to the next new scent. Along we strode, faster than ever, then suddenly they'd stop to examine a particular bush, then off again. Their high enthusiasm took me out of myself, plus it was all I could do just to hang onto them!

Choosing a new environment was stimulating for me too. The waves were huge and the wet-suited surfers were out in force, some flying down the front of the waves, while others popped above the breakers. There was something of a carnival atmosphere as there were so many people about; spectators, walkers and joggers. We power-walked along the sandy path next to the breaking surf. After some time, I felt my heart growing lighter.

After a couple of miles at this energetic pace, we stopped under a shaded picnic arbor and watched the surfers. River and Dixie were tired by then and happy to sit quietly. It gave me a chance to think about Lacey, of all the fantastic adventures we had had across her almost ten years. I smiled remembering when she was a puppy and I chased her all over the yard trying to get a dead rat out of her mouth! I pictured her patience with our cat, Beauty, who enjoyed lying on Lacey's head. I recalled how precious it was that she always wanted to carry her leash in her mouth on the way home from our outings. I thought what a truly good girl she had always been, and how much I loved her.

Before long two college girls came by to pet Dixie and River. The dogs loved the girls' attention. After a bit one of the girls shared that she had recently lost her golden retriever. That prompted me to confess about Lacey. We chatted easily about dogs and the intimacy that can develop between a pet and its' human. It was a nice exchange, a respectful sharing of feelings. It reminded me how "dog people" sort of get each other.

River, Dixie and I took our time sitting there. We savored the warm October morning, the sea gulls squawking overhead, the antics of the surfers, and the lively vibe of people going about their business; chatting in pairs, jogging, sipping coffee and enjoying being alive in the world.

I thought again about Buddha. He once said that "Everything heals. Your body heals, your heart heals. The mind heals. Your happiness is always going to come back." I know that it is true. I know how fortunate I am to have had my devoted companion for all those years.

Ken came into the room as I was writing this to you. He asked what I was doing and I told him. He looked at me, picked up the calculator. "Donna, Lacey was with you for over five million minutes. How truly blessed you are." Truly I am.

For Whom the Bell Tolls

February 20, 2017

On the stormy Friday just past, the wind was howling through the Mission San Juan Capistrano courtyard; as a docent-in-training (a tour guide of history), I was following behind a group of 4th graders

4th Graders on blustery Friday on their school field trip. The rain began to fall and the children opened their colorful umbrellas, when suddenly, the mission bells began to toll. It was 11 a.m. For the past 44 years our family has enjoyed the tolling of the church bells heard easily across the valley. They ring on a regular schedule for Mass or for special reasons. As I realized that the bells were not ringing at a regular time, the tiny hairs on my arms stood at attention. Serra Chapel was closed to our tour. It was in use. I understood that the bells tolled for someone in our community who had passed away. My memory flashed on the 3:15 p.m. ringing on the day that Tony Forster, an important leader in our town, died in 2007. I stood for a moment as that memory washed over me, made keenly aware of the unstoppable passage of time.

My thoughts focused on what it is to be inside a "living museum," a place with a working church. I was walking in the footsteps of the past, a center of human activity for 240 years, during California's entire recorded history. Our docent class has been studying Don Juan Forster, Tony's forefather, who owned and lived in the mission from 1845-1864. My children and grandchildren have attended Marco Forster Middle school, more of Tony's relatives. In fact, Tony's family continues to live here. History is alive. It is not gloomy words on pages in old books. I was standing where Don Juan had stood, and before him, where Father Serra and the early mission pioneers had worked hard to build something for our future. To study the mission is to respect its history and that of the peaceful Native Americans who lived here quietly for thousands of years. If you look closely, evidence of the Indians' lives can be found in many places of California. When our children were young we were having a snowball fight along the Santa Ana River headwaters, not far from Big Bear, when they yelled to us. They were excited to show us that they had found an Indian grinding stone from prehistoric days! A few years later we discovered an even bigger grinding stone further down the river. When our son, Dan, was a little boy digging around in the rain run-off behind our San Juan Capistrano home, he found an arrowhead. It was thrilling to think we lived where the natives had hunted. It is still fascinating to

understand what we have inherited. If we take time to reflect on this: the Mission system, the Spanish, Mexican, Russian, English, and Indian influence on our way of life, one can perhaps appreciate the depth of our local history. For me, I am falling in love all over again with "place."

Personally, I notice that I am once again reinventing myself. Maybe that's what we need to do as time passes. Nothing stands still. I am energized and excited over my recent mission studies. Perhaps one of the keys to human happiness is appreciation and gratitude. It may be that novelty fits in there as well; something new to think about. I sat with a new person at a luncheon the other day. As I explained about my grief work and life coaching, she asked, "So what is the most important thing that you teach?" I said, "To live in gratitude." She smiled, "ah..." I also believe that if we can discover new things to fall in love with our lives will be richer. Right now, I am deeply researching where the first site of the Mission San Juan Capistrano actually was before it was moved to its present location. It was right around where I live right now, writing this note to you........where exactly? Hmm. Records from the National Museum in Mexico say: "This mission was founded November 1, 1776 but because of water failure at the place where it was first founded, the site was transferred to that which it occupies today...it is located about three fourths of a league (about two miles) distant from the original site." (Two Hundred Years in San Juan Capistrano, Hallen-Gibson, p. 20, 1990). There is a brass marker in Reata Park on Ortega Highway pointing across San Juan Creek in this direction. I will keep you posted.

I hope you are finding new areas of endeavor to excite your soul. I would love to hear what you are thinking about and working on.

Senator Lewis at Mission San Juan Capistrano 1928

Being Alone with Ourselves

September 22, 2015

In the dark of early morning today, I poured a steaming cup of coffee and sat on the love seat on my second story deck to escape my too hot house and to enjoy the inky quiet. It wasn't quiet for long, the dogs had just resettled around my feet when the shadow of a big bird flew into the branches above my head. Soon the air was filled with its low "hoo hoo." I leaned my head back and stared at the stars, relaxing to the humming of "hoo hoo."

Sitting there, I identified my favorite constellations and my thoughts skipped to an essay I am enjoying by Pulitzer Prize winning journalist Anna Quindlen. She writes about how important it is to be alone with yourself; that it is sometimes valuable to be in a state of boredom. She thinks that time-outs from our hectic schedules, including feeling bored, allow our engines to recharge, allow true creativity to bubble forth into consciousness. She also believes that our children are overly programmed with little time off for play or being alone with themselves.

Lately I have been playing a bit of scrabble on my phone (clearly a statement of technologic time-filling), but it speaks to my need for a break. While at this, I am noticing that my inner creative person is poking up into my consciousness. That person is getting itchy, maybe wanting to write the next novel, wanting to research Bipolar Disorder for one of the novel's characters. I notice that she has dragged out her watercolors and that paintings are showing up all over the house. That inner Donna is also thinking about stepping up into a more intense exercise regime. It's interesting what can result from some Scrabble on your cell phone...

Perhaps Anna has something about us being alone with ourselves. I am still processing the regret she describes in her book, Loud and Clear, that while she was raising her three children SHE DID NOT ALLOW HERSELF TO BE MORE IN THE MOMENT. She writes that she was too "other" focused. Now those children are long gone, removed from her into their adulthood. She writes that she studies old photos with little recognition, wishing she had paid more attention. Living in the moment.

For many of us our lives are on turbo thrust. I'm blessed with a busy happy life, but sometimes busy is just busy. Maybe we should heed Anna's sage thoughts, perhaps we need more time to be alone with ourselves and to strive to live more in the individual moment. It would be a shame to miss out on some of the best parts of our own lives.

The Power of Reinvention

September 12, 2014

New Beginnings: School has started, Fall is closing in and for many of us there is a sense of getting back to our "normal" lives. But sometimes being "normal" gets us stuck in an unsatisfying routine. So I've been thinking about that: can we afford to be "normal?"

Last Tuesday evening, CNBC journalist, Jane Wells, addressed our Womansage group. Her talk centered around her ability to sustain a thirty-plus-year career on-camera in the competitive world of television news. She was funny and delightful, but her message was clear: she keeps reinventing herself. She told us that whatever the network needs, she is ready. Joan Rivers was also a master at reinventing herself. The vast media coverage surrounding her death illustrated her genius. Imagine going from stand-up comedy to late night host, to the Red Carpet, to Fashionista and more, staying in the spot light for decades! She was constantly evolving.

When asking how do we get "unstuck?" The answer has to be about living mindfully and looking at our lived experience as a creative challenge. You know I do a lot of crazy stuff, and today I am icing my shoulder as I write this, because I fractured it last month in the Galapagos Islands with some of our grandchildren. I was on the trip because I imagined it happening and made it so, the shoulder, hmmm, not so much!

The life we are living today is a direct result of the choices we made in the past. If life is not quite pleasing you, then make new choices now. Get out of living on "auto pilot" and take a hard look at what is not working . A tool that my clients find helpful is creating a "Goals Book." The assignment is to list 10 things you want to DO, BE, AND HAVE more in life. It's fun to illustrate some of these dreams with pictures out of magazines. This book can provide a way to a get a handle on our dreams. It can be a starting point. Then simply choose one of these desires and begin to work toward it. Setting reasonable goals and taking action toward accomplishing them every single day will lead to changing things up and getting unstuck.

We cannot not change. We age. Life moves forward. Albert Einstein liked to talk about how important imagination and creativity are. I like to think of my life as my canvas, and the way I am living it, as my creative endeavor. There is a great big world out there just waiting for you. What more do you want to do? What more do you want to be? I'd love to hear about it. Right now, though, it is time to change my ice pack!

The Power of 'Yes' *Trang's Graduation Party*

June 17, 2021

Greetings! Across the years you might have noticed that some of my favorite themes in life seem to be marinating myself in serendipitous situations. I practice noticing the small everyday happenings, and perhaps saying yes, when it would be just as easy to say no.

Well, last Sunday was just such a day. As my husband Ken winds up his girls' wrestling season at high school, he has been invited to some of the senior girls' family graduation parties. Last Sunday, he wondered if I would like to join him at one of them? Up for a new experience, but not holding any particular expectations, I joined in for what turned out to be such a thought provoking and sensational feast that days later I am still thinking about it.

We arrived at a beautiful Spanish colonial house on a hill in San Clemente, greeted by Trang, the wrestler and her father. We met a few other guests in a room with about ten people who had also arrived right on time. Within a few minutes, Trang's mother, Linh, came up to me and said, "The food is ready!" I could see that the thing to do was to grab a plate and get started. As my eyes took in the expansive offering of, perhaps, a dozen Vietnamese dishes, I caught my breath. Incredulous, I asked of the hostess, "Did you cook all day?" Smiling she confessed that she and her daughter indeed had cooked all day, perhaps even some the day before.

Her commitment to her daughter, the party, and the guests, filled me with awe. I understand Dr. Gary Chapman's Five Love Languages and to see the language of Acts of Service performed by Linh for her wonderful family warmed my soul.

As the first guest to be invited to the food buffet that dominated Linh's kitchen island, I was so stunned by the presentation that I asked if I might take a photo. Not having my phone with me, she offered to take some for me. I pulled her family into the picture as we posed in front of the colorful dishes. Seeing my enthusiasm she explained some of the what was offered.

Fascinated, I asked further, learning that she had been a sous chef at the Riverside 3 Hotel in Da Nang City where she met her American husband, a retired Marine. I did not know what all of the many dishes were, but I identified chicken parmesan, tender beef ribs, a meat skewer, barbecue pork spring rolls with rice paper (goi cuon), salads, homemade cream puffs, homemade cheesecake, and cut up melon. Following up the next day, I texted Linh my questions about the food. I learned that there was a pasta salad and a banana flowers salad with chicken.

With my plate full of a sampling of most of it, I found a seat at a long table and joined the others, who by now also had plates. The conversations were easy and I enjoyed making some new acquaintances, but what has lingered with me is witnessing Linh acting out her devotion to her family.

She has invited me to coffee and she is offering me her story. For now I know that she with her two daughters, and her new husband, arrived in the US in 2017. Upon arrival, Linh and her teen girls had little English. I admire her bravery to take on a new land, new culture and new language. I know that her daughter Trang is an A+ student with a bright future at the University of Arizona. Linh and I are planning on becoming friends. I feel energized by having had a cultural adventure. When we meet for coffee I will learn more of her life.

I'm still smiling about that day. I said yes, wandered out of my comfort zone by the fact that I knew no one at that gathering, and I was honored to get to be a part of something very special, just because I said 'yes." Maybe this is something for all of us to think about as our global seclusion comes to an end. Maybe it's time we simply wander outside of our comfort zones and put ourselves in the path of new opportunities. This is our precious time on the planet, and it just seems like we should make the most of it. For now, I admire the courage of this one mother of two who came to a new land.

Love Never Dies

March 29, 2016

You know my posts often reflect precious happenings, however within the past fourteen days five people in my friendship circle, dear to me, have passed away. Ken and I will be attending two different celebrations of life this week: up front and personal reminders of this unavoidable, natural transition in life. In our Loss Support Group we never talk about getting "over" the passing of a loved one, we work on learning how to live with it as we acknowledge the comfort talking about our cherished one brings us.

Social media allows a place for this. My grief-stricken friends are posting photos, memories, and heartfelt thoughts about their loved ones. These postings invite us to share their feelings. As I look at the pictures and read the poems, I am humbled by their willingness to allow us inside. I admire their courage as they draw us into their private agony. As I witness this process, I understand that they are reframing their pain into joyful memories of love.

Neuroscience teaches that we can "train our brains," that we can grow new neurons, that it really is possible to learn new ways of being. For those of us haunted by grief and anxiety, we can learn to become more fully mindful by striving to control our thoughts. Right now I am a part of the support of those left behind who are choosing to think of their loved one with joy and gratitude for the life they shared with them. They are purposefully choosing to reframe the loss into an opportunity to celebrate the love and times they shared. This positive thinking functions to "calm" the mind. When grief comes, it is essential to take the best care of ourselves as possible.

As I grieve with those left behind, I think of this poem one of them posted,

"If the people we love are stolen from us
The way to have them live on
Is to never stop loving them--

Buildings burn
People die
But real love is forever."

Death cannot be avoided, but when we stay mindful and see that through the pain we can more than ever appreciate all of God's gifts. We can rejoice in the magnificence of a full moon, a magenta sunset, a surprise splash of colorful flowers along a mountain trail, the peals of joy in a baby's laughter, or the gentle purr of a beloved kitty.

Life requires us to be courageous. I believe it is in us to meet the challenge. I see that my friends are doing just that.

On Being an Encouragement Machine

October 26, 2014

I keep thinking of my sister Diana's blog a few weeks ago about boogie boarding with her young sons. She tells of watching a grandmother supervising a child from the shore, but the lady was riveted by my joyous sister and her sons thrilling to the foamy surf. Finally Diana called to her, "hey come join us, the water's great!" The lady looked at her, her eyes grew bigger as she considered this new idea.

Before long, that grandmother grabbed a boogie board and joined in the fun. She wasn't very good at it, but when she finally caught a wave they all laughed in delight. Diana's point was that happiness is contagious, but I see another aspect of this story and that is THE POWER OF PERMISSION. Diana gave the lady "permission." We all hold that power if we choose to exercise it.

My husband and I are very involved with the Boys and Girls Club which teaches youth to think big. Last year I coached a Club teen who was competing for Youth of the Year. He worked hard and after many competitions got to meet the president of the United States! This is a boy who grew up sharing one room with his whole family while he slept in the closet. When he began kindergarten he did not have enough English to ask to go to the restroom, now he is a student at UCI. He was encouraged to think big.

One of my sweetest memories is of a former student, a previous gang member, who came back to my college to find me. He wanted me to meet his wife and baby, and to see his UCLA Law Degree. He came to thank me for encouraging him.

Sometimes we do not understand the power of a few little words. I recall one evening, after one of my presentations, a woman came up to me and said, "I did it! I got my MFCC. I am a therapist!" I did not know what she was referring to. I listened as she explained that she had once been in one of my training sessions at Laura's House and had asked me if I thought she were too old to get her therapist license. She explained that I had said, "of course not!" She went on to tell me that those words changed her life. I did not know her, and I still do not, but it shows the power of a few simple words.

There are endless stories of our friends and loved ones wondering if they dare to go back to school, take up writing a memoir, train for a 10K race, climb a mountain, or adopt a puppy. You have the power to encourage others to do more, to reach further. I am privileged to be the life coach for the Womansage Transition Program. The program is an engine of possibility. It supports and inspires women to move forward, to change, to dare to think bigger.

Who in your sphere needs encouragement, needs for you to believe in them? I challenge you to exercise your power, and to work to negate the effects of the CRITICISM MACHINES which surround us. Become the voice of support, become an encouragement machine. I'd love to hear about it.

A New Perspective for 2013

January 3, 2013

Determined to join our family for the long New Year's weekend, Ken and I drove through a snowy winter storm. As we very carefully made our way on slippery mountain roads, the Kris Allen song, Live Like You Are Dying, filled our car reminding us to do just that, that each day is precious. With that I recalled a news clip I had just seen in which the presenter was encouraging his audience to imagine that it was their last day of living, that they were meeting their maker who queried them: "Are you happy with the way you lived these last ten years?"

That question has stayed with me as the new year is upon us and we again have a chance for a fresh beginning. I think it is important that we become more conscious of the moods and messages we allow ourselves to have, that we stop the negative narrative that many of our human brains seem to automatically run. The problem with negative thoughts is that they allow cortisol, the primal survival hormone, to be pumped into our blood stream which breeds anxiety. As we ring in this new year let us have the awareness to live with the best choices possible. Let's more fully control our brains and aim to train ourselves to see the positive in situations.

Ken and I hosted some friends last Friday night whom we had not seen for a long ti me. They are in a difficult situation in that his construction manager job has him living away from his wife as he works near the Mexican border. He can only come home one weekend in three but even with that hardship, they exude love and joy. They are making positive choices in a difficult situation. He is filling his time writing a novel, something he never dreamed of, while she works at her art cards and enjoys their grandchildren. On the weekends when they are together they have taken up waltz lessons.

As we ring in this new year let's commit to live with the best choices possible. Why not resolve to take a clear action to see the "silver lining" and stop the negative thoughts. We can become clearer on the fact that the life that we are living right now is the result of the past choices we have made. We can turn things around quickly if we are not satisfied with our current situation. We control our choices. I am often asked, "Why do you seem so happy?" I used to be stumped by that question, but after studying human happiness, I get that I love what I do. I loved the teaching and now the life coaching and volunteering. So are you making the best choices? Will you answer that you lived these last ten years to the fullest? Will you make the effort to reach new goals of happy accomplishment in the time ahead?

That Time of Year

November 13, 2017

Last Friday, on Veterans' Day, my husband and I said goodbye to a greatly admired friend who, along with his wife, has been an integral force behind the successful passage of important national victims' rights laws. It was a beautiful service with military honors. We could not help but ponder the meaning of our individual lives; how the best of us endures in the hearts of others. During the sixty-mile drive home we received word that the baby girl we had been waiting for had just arrived. She is the first child of young parents with whom we are close. As we barreled along the 605 Freeway heading south we were more aware than ever of the rhythms of life all around us; of the precious nature of our mortal selves. We knew also that in two days we would again be celebrating the passing of a wonderful lady, who has been an important part of our small town community. It seems essential that we honor our personal losses and take solace in the fact of having had such special people in our lives to begin with.

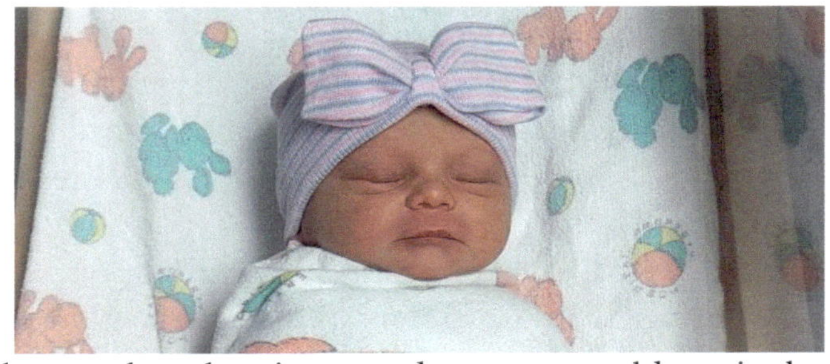

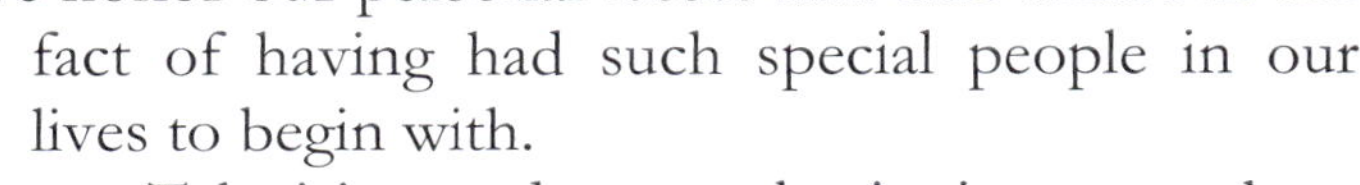

Television ads are beginning to show glittering holiday decorations and a trip to Home Depot is almost a walk into Santa's Village with the dozens of decorated trees and brightly lit lawn decorations demanding attention. It might be important to remember that for many this season can be loaded with emotional landmines. Even the most positive of us may succumb to feelings of anxiety or depression. The enormity of gifts to gather, a house to decorate, or delicacies to prepare, could cause the most hearty of us to feel a bit overwhelmed! Memories of past years, perhaps with one's original family, or the loss of a loved one, could also trigger the grief response. Some of the participants in my Loss of a Loved One support group last week expressed the idea that they are preparing to white-knuckle it through the holidays. Truly it

can be a tough time. One lady brought me a Holiday Bill of Rights from Memorial Care Hospice. Among the many "rights" were these: You have the right to be kind to yourself, You have the right to create rituals that honor your loved one, You have the right to change your mind at any time, You have the right to do something totally different from in the past, you have the right not to celebrate if you feel it will be too painful, You have the right to cry, You have the right to make your own decisions, You have the right to laugh and have fun without guilt, You have the right to go out of town, or stay at home, You have the right to plan ahead.

Recently I heard the statement that "without adversity we would not be able to cultivate our resilience." In a grim way it puts a positive spin on agony. It's like reframing the situation, seeing something from a different perspective. Without the downside of life, we could not truly appreciate the upside. So we need to "cultivate" our strengths and dig down deep into our wells of perseverance. For sure, we can help ourselves by scaling back and not letting the holiday traditions run away with us. We can come up with a new plan, something delightful in the future to do. Happiness is a lot about having something to look forward to. We can search out joy in new corners of our lives. It is more important than ever during this season to take extra good care of ourselves; being around loving, supportive people, eating properly, getting enough sleep, and always taking at least twenty minutes a day for exercise. I can still hear my grandmother's wise words in my head, "Donna, no one can take care of you besides yourself."

Sheryl Sandberg's Option B book about finding joy through adversity is all about making the most of what we have. For her, Option A, having her husband by her side to raise their children, is not available. She is choosing Option B, moving forward as best she can in gratitude for what she does have. I know that with the attitude of gratitude we can celebrate each day we are alive on the planet, knowing that it is a gift.

Be Brave

May 16, 2017

Greetings! I hope you are enjoying our colorful spring after the recent heavy rains. While riding with my friend Christine Baumgartner, on our horses today we identified 20 different types of wild flowers growing. The cactus flowers are especially colorful. As we quietly rode our horses through the winding paths along the waters of San Juan Creek, my thoughts floated back to last week in our loss support group. One of the new members shared poignant last words from her husband when he passed away in January. He had been suffering dementia, and no longer knew her, but at the last critical moment he somehow forced his mind through the tangles of that terrible disease, and said to her, "Be brave." Then he was gone. Listening to the power of that statement sent chills down my spine. What an immense act that was; not only that he knew her for that moment, but that he gifted her with such a strong admonition.

I am sure that during these hardest early months of grief she has held on to that thought. His advice works for all of us. My friend Christine is a dating and relationship coach, and she often talks about what courage it takes to dare to risk getting back into the dating pool. Putting oneself out there and owning the changes that life forces on us can yield a new kind of being, a different, perhaps new kind of fulfillment. Yesterday, I helped host a retirement party for a colleague: a big life change for her. My husband and I again have changes as two of our grandchildren graduate this spring from their universities. Our eleven grands are mostly grown up now so I am embracing the change, and even removed my Mimi (grandma) license plates. Changes are all around us, aging, loss, retirement, health issues, demographic relocations, and in our careers. The truth is that life presents serious challenges, and our job is to find the strength to face the parts that scare us and move forward, making the best life we can.

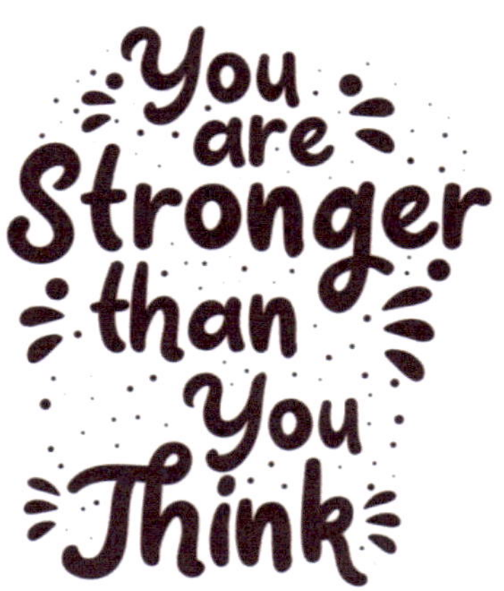

Last week I started reading Facebook chief Sheryl Sandberg's excellent book on surviving the loss of her husband two years ago. It is Option B and she talks about leaning into the "suck." Face it and move on. Cry when you have to, but know it could have been worse. Her book reinforces how truly resilient we humans are. You are resilient! I don't know what challenges are facing you right now, but I do know you have the wherewithal to handle them. I like when Mark Twain said, "Courage is the mastery of fear, not the absence of it.

A good place to start is to ask yourself, "WHAT IS RIGHT WITH ME?" (contrary to our cultural question about "what is wrong?"). Make a list. Then make a list of all the blessings in your life. Then practice gratitude thinking, marinating your thoughts in all the positive things in your life. Resilience is an active process of coping. The positive thoughts help dump happy hormones like serotonin and dopamine into your blood stream. Hardiness is about our ability to have insights into life, about being independent, using our initiative, relying on our creativity and humor, our sense of justice, and savoring our relationships and human connections.

Why not make entries into your Goals Book? List what more you want to Do in life, Have in life, and Be in life. There is something about consciously making plans, looking forward, that gets the universe to align with us.

I had a little dream niggling in the back of my brain and last January I acted upon it. I enrolled in a docent training program. By the end of February I became a certified Mission San Juan Capistrano docent. This new chapter of my life is bringing riveting rewards. My tours are mostly with fourth graders, and you can guess the fun I am having as I have the students imagine that we are all in a time machine. We pull down our imaginary control panels, adjust the dials, and we step back to the early days when the Acjachemen Indians resided in our sleepy Capistrano Valley. From there we come to 1776 as Father Serra strode into our part of the world and established a mission. The students revel in their time travels and of course I'm getting a huge kick out of teaching them! The world is a great big place with plenty of opportunity if we can just buckle up and embrace it. We don't need to be reminded to be brave, I think we are brave. I think we can go out there and create a new way of being.

In the Blink of an Eye

August 23, 2016

That's how it seems to me. It feels like two minutes ago I had a house full of tiny little grands and their sippy cups and then suddenly in the blink of an eye, grown. Yikes!!! Last week our second youngest grandchild began Middle School. We are now down to only one grandchild in elementary school. It is going so fast!!!! Too fast! Changes are all around us as school starts and Fall closes in. For those of us not tied to the school calendar perhaps it is just about getting back to normal. Maybe it's just time to take a deep breath. If your "normal" routine is not thrilling to you, now might be a good time to change it up, perhaps to become "unstuck?"

In a few weeks the Womansage Fall class of Life Transitions will begin and I will enjoy meeting a room full of women who want to do just that, become "Unstuck." I will begin the program by having the participants examine what is "right" with their lives and then we will begin to look at ways to be more fully alive. We will learn about MINDFUL LIVING and taking charge of our thoughts and dreams. The individual participants will examine their goals and imaginings in a serious way. I firmly believe that when we vividly visualize what we want we can begin to make it happen.

Last Spring when President Obama opened up Cuba to US travelers, I began to imagine myself meeting some Cuban neighbors whom we have been kept apart from since I was in high school. I imagined swimming in the Bay of Pigs. I talked to my 19-year-old granddaughter about going and she was all in and very eager to get me salsa dancing! Well that sounded intimidating and I realized I probably needed another generation in the mix. I invited her mother, my daughter, and off we went, first to check out South Beach in Miami, then to flit around the Everglades in an airboat. When we finally got to Cuba we fell in love with the people. One of the biggest highlights was swimming and chatting with the locals in the warm water of the Bay of Pigs. We never did find salsa dancing. I think we had the wrong country for that! But the point is I imagined something and because of that I found a way for it to come true. What are you dreaming of?

The life we are living today is a direct result of the choices we made in the past. If this current iteration of your life is not pleasing you, now might be a good time to make new choices; Life 2.0 or 10.0. I am always having to reinvent myself. It used to bug me, but now I get that we cannot not change. I might currently be on the 20.3 version of Donna!

Have you noticed that sometimes people get stuck in "auto pilot," as they sort of go through the motions of life? A tool to alleviate that, which my clients find helpful, is creating a Vision Board. This consists of taking a huge piece of construction board and making a collage of sayings and photos from magazines that appeal to you. It is a Right Brain activity. It can help you visualize what more you want to do or have in life. It can be a starting point. Then simply choose one of those desires and begin to work toward it. You can set a reasonable goal and take action toward accomplishing it every single day!

We cannot *not* change. We age. Life moves forward. Albert Einstein liked to talk about the important role imagination and creativity play in our daily lives. I like to think of my life as my canvas, and the way I am living it, as my creative endeavor. There is a great big world out there just waiting for you. What more do you want to do? Paint, lose ten pounds, take a trip, repaint the bedroom, make a new friend, take a class, learn a new language, plant a garden? Remember this is your life and if you are like me it is going by in the blink of an eye!

That Treacherous Goddess Habit:
Getting Unstuck

October 20, 2015

I might not remember too much from my undergrad studies of physics as I was pretty dreamy about my upcoming nuptials and signing "Mrs. Ken Friess" in the margins of my notebooks, but I do remember one important fact: that inertia is a property of matter by which something that is not moving remains still and something that is moving goes at the same speed and in the same direction until another thing or force affects it. Simply, that which is moving keeps moving and that which is still remains still. I bring this up because the biggest challenge with my coaching clients is helping them to get unstuck. For many breaking negative habits is tremendously challenging; they cannot seem to break the habit cycle. I think that Habit and Inertia are sisters. If one has the habit of not exercising, inertia keeps them on the sofa instead of at the gym. If one feels isolated and lonely, the habit of not embracing the world is held in place by inertia.

I see healthful living, such as daily exercise, careful diet, and living responsibly as HABITS. I think living the best life possible is a HABIT and it is a habit anyone may adopt for free. Some of you know that when I am not writing books, I am reading them. *The Little Paris Bookshop* by Nina George is a fascinating novel stuffed with tidbits for better living. This is what one of her characters says about habit: Habit is a vain and treacherous goddess. She lets nothing disrupt her rule. She smothers one desire after another; the desire to travel, the desire for a better job or a new love. She stops us from living as we would like because habit prevents us from asking ourselves whether we continue to enjoy doing what we do.

Powerful thoughts by Nina George! If we can look negative habits in the eye and shake them loose, a new way of living can become a daily rule. Experts tell us that after a few days of repetition an action can become a habit. If you are dismayed by the fact that in your heart of hearts there are things you want to do, why not start a new chapter today? Why not confront those negative patterns of living and begin something new?

That vain and treacherous goddess, Habit, could be working positively for you so that you live longer, feel better, and enjoy your loved ones more fully. It's a thought.

Section V

Love: The Power of Our Connections

"Where there is Love
there is Life."

~Emily Bronte, Author

A Family Affair

February 12, 2016

Valentine's Day is upon us, which causes me to reflect on something I observed over the weekend. I had a front row seat to witness the power of love. On Saturday night I assisted our daughter in hosting a pre-formal dinner party for her high school senior daughter and 45 of her teen friends. It was stunning to see the event morphing into a family affair as about thirty parents and siblings came along to wish them well and photograph the very dressed up youth. As the boys showed off their tuxedos, and the girls preened in satin and lace, I felt the tremendous connection between family members. This has left me awed. Anyone who has raised kids knows it is a messy, frustrating business, but all that was put aside as parents and siblings eagerly snapped photos of their loved ones.

An exhilarating vibe rode the air; pride, reverence and devotion. Some parents confessed to me the angst they felt pushing toward the empty nest, photographing their last child and last formal dance. My own memory scanned back to holding my newly born daughter, then to holding her newly born daughter, the center of the dinner party. It must be this, this powerful attraction, this commitment to each other that binds civilizations together, which empowers our military to risk their lives to protect our families and our freedom.

My daughter and some of the other parents kept thanking me for helping out. I thought, "Are you kidding? I would not miss being a part of this for the world!"

Re-enactors Bring History to Life in Famous Swallow's Day Parade

March 28, 2023

Always on the look-out for adventuresome ways to live life, this past Saturday March 25 in my precious hometown, I joined a doozey of a fun endeavor. It was parade day in San Juan Capistrano, its 63rd Swallows Day Parade, one of the largest non-motorized parades in America. After two years of pandemic lockdown and a horse virus that quarantined our horses, the "Back in the Saddle Again" theme was a perfect fit for our community. We were ready to celebrate!

On parade day, attired in my western get-up, I was excitedly making my way through the throngs of parade entries toward the mission's horse-drawn floats on which we volunteer docents were to ride. Slipping past two huge red dragon heads, and five teams of majestic draft horses, my breath caught as I spotted a coffin with a sign above it reading: "James Barton – Died Heroically."

I had stumbled upon a troupe of re-enactors who were staging part of one of San Juan Capistrano's most notorious murder cases, the Barton Massacre. I knew the case. I knew of Sheriff Barton. I rushed up to the costumed actors and interviewed them as best I could in the minutes before the parade began. Taking their cards so that I could follow up later, I rushed to my designated wagon, clambered up the festively decorated float.

The crowds of cheering parade goers applauded our dray as it rolled along, and my mind drifted to the Barton case. After the defeat of Mexico in the Mexican-American War in 1848, there was much social unrest. Mid-19th Century Southern California was plagued by lawlessness and violence including the tiny pueblo de San Juan Capistrano. One of the most malicious of the marauding crews was the Juan Flores-Pancho Daniels gang which was dedicated to "killing every gringo." The gang routinely held up stagecoaches and terrorized citizens between San Diego and Los Angeles.

The murderous incident which caused Los

Angeles Sheriff James Barton and six men to ride south was a particularly vicious series of raids which had occurred in San Juan Capistrano. Recently escaped from San Quentin for horse stealing, Flores was attracted to San Juan because his girlfriend lived here. One particular night the gang members robbed a local general store, killed the shopkeeper, and then blithely enjoyed the dinner the shopkeeper had prepared for himself, while the shopkeeper's body lay on the table.

The small pueblo was desperate for professional law enforcement. Answering the cry for help, on the eve of January 22, 1857, James Barton, a Los Angeles sheriff, and his men prepared to capture the gang. Unbeknownst to the lawmen, a gang member was planted as a lookout in Los Angeles. Learning of Barton's plans, the lookout quickly mounted his horse and rode out to warn the others of the Sheriff's intention.

Tired after a long ride, Barton and his men rested at Rancho San Joaquin, the area today known as Back Bay of Newport Beach, where venerable rancher Don Jose Sepulveda warned them to stop the chase. He told them that the gang was large, maybe sixty men, and that the lawmen were far outnumbered. Don Sepulveda urged that it was simply too dangerous. Also, while the posse rested and ate breakfast, it is believed that a servant, sympathetic to Flores and Daniels' cause, removed the bullets from the posse's guns which had been stowed in an out-building.

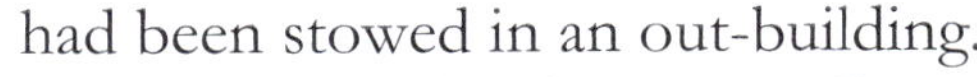

Undeterred and unaware, Barton and his men mounted up and searched the local hills and canyons to the south. Tragically when they were in the area near Laguna Canyon they were ambushed. When they tried to return fire they discovered that they had no bullets. They ran for safety. Barton and three others were murdered while two of the posse got away to tell the story. That bloody incident became known as the "Barton Massacre."

In response to the killing of the long time Los Angeles sheriff and his officers, new posses were formed, one led by General Andres Pico. Finally, Flores and 52 of his gang were arrested. On February 14, 1857,

Flores was hanged in Los Angeles with several thousand spectators attending to witness his end. Reminiscent of that hunt, there is visible today a plaque off the 241 toll way in Orange County which reads: "Under this tree General Andres Pico Hung Two Banditos of the Flores Gang in 1857." Others in the gang were rounded up and their ears were cut off and displayed as proof of their deaths. Daniels was captured the following year and hanged.

The Sheriff Barton funeral entry included 10 mourners, plus the "Widow Barton," a clergyman, as well as the "Spirit of Barton" character, a hovering shroud played by actor Barry Clark. During the parade the mourners were seen as a somber processional accompanied by mournful music. Spectators loved it as the shrouded "Spirit" moved among the mourners swooping and hovering. The "Spirit" especially fluttered and floated near the "Widow Barton" who swooned as she felt the presence of her husband's ghost!

San Juan Capistrano enjoys a rich history and The Code of the West Reenactment troupe brought some of that history to life in a most entertaining manner during the parade. The Moreno Valley Troup of fifteen members has been together for twenty years and is headed by Julia and Jon Arbough who direct and produce the historical re-enactments. They perform at many events and as a 501 C 3. They donate a generous portion of their earnings to such charities as Tunnel for Towers which helps 9/11 responders, The National Police Dog Foundation, and to Protect the Beagle Dogs. The non-profit group works out of Moreno Valley, California. In the Barton play, Joe Mortimer played the clergyman, Shelley Peters enacted Widow Barton, Julia Arbough was a mourner and her husband Jon acted as the escort to "Widow Barton."

My take-away from participating in the parade and interviewing some of the troupe's actors, is the knowledge that there are many extremely satisfying and worthwhile ways in which to invest our human energy and heart. The re-enactors have inspired me to continue my research into one of California's most important matriarchs, Ysidora Pico Forster. Perhaps one year "she" shall appear in the Swallow's Day Parade as well. Across my experience I sometimes have conversations with individuals who confide in me that they suffer "aloneness." They do not feel lonely, but they feel an emptiness, an absence of people in their lives. I encounter that sentiment more often than one might suspect. It is a situation which can be remedied if one is willing to step out of their comfort zone and enroll in some of these different groups. Truly there are friendships waiting to happen. Maya Angelou liked to remind us that A FRIEND MAY BE WAITING BEHIND A STRANGER'S FACE. This is something I am privileged to frequently experience.

Stroller Warriors Bring Sweet Memories

December 19, 2014

I'm smiling thinking of the wonderful scene I observed the other day. There was a gang of mommies whose tee shirts read "Stroller Warriors" lined up for a race along the parking lot at the beach where I was walking my three dogs. It was a blustery morning. The dogs and I paused to admire the captivating activity in front of us. Half of the eleven strollers were double strollers-a heavy load to push!

Suddenly they were off, rollerblades flashing beneath them! They seemed to fly by! I grinned. The dogs and I kept walking. An hour later we returned to find that the roller blades had been exchanged for running shoes and those energetic moms were still at it, this time jogging, high pony tails streaming behind them! I could not help but admire our cultural passion for fitness and the outdoors.

I knew I was witnessing something special and it quickly linked to a similar long ago memory of my own. My husband, Ken and I were young parents on a Sunday afternoon family outing in the Back Bay of Newport Beach. Ken was jogging while I was on my bike with two-year-old Julie in the baby seat behind me. Five-year-old Rick was riding his own bike. We had gone along for a few miles, when suddenly Julie announced, "I want to run with Daddy!" We unbuckled her and she began to jog along next to Ken. We expected her to give up after a few minutes, but she surprised us, continuing the two miles until we got back to our truck. As tiny as she was, we couldn't believe how she had just kept going, big green eyes sparkling with delight.

That day we learned something about our daughter that would prove true across the next four decades, she is dedicated to fitness and physical challenges. Not only was she an All American goalie in college, she has continued to compete in all sorts of racing events for the pure joy of it. During the years when she was the mom with young children, she could often be found pushing her big blue racing stroller, little ones buckled inside, across many miles. Last month, on Thanksgiving, she and her husband and two of their teens raced in a

10K Turkey Trot. On January 10th we will be cheering when she and her two brothers cross the finish line for the Catalina 50 miler.

I love that the Mommy Stroller Warriors celebrate fitness. It reinforces for me how important it is for us to take good care of our health, and how much pure fun it can be. Like my daughter once did, these moms, even during the hard toddler years are out there, laughing and modeling good health for their little ones. I searched online and discovered a whole national Stroller Striders movement inviting moms to companionship, support, and exercise.

As a life coach I often hear the complaints of mothers who feel isolated during the pre-school years. What an awesome way to counter that! I'm reveling in the crossover memory the mommies brought to me, of my little Julie running alongside her big daddy, of her as a mom modeling to her own children. What is niggling at the back of your imagination for you to take on? Is it exercise, joining a group, trying something new? I would love to know. We will soon have a brand-new year spread out in front of us, a perfect time to take on something new.

Paris Observations May 2014

May 27, 2014

Bon Jour my friends! I am writing to you from Paris. I knew the six day hop-over to Europe would be a good trip when I took my seat on the giant airbus last week, buckled up, and glimpsed the tenderness of a young father in front of me, gently placing his infant into a zip-in snuggly baby bed at his seat. Tears sprang to my eyes as I wondered if dads get enough of the credit they deserve.

During the subsequent days of sightseeing, I've noted many other young families, from every corner of the globe, with babes in arms, repeating the same kind of rituals; the covered Saudi mother offering her little ones juice, to the tough looking Australian man gently changing his infant son's diaper as we cruised down the Seine. This has given me fresh insights into the power of the family.

Having the opportunity to spend six days with my own daughter exploring this "movable feast that is Paris," has also been a gift. One of our favorite things was inscribing a lock, closing it around the "love bridge," making a wish, and tossing the key into the Seine, symbolizing our loves for eternity. Julie's lock was about her 20th anniversary, and mine was a celebration of my 50th year with Ken next month.

Paris can now boast three such bridges covered in gleaming gold and silver locks. The government tried to clear the locks, only for the locks to return, the peoples' choice. My bet is that in the future more bridges will be covered in locks whose inscriptions speak of love and hope.

On our first morning's power walk we came upon a bride and groom being married in the shadow of the Eiffle Tower. Even though it was rainy and cold, the bride, in strapless wedding dress, was beaming to her handsome groom as they exchanged vows. We have now counted six brides about in the city, posing, and exchanging promises in little romantic corners. I wonder how many we will discover today as take to our explorations on foot.

In the future when the conversation comes to Paris, I will think of it as a City of Love and will understand that the custom of love locks originated long ago in China and now has spread around the world, an expression of hope and humanity, connecting people across the globe with the one thing that unites us all: love.

These Birds Get It!

February 28, 2020

This morning after a walk at Dana Point Harbor, I stopped by the local feed store to pick up some grain for our horses just as it was opening. The clerk was busy rolling a white Cockatoo in its huge cage outside to be in the sun. He was squawking. It caught my interest. I followed the clerk. She went back into the dark store and from another area, rolled out a second big cage with an Amazonian Parrot in it. I asked if they were friends as she pushed the heavy cages side by side. Before she could answer, the cockatoo jumped on the side of his cage nearest the parrot, and said, "Hello" as clear as day. The parrot jumped as close as he could get and they began a very loud, animated conversation. I could see that they were thrilled to be in each other's company. Clearly they are friends.

In fact they were so happy that I could not stop myself from pulling out my phone and taking a video clip of their lively and loud exchange. (see video in right side panel) I lingered for a while. The clerk secured the cages. She was not impressed with their zeal, nor with my enchantment over them. She said that they were not hers and they were a lot of work, that they belonged to the store owner. She did share that the parrot is 42 years-old, named Cody, and the cockatoo is 20 years-old, named Baby.

I concluded my business and stood at the cages a while longer, admiring the birds and talking to them. "Hello" was exchanged many times between us.

Grinning, I got in the car, and drove home. I began thinking about them in conjunction with a class I took a few weeks ago. It was a part of USC's "Back to College Day" on the Los Angeles campus. My favorite class taught the newest brain research into human happiness. The professor said that as humans we are "wired" to be socially embedded within a group; that we need relationships to thrive. So here I was, witnessing the two birds reunited after a whole night apart, and they were beyond delighted to see one another. Clearly the importance of social relationships does not only apply to humans.

As I was driving, I basked in my own delight reminiscing about the morning's walk with a new friend. We had just enjoyed a vigorous hour-long walk around the harbor. I smiled to myself as I replayed the funny memory she shared during our walk. When we first met, a few months ago, we were strangers, standing next to one another for an all-volunteer photo shoot at Mission San Juan Capistrano. She had looked at my name tag and asked, "Are you Donna Friess?" I recall smiling yes. She jokes about it now because clearly my badge said I was Donna. She had followed up with, "I'm reading your book. We Gardening Angels are passing it around to each other."

We had introduced ourselves. The photo was taken and we went our separate ways. Later that day, I thought about how nice and friendly she was. I obtained her phone number and called her. "Hi, this is Donna. I think we should be friends!" She agreed and we settled on walking as our get-acquainted activity. This morning as we parted, I grinned saying, "A friend is a gift you give to yourself." She laughed. The fact that we had enjoyed such a fun morning caused me to think more about that happiness class and the professor's research.

He made the point that we humans are creatures of habit. I thought about the fact that for many people, as they age and their available pool of friends begins to shrink; they can fall into the habit of being relatively isolated. My work with the members of my loss support group reinforced that idea. Part of the goal of support groups is to encourage the participants to move out of their isolating comfort zones, and find new ways to become socially connected.

Columnist Helen Dennis in a recent article wrote about her own 62-year-old friendships and how rewarding and comforting they are. She explained that friendships contribute not just to happiness and feelings of fulfillment, but also to longevity. Her Orange County Register article dug into the research of social scientist, Dr. Lydia Densworth, who reported that health and longevity in primates were based primarily upon social bonds, and how well and regularly the animals interacted with other animals. Similarly, she wrote, it is the same with humans; friendships affect our physical and mental health.

During my group work with Women in Transition, "women striving to reinvent themselves," I often bring in a big chart I created. It is a huge graphic of a "Happiness Tank." I use an exercise where the participants assess how "full" their own happiness tanks are. We look at our physical, spiritual, intellectual and emotional selves. I have noticed across the classes, that early on the women tend to give themselves low scores. As the weeks progress, they come to rate their happiness tanks as more full. They also connect to one another, making friendships that often continue long after the class. I have thought to myself that it was not so much what I was teaching them, as the fact that they were in a supportive group of like-minded women, and they had a chance to bond with each other.

We are responsible for our own happiness. We cannot expect others to provide it for us, nor can we put it off waiting until a future date such as retirement. One way to keep our own Happiness Tanks full is to find new ways to connect with others, and to treasure the friendships we do have. If the parrot and cockatoo can get such a great kick out of being in the other's company, it seems like we owe it to ourselves to give ourselves the gift of a few good friends, and to see them often. Perhaps it is a matter of importance to our own health and longevity. It is worth the risk to ask: "Could we be friends?"

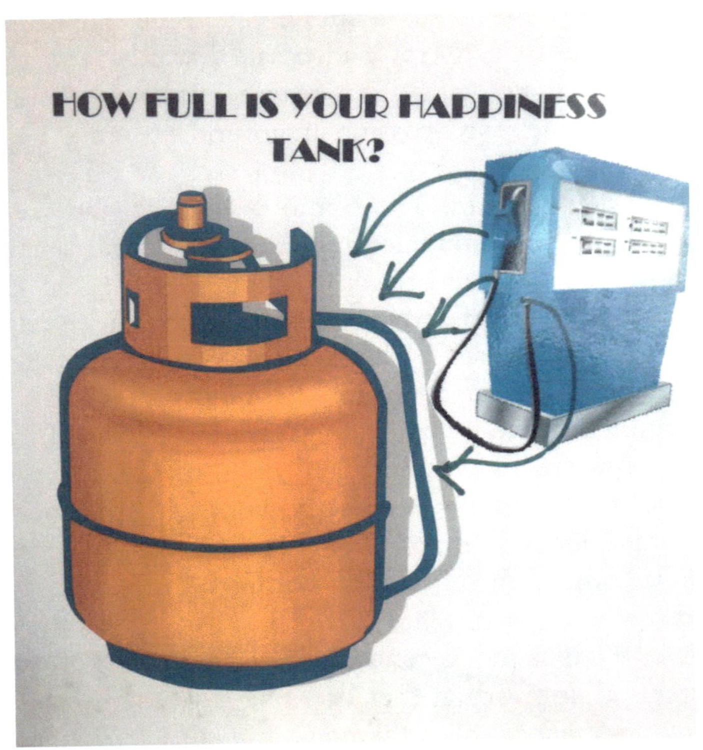

We Have the Power to Bestow a Special Gift

December 17, 2018

I got up in the dark the other morning so that I would be on time for the 7 a.m. meeting of the Monarch Beach Sunrise Rotary. I had been invited to present my talk about Horses and the Settling of California. They were a magnificent and attentive group of about 25. As the meeting adjourned at 8:30 a.m., I found a small crowd around me. Many wanted to share something from their own lives with me. I felt their urgency. One gray haired man said he had been my student in the 1980's. Another, a lady named Anita, excitedly told me that she is the descendant of one of the great ranchero dons. He was Don Antonio Maria Lugo who was born in 1775 at the Mission of San Antonio de Padua of Alta California. She said one of their family adobes is still standing. It is one of a very few two-story structures then built in the pueblo of Los Angeles. It dates to 1840. She told me more; her grandson's first name is Lugo in honor of that early Californio. She lamented that she did not know more history. I invited her to become a certified docent at Mission San Juan Capistrano, thus learning more. She beamed at the possibility of it all.

I was familiar with the Lugo name and raced home to Google more details. I exhaled in great satisfaction as I discovered rich stories of her ranchero ancestor. He once owned one of the most magnificent horse and cattle breeding ranchos in all of Southern California. More importantly, I had another, more valuable, take-away from my morning experience. I realized that I would have learned none of this from my listeners, if I had not eagerly listened to what they wanted me to know. To listen is a special gift we can readily give to others.

It seems to me that we have a precious voice within. This is a voice that does not use words. It is the intuitive inner voice that whispers to us, "step back and just listen." I believe that many whom we encounter have a deep hunger to be heard, to be seen, to feel a human connection. The good news is that we have the power to bestow the gift of our attention. We can listen.

The holidays can be very hard on some of our friends and neighbors. The music and decorations alone can be painful reminders of the past. We can reach out and connect with them. We can also be proactive for ourselves.

If we know that the holidays are going to send us spiraling down the rabbit hole, we can take action and do something about it. We can volunteer to help others by visiting hospitals or senior centers or wrapping toys for tots.

There are many ways to be of service during the holidays. Helping others can help us. Perhaps it is just as simple as gifting them our attention for a little while, by listening.

A Shiksa Goddess is Born

August 3, 2016

I found this last Friday as I was cleaning. I wrote it thirty-two years ago. Our daughter was sophomore class president and needed to provide chaperones for a class trip into Hollywood. Ken and I climbed into a bus full of San Clemente High School students going to a TV show taping.

A mother's midnight reflections-March 28, 1984.

A "Shiksa Goddess" is Born

The audience at the KCOP taping session for a popular evening television game show is brought to a hush by the handsome thirtyish host as he carefully selects nine candidates from the audience to participate in a pre-show contest. As my almost-graceful fifteen year-old daughter is drawn from the ranks of the eager contestants, my stomach tightens in wonder, will she be able to hold her own and answer correctly in front of all these people?

The chosen participants line up in front of the audience as the dashing emcee asks them to name one of the Great Lakes. As my daughter's turn approaches, the number of possible selections is diminished by each correct response. My concern mounts. I sigh in relief as I hear the huskily whispered answer, "Lake Michigan." I bask, momentarily relieved.

My attention returns to the emcee who has just discovered how lovely this young woman is. Portraying sudden adoration, grabbing his heart, he swoons as he says to her, "Well, anything you say!"

Several more questions, my apprehension continues to increase with every approaching turn. With each correct answer the young man displays ever increasing ardor toward my daughter. Finally, he explains that his deep desire would be fulfilled if only he could get to know this beautiful creature better, but alas his wife, "Moose," would never allow it! The audience laughs in appreciation of his good taste and delightful humor.

Before long, the time for the

taping arrives and the pre-show warm-up activities are rushed to a close. The contest is over. As my daughter is sent back to her seat, the young man sadly bids farewell to the "Shiksa* Goddess!"

In this moment, I am validated. My deepest convictions are publicly declared for the first time, my guess is that this is just the precursor to a thousand such incidents. As my only daughter makes her way back to her seat, I find myself thinking back over almost sixteen years to that early summer morning on which she was born. I remember the intensity of emotion I experienced as I expelled her from my protective body into the world. It was the single most powerful event of my life and I burst into tears of unbridled joy. I got my girl! Instantly the nurses were on me, admonishing me to not cry! They teamed up on me, insisting, "Dear, you will mess up your hair!" I stuffed those tears. Later, during visiting hours, I heard my grandmother's declaration that this was "the ugliest baby" she had ever seen.

Visions of that awkward girl with orthodontic braces and size ten feet on skinny legs danced before my eyes as my thoughts brought me to her intense tenderness toward animals and little children; how concerned she was the day she discovered the baby swallows who had fallen out of their nest, how she fed them around the clock for days with an eye-dropper. I always knew how beautiful she was on the inside. And now as she glides to her seat, I see that the feet easily fit the tall firm young frame, that the lush blonde hair flows around her arrestingly beautiful heart-shaped face, set off by tantalizing green eyes which sparkle with devilment. I know that long ago on that certain day, a goddess was born indeed!

*Def: a non-Jewish girl or woman

Bathed In Love

July 17, 2019

Last week I had the honor of being asked to eulogize our fallen friend Jean. As I listened to the nine or so other speakers my heart filled with pride for learning of Jean's legacy. Many of her friends from across the span of her seventy some years stood to share their most precious thoughts about her. We heard about her independence, her feisty spirit, and her commitment to raising the children in her life; her kids, niece, and grandchildren. What resonated with me the most were all the stories of Jean's unconditional love for people.

I often write of the importance of celebrating each day as if it were our last. The truth is we just do not know. I believe that it is important to not take even a single breath for granted. Jean and her husband, Jerry, spent the night with us last March, and her health seemed fine. Then a month later, it turned and she was unexpectedly gone by the end of April. Her legacy, however, lives on. Her 19-year-old grandson Liam, in particular, talked about how lucky he was to have had such an involved and affectionate grandma; that she was foundational in his growing up years, and that she will always live on in his heart.

Once again I am reminded of the quote: People may not remember exactly what you did or what you said, but they will always remember how you made them feel. Jean had the

talent of ensuring that her family and friends felt like they were the most important people in her life, and I think they were. She bathed them in love as she listened and cared.

Jerry shared with us that toward the end Jean said that she would make herself known through a white feather. He reports now discovering a rather constant sighting of white feathers tucked in interesting spots along his path. After the memorial, he took his grandchildren to the beach. Not surprisingly, there was a white feather on the sand. Standing on the warm sand at Seal Beach, as Jerry lifted the feather, Liam exclaimed, "I'm worried about the bird from which grandma is getting all these feathers!"

Jean was one of those rare people who made you feel good just by being in the room with her. She may be gone from this earth but not from our hearts. Her passing reinforces for me once again the importance of celebrating each day we have in this life.

I am home from a vigorous trip to Japan with my son and his wife and their number four daughter, and I am resting up boogie boarding at San Clemente Pier.

Listen with Ears on Your Heart!

February 12, 2014

Valentine's Day is upon us with the attendant promotions for romantic dinners, sentimental cards, flowers, or the "perfect" diamond necklace that somehow says, "I love you!" Wouldn't it be something if your life were your valentine? It is possible. It might require a change in the way you interact with your loved ones, but the results can be life altering. Recently in one of my life transitions groups we were discussing the importance of active listening and the use of empathy. The next week one of the members gave this report. When her twenty something son began his usual long diatribe of complaints about his life, instead of trying to solve them or minimize them, as was her habit, she tried something new: she simply listened with ears on her heart. She stopped responding from her strong know-it-all Parent State, instead she relied on her feelings. The result was immediate and dramatic. Her son's body language softened and relaxed. The anger that had been boiling inside of him seemed to evaporate as he comprehended that he was really being heard.

Imagine what the world would be like if we got more into our hearts than our heads and really listened to our family members, friends and coworkers. Perhaps the angry daughters would soften toward their mothers if mother would just listen. Possibly the controlling husband would have a happier wife if he would actually acknowledge her point of view. Maybe the rebellious son would stop acting out if he did not have to work so hard to be seen. Perhaps our relationships would become more authentic, less about keeping up appearances, or fulfilling a role.

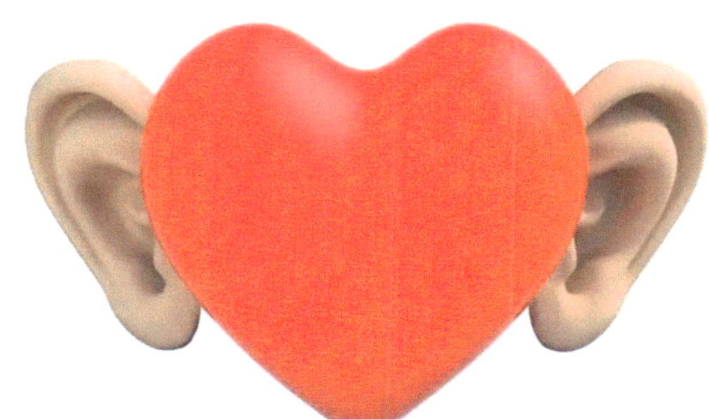

As a career communications professor, I shared positive relationship strategies with my own children as they were growing up. When they were teens, I taught them to get out of the "House of Should" and into the "House of Choice." I was trying to teach them to become mindful about their actions instead of acting on "auto pilot," doing what everyone else wanted them to do. As the years passed occasionally one of them would catch me doing something that my strong Parent State said that I "should" do, when I was not listening to my own heart. They would parrot back, "Mom, get out of the house of should!" It made me laugh to hear my own words coming back, but they helped to keep me in touch with my feelings, and not let my strong head do all the ruling. They helped to keep me real.

Starting today you could take action to make your life your valentine. You could begin to listen more fully with ears on your heart. It may require some changes; becoming a more ruthless time manager, getting enough sleep so you are not short tempered, or exercising and feeding yourself properly. It may simply mean putting this new goal into your awareness. You can become the empathetic listener the people in your life need you to be. Now is our time. It is up to us. I think we humans are amazing miracles and I believe we deserve to enjoy loving and peaceful interactions with others. I hope you will listen with ears on your heart and really hear the people in your life.

About the Author

Psychologist Donna L. Friess Ph.D., is professor emeritus, Cypress College. Donna was chosen Orange County Teacher of the Year in 2009, was nominated for the U.S. President's Service Award and is a long-time member of the U.S. Department of Justice Office for Crime Victims, Technical Training and Advisory Consortium. Donna has authored ten books and her biography appears in Who's Who of American Women, Wikipedia, and others. Her autobiography *Cry the Darkness* has been published in seven languages.

Donna is married to her high school sweetheart and they live in a noisy family filled with three adult children, eleven grown grandchildren, lots of dogs, horses and cats.

Visit drdonnafriess.com for more information.

Made in the USA
Columbia, SC
31 October 2024